Praise for *A River Lost*

"Since I moved to the Pacific Northwest a few months ago, I've read a dozen books about the region. Blaine Harden's *A River Lost* . . . struck me as the truest and taught me the most, maybe because it's the most personal and hardheaded. . . . He has a native son's feel for its people. . . . His writing is graceful, affecting, and spiced with wry humor."
—Joe Kane, *Village Voice*

"Records in fascinating detail how the well-being of those who live off the Columbia's largesse was purchased with billions of federal dollars and how one of the West's most majestic rivers was sacrificed to economic advance."
—*The Economist Review*

"Harden's acidly ironic primer about 'the West's most thoroughly conquered river' is as enjoyable as it is enraging. . . . [A] frank look at a great river's woes."
—Christopher Solomon, *Seattle Times*

"A hard-nosed, clear-eyed, tough-minded dispatch on the sort of contentious subject that is almost always distorted by ideology or obscured by a fog of sentiment."
—Hal Espen, *New York Times Book Review*

"Harden's research is admirably thorough. . . . A cautionary study of the cultural and environmental price too often paid for progress."
—*Booklist*

"[Harden] examines the changes—sociological, environmental, economic and aesthetic—that the taming of this great river wrought. [A] wonderful account. . . . A sensitive and thoughtful examination of a complex situation."
—*Publishers Weekly*

A River Lost

Also by BLAINE HARDEN

Africa:
Dispatches from a Fragile Continent

Escape from Camp 14:
One Man's Remarkable Odyssey from North Korea to Freedom in the West

A River Lost

The Life and Death of the Columbia

BLAINE HARDEN

W. W. NORTON & COMPANY
New York · London

The lines from "The Talkin' Blues" reprinted by kind permission of Ludlow Music. WGP/
TRO-© Copyright 1988 Woody Guthrie Publications, Inc. & Ludlow Music, Inc., New York,
NY. Stanzas from "Roll On, Columbia, Roll On," reprinted by permission of Ludlow Music.
Words by Woody Guthrie. Music based on "Goodnight, Irene" by Huddie Ledbetter and John
A. Lomax. WGP/TRO-© Copyright 1936, 1957, 1963 (copyrights renewed) Woody Guthrie
Publications, Inc. & Ludlow Music, Inc., New York, N.Y. Excerpt from "She-Who-Watches,
the Names Are Prayer" from *Seven Hands, Seven Hearts* by Elizabeth Woody (Portland, Or:
The Eighth Mountain Press, 1994); © by Elizabeth Woody; reprinted by permission of the
author and publisher.

First published as a Norton paperback 1997; reissued 2012

For information about permission to reproduce selections from this book, write to Permis-
sions, W. W. Norton & Company, Inc., 500 Fifth Avenue, New York, NY 10110.

For information about special discounts for bulk purchases, please contact W. W. Norton
Special Sales at specialsales@wwnorton.com or 800-233-4830

Composition and manufacturing by Courier Westford
Book design and cartography by Helene Berinsky

The Library of Congress has cataloged the hardcover edition as follows:

Harden, Blaine.
A river lost : the life and death of the Columbia / Blaine Harden.
p.   cm.
Includes bibliographical references and index.
ISBN 0-393-03936-6
1. Economic development—Environmental aspects—Columbia River Region. 2. Economic
development—Social aspects—Columbia River Region. 3. Water resources development—
Columbia River Region—History. 4. Environmental degradation—Columbia River Region.
I. Title.
HC107.A195H37   1996
333.91'6215'09797—dc20   95-38618

ISBN 978-0-393-34256-7 pbk.

W. W. Norton & Company, Inc.
500 Fifth Avenue, New York, N.Y. 10110
www.wwnorton.com

W. W. Norton & Company Ltd.
Castle House, 75/76 Wells Street, London W1T 3QT

1 2 3 4 5 6 7 8 9 0

For Lucinda and Arno

Contents

PREFACE TO THE REVISED EDITION   13

INTRODUCTION   19

1: Slackwater   29

2: Better Off Underwater   50

3: Machine River   65

4: The Biggest Thing on Earth   83

5: The Flood   108

6: Ditches from Heaven   127

7: A Noble Way to Use a River   145

8: Wild and Scenic Atomic River   157

9: Born with No Hips   187

10: Slackwater II   198

11: The River Game   227

EPILOGUE   254

NOTES   261

ACKNOWLEDGMENTS   273

INDEX   275

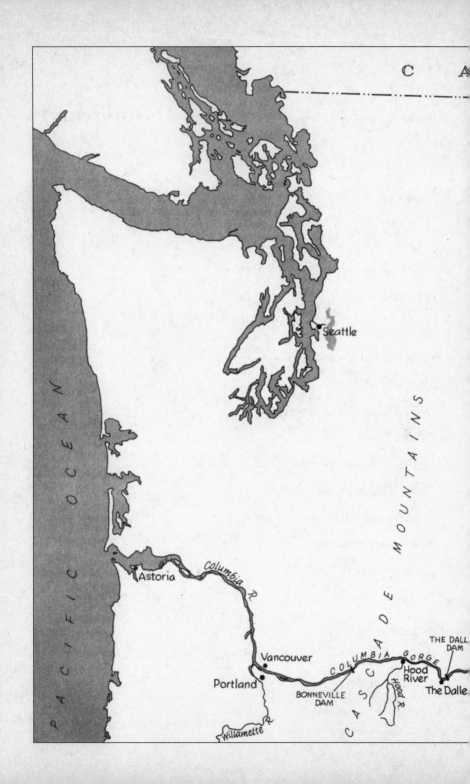

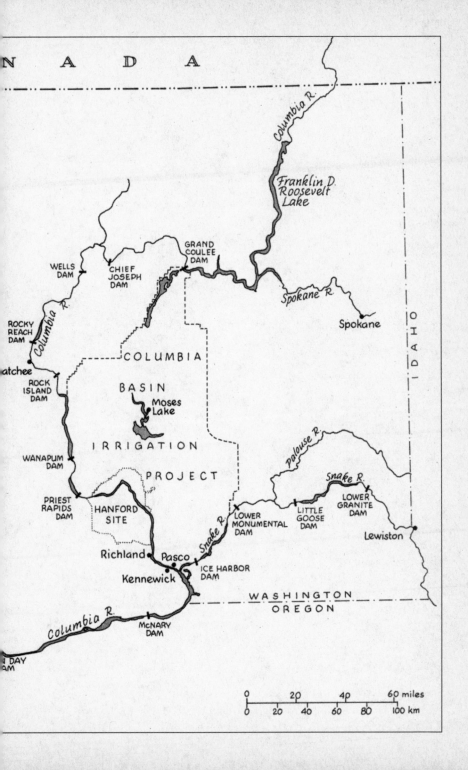

Preface to the Revised Edition

HERACLITUS WARNED that nobody steps into the same river twice. And nobody frets about that warning more than an author revising a book about a river. Still, Heraclitus had it wrong when it comes to the essence of a river like the Columbia. You can step into the same dammed river twice.

The mainstem of the Columbia is plugged by fourteen fat slabs of concrete that, barring a seismic cataclysm, are not going anywhere. The fattest and most famous of them all, Grand Coulee Dam, was the largest structure in North America when my father helped build it in the late 1930s. It got even bigger when I (briefly and ineptly) helped expand it in the 1970s. Far into the future, it is almost certain to remain the largest and most important hydroelectric plant in the United States.

Throttled by concrete, the Columbia has undergone no fundamental change since *A River Lost* was first published in 1996. The river still doesn't flow; it is still operated on a minute-to-minute schedule, with less spontaneity than the faucet in your kitchen sink.

But the context in which that exceedingly large faucet functions has changed substantially. In the past fifteen years, as the United States has stumbled into an era of climate change, soaring energy prices, debt-crippled government, and global food scarcity, the mechanized Columbia has become more valuable—perhaps even more virtuous—than ever before.

14   With almost no new investment, it continues to produce vast quantities of low-cost electricity, more than half of all the power consumed in the Pacific Northwest. In Washington and Oregon, where environmentalism is a moral imperative and a potent political force, that electricity is more than just an economic blessing. It is increasingly perceived as a social benefit: clean, green, and good for the planet. Its generation does not release the carbon emissions that cause global warming. No other part of America has such a monstrous, renewable, nonpolluting, and highly efficient power source already in operation.

Wind has joined forces with the river in the past decade. Towering wind turbines have been erected by the thousands throughout the Columbia Basin. They cluster where the wind rattles through gorges and valleys carved by the river and its tributaries. High-voltage transmission lines that extend out to remote dams on the Columbia provide a convenient tie-in, allowing wind turbines to plug into and sometimes overwhelm a power grid that has not yet expanded enough to keep up with new wind generation.

When the wind blows, the Northwest's need for hydroelectricity declines and the river, in effect, becomes a battery, storing energy (as unspilled water) in reservoirs behind dams. Should the wind wane or demand for power increase, electricity is instantly available from dams. This synergetic marriage of wind and river—together with electricity generated by solar plants and electricity saved by conservation—has prompted predictions that over the next two decades there will be enough green power in the Northwest to phase out the use of coal to generate electricity.

A shifting global context has also injected new value into the Columbia Basin Project, the largest all-federal irrigation project in the United States. For nearly six decades, the U.S. Bureau of Reclamation has funneled water from the Columbia into fertile but arid land in eastern Washington. Massively subsidized by taxpayers, the project focused its benefits on a relative handful of farmers and often produced crops that were surplus to the country's needs. The irrigation scheme never expanded to its planned one million acres because economists determined that it devoured more wealth than it produced. But as climate change contributes to crop failures from Texas to Ukraine to Australia, global demand for food has surged, making the vast irrigation scheme look increasingly prescient. For the first time in more than a generation, there are state and federal plans to expand the project.

Since the publication of *A River Lost*, the Columbia's remarkable capacity to make cheap electricity has been discovered and is being aggressively gobbled up by an entirely new category of user: goliaths of the Internet. Google, Amazon, and Microsoft have rushed down to the river in eastern Washington and Oregon to build "server farms." These huge data centers—air-conditioned warehouses filled with thousands upon thousands of power-hungry servers that communicate with Internet users around the globe—now give nearly everyone on Earth who sends e-mail, uses a smartphone, or streams video a personal stake in the damming of the Columbia.

Dams have operated in the Columbia so effectively and for so long that there is a fairy-tale tendency to think of them as part of nature, as inescapable as rain and wind. George W. Bush was the first American president to try to turn this kind of magical thinking into federal law. His administration concluded in 2004 that federal dams on the Columbia and its primary tributary, the Snake, had become part of the river's "environmental baseline."

This is a self-serving fantasy for the Information Age. It protects the reliability of the hydroelectricity used by server farms—and insures that your video streams are instantly available. It guards the interests of politically influential river users, such as utilities, irrigators, and barging companies. But it also allows the federal government to dance away from the costs and consequences of damming the Columbia. These include the destruction of the world's preeminent salmon river and the torment of Indians whose economic, nutritional, and spiritual lives were built around salmon.

The Bush administration argued that the dams did not jeopardize endangered salmon because they were built before Congress passed the Endangered Species Act. It also argued that hatchery-bred salmon, 150

16   million of which are dumped into the Columbia each year, should be counted as wild fish when it comes to assessing how many wild salmon the dams have killed.

In his courtroom in Portland, Oregon, U.S. District Court Judge James A. Redden has spent the last decade shredding the logic of these arguments. He characterized the federal government's reasoning as "a cynical and transparent attempt to avoid responsibility" for dams that continue to kill vast numbers of fish and push thirteen species of salmon and steelhead toward extinction.

Under President Barack Obama, the federal government has behaved very much as it behaved under Bush, Redden made clear in an acidly worded ruling in 2011. He said the government continued to "resist" efforts to operate the dams in a way that would keep more salmon alive.

The judge concluded that since the federal government has a shady history of abruptly changing its mind on the Columbia, abandoning previous commitments, and failing to follow through on "hydropower modifications proven to increase [fish] survival," the federal courts have no choice but to continue to police the river. He ordered the government to come up with new plans to protect fish that should consider "aggressive action," including removal of dams.

Ripping dams out of rivers has become a formidable trend in the United States, with nearly five hundred removed or scheduled for demolition. Most of them are relatively small structures, but work began in 2011 to remove two large dams on the Elwha River in western Washington and open up a major salmon ecosystem that had been blocked for more than a century. In what will be the largest dam removal and river restoration project in world history, a plan was approved in 2009 to take four big dams out of the Klamath River in Oregon and California. It would restore more than three hundred miles of fish habitat and could resuscitate a river that before dams had supported the third-largest run of salmon on the West Coast.

Many Indians, fish biologists, and environmentalists have come to regard Redden (who was eighty-two years old in 2011 and who has announced that he will soon retire) as a national treasure—a fearless protector of the river and what's left of its natural wonder. Still, when a federal judge raises the possibility of removing federal dams from the Columbia and Snake, there is always ferocious political blowback. Some elected officials who look out for the interests of utilities, server farms, irrigators, and other river users view Redden as an interfering, overstepping environmental zealot.

"Once again, a federal judge is trying to run the river with blatant disregard for the critical needs of the Northwest," the all-Republican Idaho congressional delegation announced after Redden's decision.

"Reason and common sense need to prevail over an activist judge who is intent on keeping dam removal on the table and keeping this issue tied up in his courtroom for years," said Congressman Doc Hastings, a Republican from eastern Washington.

For the foreseeable future, then, a clash of economic interests, biological imperatives, and environmental values has been set in concrete on the Columbia. That clash was the primary focus of *A River Lost* when I wrote the book in the mid-1990s. Heraclitus notwithstanding, it remains the focus of this revised edition.

While conflicts in and around the river are as enduring as the dams, the people who fight them are not. Several of the principal characters in this book, including my father and mother, have passed away. Many of them—dam builders, Indians, irrigators, river barge owners—were elderly when I talked to them. Most were present at the creation of the machine river and their viewpoints remain essential to understanding the problems that continue to roil the Columbia. In revising this book, I have stuck with their remarkable and revealing stories while updating what of significance has changed on and around the river.

Blaine Harden
Seattle, Washington, 2011

The land around here's mighty poor,
We don't own the place no more—
You work all year on a place like this,
And you ain't got change for fifteen cents.

　　　　　　　—WOODY GUTHRIE
　　　　　　　"The Talkin' Blues"

IN THE LATE summer of 1932, my father, Arno Harden, hopped a boxcar in Great Falls, Montana. He was twenty-one, alone, fresh out of work, and heading west. His traveling bag was a pillowcase. He had one pair of shoes, the work boots on his feet, a plaid wool mackinaw, and a black leather cap with flannel earflaps. Two months of bucking hay for a farmer who let him sleep in the granary had earned him eighty dollars. He had saved most of the money and it was in his pocket, along with a sandwich he bought in a rail yard cafe. My father also carried a letter—from his father.

The letter told him not to come home. It said there was nothing to come home for. His mother had died in the spring of liver cancer at the age of forty. Drought had ruined the family farm in northeast Montana. Three hundred and sixty acres of wheat, barley, and corn had failed, and the topsoil was beginning to blow. The livestock had nothing to eat for winter. His father was trying to sell 2,500 head of sheep, 60 cattle, and 25 horses. For the third time in three decades, the Hardens had bet their life's savings on rain in a dry country. For the third time, they had lost.

The letter instructed Arno, the oldest of eight children, to find his way out to Washington State. It said Joe Harden, an uncle who worked in an apple-processing town called Wenatchee, might know of a job. It

20   was understood that my grandfather, when he could sell the livestock, would give up on Montana, load the rest of the family in a four-year-old Oldsmobile, and follow my father west.

Uncle Joe, as hoped, came through with a job. My father went right to work at Columbia Ice & Cold Storage in Wenatchee, wrestling 150-pound cakes of ice into boxcars packed with apples. The rail yard was down by the Columbia River, and my father arrived on its banks just as the federal government was beginning to spend prodigious amounts of money to transform that huge, cold, swift river into the world's largest electricity machine. For my father, as for almost everyone who wandered into the Columbia Basin in the wake of the Great Depression, the harnessed river offered up a radically different version of the American West. In this version, my family's dismal cycle of westering dreams, dry-land failure, and bankrupt flight was suddenly and permanently broken.

My father secured a job at Grand Coulee Dam when it was built in the 1930s and again when it was expanded in the 1970s. He also worked at Wanapum Dam on the Columbia, and at Hanford Atomic Works, the federal plutonium plant built beside the river. He and my mother raised four children in a prosperous little farm town called Moses Lake, whose very existence in the desert outback of eastern Washington depended on a gargantuan federal irrigation project that funneled in cheap water from the dammed-up Columbia. For most of his working life, my father was a high-paid union welder whose work was linked to the river and whose wages derived from federal contracts. My parents (my mother worked as a supermarket checker) could afford a lakefront house with a bedroom for each of their children. Every few years, there was a new car in the driveway. By the time I graduated from high school, there was money in the bank for a private college.

I left the Northwest for the East Coast at age twenty-two. Aside from hurried visits to see my family, I did not return for nineteen years. I became a reporter and foreign correspondent for the *Washington Post,* in Africa and Eastern Europe. While I was away, I remembered/imagined the Columbia Basin as a soothing version of Garrison Keillor's white-bread America—friendly and well scrubbed like the Midwest, but more handsome, with high mountains, low humidity, mild winters, and good fishing. The defining event of daily life in Moses Lake was a large supper featuring boiled potatoes. The defining event of weekly life was feeling guilty about dozing off during Pastor Braun's Sunday sermons at Emmanuel Lutheran Church. Our social life revolved around potluck dinners at the church, PTA at the school, and monthly meetings of the Sons of Norway. Most everyone in the Columbia Basin, as I recalled, was white, Christian, politically conservative, and scrupulously paying off a loan on a pickup. Physical work was the highest earthly value, emotional outbursts were discouraged, and ambition was stifled by self-doubt. Big government was bad, unless it was helping us make money off the river.

When I told my father that I would be going abroad as a foreign correspondent, he was puzzled. "Why do you want to do that?" he asked. "Those people don't care about you." While struggling to fall asleep in a Sarajevo hotel as Serb artillery ripped apart the city, I finally conceded his point. I decided to go home, get to know my family again, and try to figure out where I came from.

The Pacific Northwest to which I returned bore little resemblance to my boiled-potato, Pastor Braun recollections. The region had devolved in my absence from a Lake Woebegon with dams to a natural-resource war zone. The builders of dams, people like my father, stood accused of killing the Columbia River and wiping out its phenomenal runs of salmon. Hanford, which had paid my father handsomely, had become the single most polluted place in the Western world. Some of its radioactive waste leaked into the river and some of it threatened to explode. Environmentalists, having closed down federal forests to save the spotted owl, had sued to protect creatures ranging from woodpeckers to caribou. Farm families that lived downwind from Hanford suffered from tumors, harbored conspiracy theories, and sued a government that had secretly salted them with radiation.

There were hearings in towns across the Northwest. Federal and state officials gathered in school gymnasiums to shuffle their feet, blink nervously, and listen to citizens denounce them as liars.

Federal technocrats admitted that it had been a mistake to "develop"

22   the Columbia so thoroughly, to pour all that concrete and spill all that waste, to kill all those salmon and dispossess all those Native Americans, to flood all that land and transform the river into a chain of slow-moving puddles.

At the same time, river users were determined not to lose the federal subsidies on which their profit margins depended. Simultaneously dependent upon and contemptuous of the federal government, their creed, as historian Bernard DeVoto once described it, was: "Get out and give us more money." Irrigators, utilities, barging firms, and river towns had joined together to convince politicians and consumers that if environmentalists had their way—if too much was done to deconstruct the engineered river for the sake of salmon—we would all starve in the dark.

Yet subsidies were drying up. Political power in the Northwest had long since shifted to the chain of suburbs that runs from Vancouver, British Columbia, down through Seattle and south below Portland. These high-wage, smart-work people hoped to have it both ways, complaining about ecological decay and development excess even as they clung to the subsidized river system that gave them cheap electricity.

The Columbia represents an American West that for most of the past two centuries has summed up progress, patriotism, and virtue in a single word: conquest. When I returned home, I set out to follow the self-righteous rise and disputatious fall of the West's most thoroughly conquered river. In particular, I went searching for myths that users of the river made up about themselves, myths of western individualism that had been sustained by other people's money.

I have written this story from the inside out, as a legatee of the conquered river. For I was as sustained by federal largess as any river user. The federal dollars that rained for decades along the Columbia gave me and my family work, water, electricity, and pride in ourselves. When I returned home, I could not help but bridle as people in Seattle and Portland sneered at the Columbia Basin as an environmental wasteland populated by cowboys on welfare.

Yet, the more I saw of the puddled remains of the river, the more I felt like a stranger looking in on a foreign way of life. The familiar landscape was deeply unsettling. The community I grew up in seemed contaminated by self-deception.

This book is about the destruction of the Columbia by well-intentioned Americans whose lives embodied a pernicious contradiction. They prided themselves on self-reliance, yet depended on subsidies. They distrusted the federal government, yet allowed it to do as it pleased with the river and the land through which it flowed. As long as there was federal money, they did not mind that farmers wasted water, that dams pushed salmon to extinction, or that plutonium workers recklessly spilled radioactive gunk beside the river.

Users of the Columbia—the generous and God-fearing westerners among whom I grew up—remained locked in old habits of pride, denial, and dependence. My story of the river is a memoir, a history, and a lament for a splendid corner of the American West that maimed itself for the sake of subsidized prosperity and that continues not to understand why.

To explore the river and befriend those who collaborated in its destruction, I traveled on a big freight barge sailing west from Idaho. The pilots and deckhands on that barge, like most of the people I encountered on the river, were furious. Their livelihoods depended on subsidized slackwater, the sluggish navigable ponds between dams. They felt betrayed by schemes to remove dams, ground barges, and save salmon.

At the confluence of the Snake and Columbia Rivers, I got off the barge to see what had happened to the salmon-choked river that Lewis and Clark had discovered in 1805. The waterway I found was a remote-controlled "pool," the level of which fluctuated to meet electricity needs on a grid that reached to southern California. In the bathtub river,

24   dwindling numbers of salmon were distilled from the water, sorted by computer, and hauled to the sea in trucks and barges.

To follow what the Columbia has become, I could not simply ride downstream in a barge. I bought a car from a farmer who was having trouble with his payments, and drove twenty thousand miles up and down the river. I drove north to Grand Coulee Dam, where my father worked, where I worked (before getting fired), and where the river was harnessed for the sake of jobs, electricity, and irrigation.

From the dam, I tracked a wholly artificial, concrete-lined branch of the river back to my hometown. Irrigators around Moses Lake enjoyed a half century of deeply subsidized security before outsiders—salmon advocates in the Northwest and budget cutters back in Washington—began to question giving so much water and so many below-cost benefits to members of the middle class.

From Moses Lake, it was an eighty-minute drive to Hanford, where the Columbia skirts around America's largest nuclear dump and where federal dominance in the Columbia Basin, nurtured by decades of secrecy, reached its toxic apogee. Back on the barge below Hanford, I floated west out of the desert, through the Cascade Mountains, and into the rainy, crowded, and affluent West Side of the Pacific Northwest. There, the majority no longer engaged in resource extraction. More people wrote software than felled trees. They went outside to play, not to make a living.

On the west side of the mountains, the integrity of the Columbia River and the survival of its salmon had become lifestyle concerns. The river was a major attraction in the giant civic park that the Pacific Northwest had become. Accordingly, the West Side majority favored spending a moderate amount of money to save salmon. They wanted to re-machine the Columbia so that it could resemble, at least during salmon migrations, a living river.

When I began my travels it seemed both logical and inevitable that the West Side—the world of high tech and hiking boots—would win control of the Columbia. But the more time I spent on the river and the more I learned about what was at stake, the less sure I became. The West Side was not losing sleep over the fate of the Columbia. When its residents did pay attention to the river, they behaved like dilet-tantes, motivated by a passing desire for a pristine playground or by abstract notions of saving endangered species. River users, however, were fighting for their jobs. They were defending a subsidized status quo that they believed to be their birthright.

Size is not the most meaningful measure of the Columbia River. It is, of course, big: 1,214 miles long and nearly 10 miles wide as it nears the sea. Snaking south out of the Canadian Rockies and flowing west to the Pacific, it drains an area larger than the Eastern Seaboard from Maine to Virginia. Its annual discharge would spread a foot of water across all of California and Arizona. The river jabs a four-hundred-mile finger of freshwater out into the Pacific. There are three bigger rivers in North America. The Mississippi, the Mackenzie, and the St. Lawrence all travel farther and discharge more water. But none of them even comes close to the Columbia for muscle.

For a principal river of the world, it has an astoundingly steep drop. The Columbia falls nearly twice as far as the Mississippi—in about half the distance. The greater a river's drop, the greater its power. Every half hour the Columbia expends as much energy as was released by the explosion of the Hiroshima bomb. The river possesses a third of America's hydroelectric potential.

When Franklin Roosevelt saw the Columbia from a train window while campaigning for the vice presidency in 1920, his first instinct was for control. "As we were coming down the river today, I could not help thinking of all that water running unchecked down to the sea," he said as soon as he got off his train in Portland. "Those great stretches of physical territory now practically unused" along the river must be "developed by the Nation and for the Nation."

By the mid-thirties, the four largest concrete dams ever built were going up in the West. Two of them (Bonneville and Grand Coulee) were on the Columbia River. At the time, no river with the Colum-bia's power had been dammed anywhere in the world. Over the next forty years, as the Columbia was transformed from America's largest

26 free-flowing stream into its most elaborately engineered electricity-irrigation-transportation machine, there would be twelve more big dams on the mainstem of the Columbia and more than a hundred others on its tributaries.

The engineered West offered its inhabitants a superior brand of life, particularly in the far northwest corner. Dams gave people who lived in the Pacific Northwest the cheapest electricity in the country. They turned the deserts of eastern Washington and Oregon into gardens. Their power made aluminum for the airplanes and fuel for the atomic bombs that helped win World War II. Their locks turned a town in Idaho—a town 465 miles from the sea—into a major seaport. The Bureau of Reclamation made no secret of what it was doing. Its official slogan was "Our Rivers: Total Use for Greater Wealth."

The sum total of the concrete miracles, over half a century, transformed Washington, Oregon, Idaho, western Montana, and the Canadian province of British Columbia from a boondock into a high-tech, high-wage region whose gross national product ranked tenth in the world.

As river stories go, most everything on the Columbia happened quickly, in little more than fifty years. The river ran free when my father arrived in Washington State. It is worth remembering, as you travel with me on the river, what he and many Depression-era newcomers did *not* understand when they began working together to stopper up the Columbia.

He knew next to nothing about salmon. He had never eaten or fished for one. He did not know the Columbia teemed with them. He did not know that the local Indians centered their lives on them. The first time he walked down to the bank of the river in Wenatchee, he saw what he thought was a silvery log in the shallows. When he kicked it, it came alive.

"Scared the hell out of me," my father remembered. "Never seen anything like it. Nobody talked about fish then. I never seen anybody fishing. Not very many people ate fish, I never seen them anyhow."

People born and raised in the Pacific Northwest are often said to have some special affinity for salmon. Public agencies often describe the fish as "our most potent symbol of endurance and vigor." But if you grew up in irrigation country, that is nonsense. I never had any feeling for the fish. We did not fish for salmon, we could not afford to buy them, and we did not have the foggiest idea when or where they migrated, though the Columbia was less than an hour from our house. In twelve years of public school and four years of private college in the Northwest, the issue of salmon dying for cheap electricity never came up. I dimly remember hearing that dams killed salmon, but it seemed unimportant, especially compared to the mystery of having enough water to live in the desert.

It is also worth remembering, as you consider what has happened to western rivers like the Columbia, who these people were who built and believed in and benefited from dams. A lot of them were like my father, farm kids who came of age in a rawboned West where cowboy myths about self-reliance had a firm grounding in fact.

Before the Depression forced him to flee Montana, my father broke wild horses, hauled lignite coal in an open wagon through prairie blizzards, and took lickings from a father who was quick with the razor strop. He boxed nearly every Sunday in the living room of his house against relatives and neighbors.

Like many beneficiaries of the engineered river, my father and our family savored those hardtack memories—even as we became middle-class cheerleaders for federal subsidies. Applying a brand of logic peculiar to westerners who prosper with the help of federal money, we understood the government-planned, government-run, and government-financed damming of the Columbia as an affirmation of our rugged individualism. We incorporated the harnessed river into our mythic West.

It was an enchanted place where, in memory, a man could break wild horses and box on Sunday with his neighbors. But where, in fact, he and his family would never again have to swallow their pride, pack up their belongings, and move on.

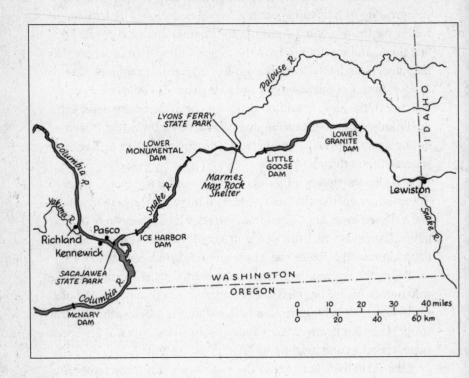

1

 *Slackwater*

There is something . . . thrilling about a river. . . .
—WALLACE STEGNER
Beyond the Hundredth Meridian

W E SAILED WEST from Idaho at sunset on water the color of dark
chocolate. The sun disappeared slowly into the downstream
distance, notching itself between puffy, bald hills and burning out in a
long tomato-red smear. The river smelled of the farms it irrigates and
erodes, a swampy perfume of mud and fertilizer, algae and a hint of
dead fish.

Down in the galley, groggy from afternoon naps, a fat tugboat
skipper and a muscular deckhand were playing a quick hand of black-
jack, yawning, smoking, drinking coffee, scratching themselves in
manly places, and preparing for a six-hour shift of squiring twelve
thousand tons of peas, lentils, wheat, computer games, wood chips, and
polyurethane-coated milk cartons out of the hinterlands of the West
and off to the consuming capitalists of the Pacific Rim.

On the splendid September evening that we lumbered out into the
middle of the Snake River, the principal tributary of the Columbia,
the tugboat *Outlaw* pushed six barges. The tow, as the row of ungainly
barges is called, was longer than two football fields and weighed more
than a medium-sized office building. Unable to stop in anything less
than a quarter mile of still water, too long and too heavy for any other
American river, it was a captive of the engineered rivers upon which
it plodded.

So, too, were the two men I introduced myself to down in the galley,

30   the fat skipper and the muscular deckhand, the ones playing black-
jack and scratching themselves. Without federal dams and locks on the
Snake and Columbia, they had nowhere to go on their boat. Without
slackwater, they did not have a job, a marketable skill, or a future.

They were, therefore, suspicious of all those they took to be agents
for, promoters of, or sympathizers with free-flowing rivers. Their long
list of enemies, as I was to learn, included environmentalists, Indians,
fish biologists, windsurfers, federal judges, federal bureaucrats, salmon
fisherman, and residents of Portland and Seattle.

As quickly as I reasonably could, I assured them that they need not
worry about me. I explained that I was like them. I was a beneficiary
of dammed-up rivers, Arno Harden's boy, clearly no fancy-pants, fish-
loving yuppie. It was true what I said, as true as anything that journalists say to ingratiate themselves, making friendships of convenience to
wheedle out information. In any case, I repeated this autobiographical
wheeze to every pilot and deckhand I met sailing west on the Snake and
Columbia, and it worked like a passkey.

The men on the river welcomed me with genuine warmth. They
fed me food my father liked to eat, boiled potatoes and beef and ice
cream and sugar cookies. They told me about their failed marriages
and showed me pictures of their kids. They told me about giving up
half their lives to the river, never leaving their tugboats for fifteen days
at a stretch, working six hours on and six hours off and always being
tired, and going home to lonely wives and confused kids and sleeping
fitfully in their own quiet beds, missing the bawl of diesel engines and
the jostle of the river. They told me about how the Snake and Columbia
sometimes freeze in the coldest winters and how the barges crunch
through the ice making a hellish noise like an endless rear-end colli-
sion. They told me about the bald eagles that lance down on the river
in winter to slaughter ducks whose legs are encased in ice. After eagles
attack, they said, the cream-colored ice is stained with feathers and
excrement and blood.

Wherever the conversation wandered during my days on the river,
it always found its way back to fear and resentment. Deckhands and

pilots were terrified of losing their livelihoods to schemes that would retool the river in favor of fish.

The lower Snake and mid-Columbia, because of federal dams, have been slowed to a lake-like one mile per hour. The more than one hundred white-water rapids that used to torment—and, on occasion, violently terminate—river transport from Idaho to the sea have been drowned. Dredges have gouged out shipping channels in both rivers to a depth of at least fourteen feet, five feet deeper than the Mississippi. The difference allows the Columbia-Snake System to float barges that are twice as heavy as those that ply the Mississippi. A bushel of wheat travels more efficiently and more cheaply on the Columbia-Snake System than on any river, highway, or railroad in the nation.

About 40 percent of America's wheat exports move down these rivers, which have been fully modified for freight since the mid-1970s. If you are a wheat grower or maker of computer games or manufacturer of polyurethane-coated milk cartons and you live anywhere near the Rocky Mountain West, federally financed river modification means that there are transport dollars to be saved by forsaking trucks and trains and even the Mississippi and sending your wares to sea in Idaho.

What saves money, alas, kills salmon. Mostly it kills them when they are young and trying to go to sea. In years when there is lots of water in the rivers, about 60 percent of juvenile salmon that attempt to swim to the Pacific from Idaho do not make it. In low runoff years, nine of ten perish. The percentage of migrating juvenile salmon that succeed in returning to Idaho as adults rarely exceeds the 2 percent level that scientists say is the minimum necessary for species survival. In 1992, just one adult Snake River sockeye survived the nine-hundred-mile trek back up the Columbia and Snake Rivers to spawn in Redfish Lake in central Idaho. He was named Lonesome Larry, and then-Idaho-governor Cecil Andrus, a devoted fisherman, had him stuffed, mounted, and displayed for visitors as a symbol of how "eight lumps of concrete" have ruined his state's heritage.

Lonesome's frozen sperm, along with the fresh sperm of a handful of other adult sockeye males who survived the river gauntlet, was used to fertilize about ten thousand eggs from sockeye females who also made it back to Redfish Lake in the early 1990s. (For all his fame, it turned out that Lonesome's sperm, after thawing out, had "low motility." It probably contributed nothing to the future of his species.)

The breeding project was part of a last-gasp effort to save Idaho's wild salmon—an effort that had paid some dividends by 2011, when several hundred sockeye returned to Redfish Lake. The part of salmon saving that terrified barge pilots and deckhands would require major modifications—or indeed removal—of the dams that make barging possible. Before there were dams on the Snake and Columbia, the stream-flow time from Lewiston, Idaho (where I boarded the barge), to the sea was about two days. With dams, it could be as long as two weeks. On the barge, the crew had heard about the possibility of a Snake River "drawdown." It would unplug reservoirs—for a few months each year during the spring and summer salmon migrations—and turn the lower Snake and part of the mid-Columbia back into something that is less like a lake and more like a river. In theory, this would whisk vulnerable young salmon to the sea, while protecting them from turbines, predator fish, and the lethal effects of slow-moving, warmish water.

Speeding up the rivers would lower water levels and halt all barge traffic on the Snake for most of every summer, the peak shipping season. It would leave many irrigation systems on the Snake and mid-Columbia high and dry, requiring costly modification. It would cost Northwest utilities tens of millions of dollars to buy electricity lost to the drawdown. The Army Corps of Engineers estimated it could cost U.S. taxpayers as much as five billion dollars to modify four Snake River dams.

A more radical fix for what stalls young salmon in the lower Snake is demolition of its four federal dams. This option has gained increasing support among scientists, Indians, and environmentalists. The federal agencies responsible for enforcing the Endangered Species Act concluded in 2000 that breaching the dams "would provide more certainty of long-term salmon survival and recovery than would other measures." Environmental groups and many fish biologists argued that dam removal was the only chance to save Snake River salmon.

But irrigators, utility companies, Idaho port authorities, grain buyers, and barge companies were implacably opposed—even as they insisted that they do care deeply about salmon. "Salmon are why we live in the Northwest. They are an environmental bellwether of our quality of life," Jonathan Schleuter, executive vice president of the Portland-based Pacific Northwest Grain and Feed Association, told me. He and other champions of the engineered river claimed they object to dam removal and the drawdown because there is no conclusive scientific evidence proving that they will really help fish. They say more basic research is needed.

In response, environmental groups saw a sinister strategy of delay. The Sierra Club claimed the Army Corp of Engineers, which built the Snake River dams, would go on testing until all the salmon were dead.

Out on the river, away from bureaucratic sniping and sham salmon sympathy and polished environmental rage, I found a clarifying absence of cant. The men on the barge did not pretend to care about endangered fish. They did not believe anyone really did. Sealed off in a bizarrely big boat for fifteen days at a stretch, missing too much sleep and eating too much ice cream, they saw salmon for what they were—the enemy.

"Nobody wants to give up anything. I don't want to give up my job. The farmers don't want to give up their water. Consumers don't want to give up cheap electricity. I ain't never seen a dinosaur, but I don't miss them. Who says it is not evolution killing these salmon? Who cares anyway?"

Greg Majeski, the muscular deckhand, explained his neo-Darwinian theory of endangered species while handing me a life jacket and leading me on a two-hundred-yard hike to the bow of the tow. It was just after sundown and Majeski, at the beginning of his evening shift, had to get out there to hook up a flashing lantern-style warning light. The thirty-four-year-old deckhand, wearing a coiled orange electric extension cord across his chest like a bandolier, grabbed the warning light and told me to follow him.

"Don't fall in the river," he instructed.

The journey out to the bow was as much an ascent as a walk. Barges in the tow rode at different levels in the river, depending on what they were carrying. The heaviest barge, with 3,000 tons of wheat, sat about four feet deeper in the river than the one in front of it, which had 1,900 tons of peas, lentils, and computer games. Majeski hopped, climbed, and shimmied between the barges with the bored nonchalance of a commuter changing trains. Trying to keep up, I slipped, bruised my knee, and sheepishly asked for a hand, all the time fretting about the Snake as it sluiced beneath us in the seams between the barges.

Most deckhands slip and fall in the river several times during their career. It usually happens when their tow is near the riverbank, picking up loaded barges or dropping off empties. Majeski fell in the middle of the river. It was at night during a 50-mile-an-hour spring windstorm. His radio went dead as soon as he hit the water. His flashlight continued to work and he tried to shine it, while bobbing in seven-foot waves, into the eyes of the tow's skipper, who sat in the wheelhouse forty-two feet above the water and about two hundred yards from the point where Majeski fell in. His skipper never saw the flashlight, but he was bothered by the oddly silent radio. The skipper managed to find his floundering deckhand by scouring the river with a wheelhouse spotlight. He turned the tow so Majeski could pull himself back on board. The deckhand changed his clothes and returned to work.

After fourteen years on the river, Majeski's job, which paid him about forty-five thousand dollars a year with overtime, had given him the body of a linebacker—hulking shoulders, tree-trunk arms, tight waist, powerful legs. Out on the barges, his primary responsibility was to tie, untie, and tighten the cables that hold the tow together. The cable was an inch and a half thick and a foot of it weighed fourteen pounds. Dragging forty feet of cable across a barge meant wrestling with five hundred and sixty pounds of not-very-flexible steel. Deckhands, as they aged, suffered from chronic tendinitis, bad backs, torn shoulder ligaments, and aching wrists. High winds on the river could snap a cable like a rubber band. A flying cable could shatter or sever human limbs. A few months before my trip a cable shredded as it snapped, shooting a sliver of steel into a deckhand's thigh. There was also the risk of getting a foot, leg, or arm caught between barges, a squeeze that could turn appendages to mush.

Out on the bow, the evening was fine and warm, with little wind. We escaped the incessant wail and vibration of the tug's diesel engines. The bow of the tow plashed, with a soothing sibilance, through a darkening, glass-smooth river. The Snake, as it enters Washington State and heads west toward its confluence with the Columbia, flows through a steep, arid, and oddly empty canyon. Its steep walls have no trees and very little vegetation. They seem, from a distance, to be covered in elephant hide—dirty gray, cracked, and gullied by long-ago rain. There are irrigated wheat fields and vineyards and small farm towns up over the canyon lips. But none of this can be seen from the river. I could see no electric lights as the last traces of the canyon disappeared in the black of a moonless evening. From the bow of the tow, night passage on the Snake was serenely disorienting. The darkness was unearthly, like sailing in a cave.

Majeski broke the spell by plugging in the flashing warning light and telling me that he had had to divorce his wife, a woman in her twenties. He said she had been seeing a number of other men while he was out on the river. "She wasn't fit to be left alone without adult supervision for fifteen minutes, let alone fifteen days," he said.

After just two hours, Majeski said goodbye to me. He fetched my suitcase and returned to the tugboat *Outlaw*. He untied the cables that hitched the tug to the roped-together barges, and I was cut loose with twelve thousand tons of export merchandise to float alone in an inky canyon of slackwater.

Drifting blind in slackwater. That is not a half-bad description of what it was like to grow up in the Columbia Basin in the age of dams. Slackwater was the amniotic fluid of my hometown. Pumped into irrigation

36 ditches and funneled south through a network of canals longer than the Potomac River, it changed everything.

When water arrived in Moses Lake in the early 1950s, the encircling scrub desert of sagebrush, cheatgrass, and greasewood gave way to fields of sugar beets, alfalfa, and wheat. Hot summers moderated, and dust storms eased. With sprinklers knocking down the dust, you could see a hundred miles west on summer evenings and catch the jagged profile of the Cascade Mountains etched in black against the burnt red sky.

Those mountains, which run north and south from British Columbia to Oregon, form a fundamental dividing line in the Pacific Northwest. By scraping rain from the sky as weather blows in off the Pacific, the Cascades cleave the region between wet and dry, forest and sagebrush, urban and rural, crowded and empty, Democrat and Republican. Those who live on the West Side of the mountains—the side with the ocean, the rain forest, Puget Sound, and most of the people—enjoy a freedom nearly unique in the West. Freedom not to panic about water. The East Side, the side with the desert, the dams, the irrigation ditches, and Hanford, is like every other part of the West. Too dry for comfort, always jealous of the living it wrests from the river.

Before slackwater, Moses Lake was a far-west replica of the sorry homestead country that two generations of Hardens had gone broke on back in eastern Montana. The town was notable for its large jackrabbits, plentiful rattlesnakes, and frequent sand storms. A Chamber of Commerce history tried to dress up Moses Lake's early years, but it admitted that before federal money gave us slackwater there was a certain pointlessness to the Moses Lake experience. "Out of the desert a city was built," the history said. "Some of the earliest homesteaders and settlers of the area . . . would ask, 'Why?'"

Human habitation before the turn of the century had been limited to a band of Columbia River Indians who occasionally stopped by the lake to water their horses and dig for wild onions, sweet white camas, and other roots that grew in the mudflats around the shallow lake. When white people began trickling into the area in the 1870s, the Indians were led by a chief called Sulktalthscosum. Presbyterian missionaries renamed him Moses, a christening for which poor spellers in my hometown have always been grateful. Chief Moses was a leader who would do almost anything to avoid fighting with whites. That, however, did not stop the U.S. Army from packing him and his five hundred followers off to a reservation.

Land around the lake that came to be named after the renamed chief was not extensively settled by whites until 1910, when farmers were lured to the area by a few years of above-average rainfall. It was a chronic miscalculation of the arid West. Ill-informed settlers figured that if it rains for a couple of years, it will rain forever. When the rains returned to normal—about eight inches a year, less than a fifth of what falls on the East Coast, less than a tenth of what falls over on the west side of Washington State—most settlers gave up and moved on.

The New Deal broke the cycle, building Grand Coulee and giving us water. The pork-barrel labors of Washington State's two long-serving United States senators, Henry M. Jackson and Warren G. Magnuson, flooded our desert not only with irrigation water, but also with dollars. It amounted to 10 percent of the nation's entire public-works budget, and it was spread over a region with 0.4 percent of the nation's population.

With a seemingly inexhaustible supply of water and federal money, Moses Lake won itself a future and a factory. A sugar-beet plant was built on the east side of town. Every Easter, we children were invited by the U&I Sugar Company out to the beet fields surrounding the factory to hunt for coded eggs that could be traded for candy. Irrigation also made life sweet for those who hunted with shotguns.

The state fish and game department imported Chinese pheasants and set them loose in the irrigated fields, where they thrived beyond all expectation. For a time, the big, noisy, succulent-eating game birds were almost as common as sparrows. I flushed them from vacant lots on my way home from school. My older brother, handy with a shotgun, shot several a week during hunting season. For a time, my mother cooked more pheasants than chickens.

The state fish and game department also planted large numbers of trout, bass, crappies, and perch in Moses Lake, a body of water that itself was perked up every spring by an infusion of water from the Columbia.

38   For a time, the planted fish, like the planted pheasants, thrived in the lake and in the Potholes Reservoir south of town. Tens of thousands of city people from the rainy West Side flocked over to the well-watered desert to shoot our pheasants, catch our fish, and spend their money.

My earliest memories in Moses Lake are of weekend afternoons in the summer, when my mother and father took the family to irrigation canals to swim. It was before we had air conditioning. By mid-July, with the temperature often near a hundred degrees, the lake turned fetid, as farm runoff rich with chemical fertilizers inspired a malodorous bloom of turd-like clumps of algae. Canals were the one clean place to cool off. Adding to their allure, the canals were posted by the federal government and surrounded by cyclone fence. Signs said the water was deadly and the Bureau of Reclamation would not accept responsibility if you drowned. My little sister, Debbie, and I wore life jackets, at my mother's insistence. We also wore sneakers so as not to cut our feet on sharp rocks and broken beer bottles. Holding our noses and closing our eyes, we jumped into the canals from low wooden bridges, and the boiling current whipped us twenty or thirty feet downstream before we dared breathe or open our eyes. The water was pristine and, no matter how many times we jumped in, astoundingly cold.

I did not know then, of course, that it came from the Columbia River or that the federal government built the multibillion-dollar system that delivered it. I assumed that cold-water ditches in the desert were part of the natural order, one of God's gifts to the chosen people of the Columbia Basin.

My solitary drift in the Snake with twelve thousand tons of cargo lasted only about three minutes, the time it took for the tugboat *Outlaw* to untie itself from the barges and back away, and for the tugboat *Defiance* to move into position and tie up. The Tidewater Barge Lines of Vancouver, Washington, my host for the river journey, controlled 80 percent of the shipping on the Columbia-Snake System and operated sixteen tugboats. They routinely switched barges in midstream.

A new deckhand appeared, grabbed my suitcase, and led me to my cabin on the *Defiance*. Then he ushered me up two flights of stairs to the wheelhouse. It was movie-house dark but for the glow of a color radar monitor that tracked the tow's position in the river. All four sides of the wheelhouse had large windows, affording the skipper a panoramic view of the encircling blackness. In the glow of the monitor, I could just make out the back of the skipper's crew-cut head.

"By the time you get to Portland, you are going to be bored shitless."

In this way, without getting up, Steve McDowell introduced himself. He told me to sit down, asked if I was hungry, spat a plug of chewing tobacco into a paper towel, tossed it neatly into a plastic trash can, and launched into a dyspeptic disquisition about life on the river.

McDowell had begun barging at the age of twenty-three, after going bankrupt in the coin-operated Laundromat business in his hometown of Vancouver, Washington. He worked as a deckhand for ten years before winning promotion, fourteen years ago, to river pilot. At age forty-seven, he still had the shoulders and arms of a man who can wrestle steel cable. But his stomach was headed south at a gallop, straining at his T-shirt. He pointed pridefully at the bulge.

"They call it Tidewater belly, wheelhouse gut. You see a lot of fat people out on these boats. The only entertainment we got is food," McDowell said. He had tried jogging and even bought a rowing machine, bringing it on board the *Defiance*. "I gave up the jogging a few years ago. So far, I look at the rowing machine and it looks at me and nothing happens."

The crew on a Tidewater tow consists of just four men, two pairs of pilots and deckhands. One pair sleeps while the other works. As senior pilot on the *Defiance*, McDowell was also the tug's skipper. Tugboat pilots and skippers steer, eat, and sleep. That is pretty much it, except for their twice-daily climb from their bunks up two flights of narrow stairs to the wheelhouse. Once there, they mostly sit in a large reclinable black leather captain's chair. Deckhands cook their food, clean their toilets, do their laundry, repair their engines, and bring them coffee and cookies.

The tow was a time capsule from Grover Cleveland's America. Fat, out on the river, meant prestige, prosperity, and power. When deckhands win promotion to pilot they separate themselves from their subordinates and their muscle-bound, backbreaking past by dressing up in a wheelhouse gut. When an experienced pilot hires on with Tidewater Barge Lines from another outfit, his lack of seniority can force him to work as a deckhand and suffer the indignity of shedding weight. Dave Faulkner, the deckhand working on McDowell's shift, the one who picked up my suitcase, was losing status as we sailed west. Faulkner, for ten years a tug pilot on the Bering Sea in Alaska, had shrunk from a thirty-six- to a thirty-two-inch waist in eight months on the *Defiance.*

Waistlines are not the only part of a pilot's life that can come undone on the river. Divorce is a chronic problem for them, as for deckhands. Crew members, having little else to talk about during their fifteen days' confinement on the river, gossip so much and so often about each other's marital problems that they call their discussions "As the Barge Turns." Everyone seems to know intimate details of everyone else's sex life. I mentioned to McDowell what Majeski had told me about his young wife. He nodded knowledgeably. For him it was old news.

"Barging does put a strain on marriages. It is especially hard on these young guys who haven't developed their relationships yet," said the skipper, once divorced since coming to work on the river. McDowell said he has managed to keep his second marriage together, in part because he and his current wife own a house overlooking the Columbia. He cruises past the house in the *Defiance* a couple of times a week, waves to his wife, and chats with her on a VHF-band radio. He says it keeps them both from feeling isolated and resentful. Cell phones, of course, could do the same service for pilots and deckhands alike. But many of them seemed to prefer two weeks of spousal silence.

McDowell said it takes the better part of a decade of getting fat and fighting loneliness in the wheelhouse before a pilot can master the Snake and Columbia. Mastery means memorizing the position of the shipping channel in 350 miles of river between Lewiston and Portland, along with the best approach to every turn, sandbar, rocky shallow, narrow bridge, and tricky lock along the way. Most important, mastery means learning how not to panic in the wind.

The Columbia is probably the most consistently windy navigable river in North America. Winds of more than fifty miles an hour blow several times a month in the river gorge that cuts west through the Cascades. The gorge, the only major breach in the mountains, is an equalizing chamber through which the radically different climates of the East Side and West Side of the Pacific Northwest are always trying to iron out their differences.

The wind blows hardest upriver, from west to east, when storms slam inland off the Pacific. But even when the coastal weather is relatively calm, temperature and barometric differences between the wet and dry sides of the mountains create a vacuum that draws moist thermal winds up the gorge.

The wind on the river abruptly reverses direction, turning tail and heading west, when a large mass of cool marine air builds up across the West Side and begins spilling over the peaks of the Cascades. That moist air, once it clears the mountains, races downhill like a flash flood after a big rain. The "drainage wind" follows creeks, streams, and minor rivers on the East Side until it gathers together on the surface of the Columbia itself, turns west with the river, and pushes through the gorge toward the sea. It is not uncommon for winds of more than forty miles an hour to blow upriver all day and then reverse in the evening to blow with equal, or even greater, velocity downriver.

The reliability of these winds was the driving force behind an extraordinary fourteen-fold increase in wind-power generation in the Northwest between 2005 and 2010, as thousands of wind turbines were erected in Washington and Oregon. By 2014, wind capacity is expected to double again, to about 7,000 megawatts. That's about a third of all the electricity consumed in the region in 2010.

"Whenever you have a wreck, it is 95 percent of the time the wind," McDowell said. "Imagine holding up a piece of plywood in a 45-mile-an-hour wind. That is what it is like steering a barge on the river. Unloaded barges have to be tacked into the wind, like a sailboat. If you steer these boats for any time, you are going to hit something."

McDowell said a 60-mile-an-hour wind on the Columbia ripped his tow apart three years ago, snapping six steel cables and blowing away one of his barges. "Luckily I was near another Tidewater tug. I

42 left what remained of my tow with him, and went downriver chasing the barge that got away." On the day before he picked me up, McDowell said he was pushing a tow of empty barges up the Columbia into a gusting 50-mile-an-hour headwind that snapped a cable and sent spray more than two hundred yards in the air. Lofted up by the bow of his tow, the spray whipped in the wind until it splattered against the wheel-house windows of his tug.

"Used to be we didn't tie up over nothing. Now if you are running upriver with oil in the wind, and you pass up a place to tie up, and you spill some oil, you'll never work in the industry again," McDowell said. The Exxon Valdez oil spill in 1989 in the Gulf of Alaska changed the willingness of skippers like McDowell to challenge the wind. Since the spill, he and other Tidewater skippers have had to attend courses on hazardous-material cleanup. Tidewater Barge Lines has stationed emergency cleanup rigs at intervals along the Snake and Columbia.

Worse than the wind, in McDowell's view, are the wet-suited "clowns" who play in it. The Columbia Gorge was discovered in the 1980s as the best windsurfing site in the continental United States. Before long, windsurf tourism became the dominant industry in Hood River, Oregon, and a number of other former timber towns in the gorge. "Board-heads" from around the world put in about three hundred thousand windsurfing days a year along a forty-mile stretch of the Columbia. The most adventurous of the windsurfers come out on the river in the severe winds that snap barge cables.

"They are going to send me to an early grave," McDowell said. "When it first started, I thought it was just a passing fad. I never believed it would develop into the nightmare that it is now. It has added a lot of stress to this job. When you go through the gorge, there are so damn many of them that you can't pay attention to them all. There are always one or two thrill-seekers who have to have that one last pass in front of you. When they do, you just hold your breath. They disappear in front of the bow and you just pray they come out."

McDowell's house on the Columbia is in the gorge, not far from Hood River and its windsurfing boutiques. "I just hate to go there during the windsurfing season. All these trust-fund babies come in and money is no object to them. I've seen more people in spiky hair and rubber clown outfits than I ever thought I'd see in my life. I went into what used to be my favorite bar, and one of these weirdos asked me to sign a petition. It called for an immediate ban on barging in the Columbia."

As hours passed and we chugged downriver on the black windless Snake, whose rocky shallows McDowell had long since committed to memory, the skipper leaned back in his big leather wheelhouse chair, filled his mouth with chewing tobacco, and directed my attention to the real aggravation of working on the river. Obesity, marital discord, windstorms, oil spills, and even windsurf weirdos were nothing compared to the torment of endangered salmon.

McDowell pointed to the radar screen and asked sarcastically if I could spot "the last sockeye" floating dead in the Snake.

Before I could think of a clever answer, he launched into an angry (and historically questionable) lecture. He said that the Idaho Department of Fish and Game decided in the 1960s to kill off all the sockeye by poisoning the central Idaho lakes where they spawn. He added that when dams on the Snake River were built in the sixties and seventies, no state or federal fish agencies attempted to protect the fish.

"They want to destroy our industry to save this fish that they used to kill," McDowell said. "How important are these salmon? How important are we? To change everything around for a few lousy fish don't seem like it is real smart."*

---

*Like a number of salmon myths I heard out on the river, McDowell's story about the poisoning of all the sockeye in central Idaho exploits a nugget of fact to tell a misleading and self-serving untruth. The real story is neither as appealing nor as appalling as McDowell's version. The Idaho Department of Fish and Game did poison three high-mountain lakes in the late 1950s and early 1960s. It did so with the intent of killing trash fish, thereby allowing the lakes to be stocked with rainbow trout, a game fish that officials hoped would attract tourists to Idaho. At the time of the poisonings, state fish counts showed no sockeye population in any of the three lakes. Later investigation found that the lakes might have been spawning territory for as much as a quarter of Idaho's sockeye population. The fish and game department, however, never poisoned and never considered poisoning two lakes where fish counters had located healthy populations of sockeye. Dexter Pitman, manager of Idaho's salmon and steelhead program, said the story of the poisoning is told by river users "to justify not taking any action to protect the fish and to belittle the sanity of fish biologists."

When I bailed out of eastern Washington in 1974 for graduate school on the East Coast, users of the engineered river had not yet begun to whine. All was well in the slackwater empire. Failure in Vietnam (where my brother, James Arno Harden, was killed in a helicopter crash) and the squalor of Watergate may have rattled the nation's faith in itself. But in eastern Washington we still believed in the purifying power of "total use for greater wealth." Progress was still conquest over nature, and the highest form of conquest was still pouring concrete into the Columbia. The chairman of the committee on ecology in the Washington State legislature, a man born and raised in the Columbia Basin, announced in 1974 that "we must not tie up needed developments with needless red tape."

Grand Coulee Dam was tripling its electricity output with the addition of six new turbines, each of which was capable of ingesting the equivalent of a Colorado River. A landmark treaty was signed with Canada that, in effect, turned the Columbia inside out. Before the treaty, the river spent most of its power in the summer. The dry-season flow pattern—an oddity among big North American rivers—was caused by the peculiarities of the upper Columbia Basin, which drains mountain snowpack and ice fields. The summer melt had, for more than ten thousand years, made the river a reliable salmon highway from April to September. But international law and three new dams north of the border conspired to hoard much of the Columbia in reservoirs until winter, when consumers most wanted its electricity.

Farther south, the Snake River was being outfitted with its own network of dams, locks, and reservoirs so it could give a seaport to Idaho, a state that lies mostly in the mountain time zone.

Hanford was busier then ever churning out plutonium for the cold war. A Hanford scientist confidently told a local congressman that the secret federal reservation would one day open up to the business community as the world's first "nuclear power park." It would attract, he said, a lucrative cluster of breeder reactors to produce both weapons-grade fuel and electricity. It would also attract companies that reprocessed spent reactor fuel and stored toxic waste. The congressman thought it was a fine idea and so did the newspaper that reported it.

In the Columbia River itself, wild salmon were already in dangerous decline. But fishermen did not blame the instruments of greater wealth: dams, locks, irrigation diversions, clear-cut logging around salmon habitat, or the wholesale transformation of the Columbia into a stair-step lake. They blamed Indians.

A federal judge set off the closest thing to civil war that the Pacific Northwest has known when he ordered in 1974 that, based on treaty rights and historical practice, Indians had a right to "half the catch." Whites in Washington State shot Indians and cut their nets; state and local police raided and tear-gassed an Indian fishing camp. Fishermen and police refused for years to obey the judge's order. The judge was burned in effigy, accused of having an Indian lover, and threatened with death.

Farmers around my hometown, with wheat prices at record highs, were pressing to expand their acreage and pad their profits. They were furious when state and federal water officials tried to enforce regulations limiting the use of unlicensed wells for irrigation. Moses Lake farmers derided worries that groundwater might run out, arguing that they would never accept federal infringement on their property rights. "We don't have to tolerate people in the government who use their position to strip people of their very means of making a living," one irrigator said. He added that the feds could control the water under his farm only if they paid him rent for keeping it there.

Odd as it may seem growing up in a place that owed its very existence to federal money, I cannot recall anyone ever saying anything good about the government. In our house, my father explained that the federal government was run by "a bunch of thieves. They ought to take those bastards outside and shoot them." This was not just my father's opinion; it was a sacred incantation in irrigation country.

We were federal-dependent and federal-hating (except for the sainted memory of the great rainmaker FDR, and our appreciation of the pork-barrel artistry of Magnuson and Jackson) and we never gave

46   it a second thought. As I think back on those years, there was an even higher level of paradox—and delusion. However much we resented the federal government, we never seriously challenged what it was doing, to the Columbia River, at Hanford, or anywhere. Although we never talked about it, never heard about it at school, and never acknowledged it even to ourselves, the price we paid to prosper in the engineered West was powerlessness.

Faceless experts from the Bureau of Reclamation, the Army Corps of Engineers, the Atomic Energy Commission, and the Department of Energy did what they wanted and kept as many secrets as they wished. They operated without local challenge or local understanding. All they had to do, in return, was give us regular work.

The way we lived, the way working people lived across the engineered West, has been described as the "managed oasis life." In *Rivers of Empire*, historian Donald Worster writes that "their conformity, their lack of self-confidence, and their thirst outweigh any resentment they may feel toward those in power. . . . The masses will, in gratitude, agree to make no trouble. . . . The rewards of acquiescence are so high."

We acquiesced to a power elite of a kind that ruled everywhere in the engineered West. Its structure was so consistent and so ubiquitous that western historians called it the "Iron Triangle." It was a club with membership limited to growers (and other major users of power and water), federal bureaucrats, and senior politicians.

In the Columbia Basin, the Iron Triangle worked like this: Technocrats from the Bureau of Reclamation and the Army Corps of Engineers spent large amounts of federal money to build and maintain dams, locks, and irrigation canals that subsidized a network of moneyed interests. Those interests included utilities, aluminum manufacturers, shipping companies, food processors, and irrigators. Grateful growers and industry executives contributed generously to the campaigns of Jackson, Magnuson, Representative Tom Foley, and other politicians, who in turn appropriated money to make sure that technocrats continued to deliver cheap power and cheap water to the tight circle of well-heeled contributors.

One wrinkle in the Iron Triangle peculiar to the Columbia Basin was Hanford, the plutonium plantation on the banks of the Columbia. Unlike the dams and the irrigation schemes, Hanford was not sold to the public as a scheme to benefit the West. It was a bulwark against communism, too important to national security to be understood, doubted, or even discussed. It employed many thousands of people and paid them well. If we talked about Hanford at all, we said we were lucky to have it.

When I came home to follow the river, the managed oasis life was going to hell. The cappuccino cognoscenti on the West Side of the Cascades were making jokes about the Depression-era mentality that had served my family so well, the mentality that defined dependence as self-reliance, passivity as patriotism, and not-knowing as wisdom.

"The East Side is populated by a generation of people who believe there is a free lunch. Why are we subsidizing them and their myths about individualism? I tell these intolerant people that you are welcome to play cowboy, but you don't get to do it on the government dime.

"These people in rural areas have hung out for forty years in the Eisenhower administration and now they are going to have to pay. In the end, it won't make any difference what they do. Time and demographics are on the side of environmentalists, if not the environment. Most people who believed the world is flat didn't change their minds. They died."

So said Andy Kerr, an environmental activist in Portland who was often quoted in the West Side newspapers as an oracle of the New West. Thrilled by the sound of his own voice, Kerr told me that westerners had to wake up to the fact that they had outgrown cowboy stories.

The most misleading of those stories, demographically speaking, was about where most westerners actually live. Odd as it may seem, urban density is the rule, not the exception, in the wide-open spaces of the West. Deserts, badlands, mountains, huge tracts of federal property, and chronic water shortages (which climate change seems certain to make worse) combine to render much of the region unlivable. As such, the West has remained the most rural part of the United States

48   in terms of land use while becoming the most densely urban in terms
of where people actually live. By 2005, ten of the country's fifteen most
densely populated metro areas were in the West, where people moved
to newly developed land at twice the per-acre density of any other part
of the country. The urbanized area in and around Los Angeles had
become the most tightly packed place in the continental United States,
according to the Census Bureau. Its density was 25 percent higher than
that of New York, twice that of Washington, D.C., and four times that
of Atlanta, as measured by residents per square mile of urban land.

The history of this New West was being written not by resource-
sucking East Side whiners, Kerr told me, but by winners, people like
himself and other highly educated, well-heeled urban city folk.

The behemoths of Northwest capitalism, Microsoft and Boeing,
Amazon and Starbucks, Nike and Costco, did not make money by
clear-cutting forests or damming rivers. Their economy was made
of high technology, manufacturing, and aggressive international
marketing. Washington State led the nation in per capita income from
foreign trade. The West Side was an archetype of what Bill Clinton said
the entire country should become, "a high-growth, high-wage, smart-
work society." Managers in Seattle and Portland had a bottom-line
stake in recruiting the best young minds in the country and keeping
them happy in the Northwest. Environmentalism, for them, combined
good public relations with sound employment policy.

Around my hometown, the imported Chinese pheasants had mostly
disappeared, the fishing had gone bad, and the sugar-beet factory had
exploded and closed down. The Easter egg hunt was a fading memory.

The Columbia itself, despite its huge flow and pristine headwaters,
was becoming polluted. A joint Washington-Oregon environmental
report described dangerous levels of toxic chemicals in the river,
mostly from pulp mills. The presence of dioxin and other industrial
poisons periodically rose to worrisome levels in river trout and walleye,
prompting state warnings that fishermen should not eat more than
twenty fish meals a month. Biologists from the University of Washington told Congress that "watersheds and rivers of the Pacific North-

west are presently moving toward a level of biotic impoverishment that will be in large part irreversible."

American Rivers, a Washington-based environmental group that monitors rivers across North America, had placed the Columbia at the top of its annual list of the country's ten most-endangered rivers.

Shortly after coming home to Moses Lake, I drank coffee in a pancake house with an irrigation farmer who insisted that *he* was an endangered salmon. The farmer was Bernie Erickson, a big-boned wheat grower who flew his own airplane. The salmon metaphor swam unexpectedly to the surface as Erickson toyed with a packet of Sweet 'n Low and struggled to convince me that something was going terribly wrong in the West.

The feds forgot, he said, that "all wealth comes from the earth." He said irrigation farmers, like salmon, die without cheap water, adding that farmers also need subsidized electricity to pump the water and crop subsidies to guarantee profits for whatever they grow. He blamed environmentalists for tricking urban Americans into seeing salmon as "sacred" while viewing farmers as "greedy people who are raping the earth."

Along the Columbia, I heard countless variations on Bernie Erickson's theme of the resource-using westerner as endangered species. Utility executives and farm wives, dam operators and river dredgers complained of a conspiracy to destroy the "working river," ruin their livelihoods, and sabotage what was good and godly about life in the West. Most of these people sounded furious and seemed afraid. Everywhere they looked they saw the dark hand of the federal government and the arrogant, interfering ways of high-salaried city people. They believed the urban majority was trying to turn the Columbia River—along with the forests, mountains, and deserts of the entire West—into a theme park where the only jobs would be menial and minimum wage.

2

A FENCE OF LIGHTS took shape in the downstream river. McDowell slowed the tow from eight to two miles an hour and eased it across the face of Lower Granite Dam, the first of the four lock-equipped federal dams on the lower Snake. Since it was late at night, with temperatures across the Pacific Northwest neither cold enough for heat nor warm enough for air conditioning, the dam's turbines were not sucking in the river to make electricity. Nor was water spilling over the dam, it being late summer, long past the spring freshet.

With the river turned off until morning, McDowell had no current to fight as he steered toward the right bank and gingerly poked the tow's snout into the lock. We moved at the speed of a slow walk, with the deckhand, Dave Faulkner, out on the bow and on the radio, talking McDowell in. The tow touched the wall of the lock with a gentle bump that was imperceptible up in the wheelhouse.

"You go slow, but you go slow for a reason," McDowell whispered.

His eyes patrolled up and down, scouring the water around the tow, hunting for logs that might be drifting into the lock. In the Snake River, locks are just two feet wider than the tows they hoist up and down. In such a narrow elevator, an overlooked log can disastrously compromise two hundred yards of roped-together barges. It happened in this lock three months earlier. A Tidewater Barge Lines tow carrying wood chips (and not piloted by McDowell) was descending in the lock when a log got wedged between it and a concrete wall. Several thousand tons of wood chips spilled, one barge overturned, and the tow remained stuck in the lock for more than a week, closing down the Snake River for navigation.

We did not get stuck. Safely below the dam, the tow crept back out to mid-river. It was midnight, the end of McDowell's shift. He repaired to the galley for a supper of fried eggs, hash browns, leg of lamb, and ice cream.

A few days before my barge journey, a scheme surfaced in Idaho to rescue endangered Snake River salmon without any sacrifice from bargers, utilities, irrigators, or port towns. The plan called for the construction of a flexible Kevlar fish tube, eight feet in diameter and 350 miles long, that would stretch the length of the Columbia-Snake System. Skirting dams, predators, fishermen, and slow-moving reservoirs, it would whisk baby salmon to the sea in water pumped at the velocity of the undammed rivers. The bottom of some sections of the flex tube would be covered with an indoor-outdoor carpet so that fish, tired from their commute, could feed and sleep. The plan was dreamed up at the federal Idaho National Engineering Laboratory, a facility best known for its work with nuclear weapons. The onetime cost of the tube was estimated at between $1 billion and $1.4 billion—cheap in comparison to what was likely to be spent on dam removal or the drawdown. Best of all, the nation's taxpayers, not local river users, would foot the bill.

The flex tube plan did not go far. Derided in regional newspaper headlines as a "fish waterslide," the plan provoked contemptuous giggles across much of the Northwest. It seemed a throwback to the discredited dam-building era, when technology was sacred and federal engineers ruled the West. There were no giggles, however, in Lewiston, Idaho, the Snake River town where I boarded the barge.

Lewiston, population twenty-eight thousand, did not have a major airport. It was not on an interstate. The town squatted in the bottom of a famously steep and treacherous rimrock canyon. Truckers routinely blew out their brakes while descending the Lewiston Hill Grade, often losing their loads and occasionally their lives. Nor was safe arrival in

52 Lewiston any particular thrill. The town stank from the nearby Potlatch paper mill. Along with its smelly isolation, Lewiston had a bitter history of greatness lost. It was named the first capital of Idaho Territory in 1863. A year later, after Idaho legislators had had a chance to think the matter through, the decision was revoked and the capital was moved south to Boise. Lewistonians, at the time, refused to lose gracefully. They issued a writ to arrest the governor, if he dared leave town with the territorial seal. He managed to get away, without the seal, in a skiff on the Snake. Residents of Lewiston sent resolutions to Congress demanding "relief from the evils and embarrassments" of losing the capital. They surrendered the Idaho seal only at gunpoint, when a detachment of U.S. soldiers burst into Lewiston, pushed through a phalanx of town sheriffs, and broke open a safe.

The town's second stab at greatness—and economic good times—dated to 1975, when Lower Granite Dam was finished. The dam was the final piece in the federally built and federally paid-for Columbia-Snake River System. It allowed Lewiston to advertise itself to the world as "Idaho's only seaport, the most inland and eastern port in the Northwest." With slackwater came barges and growth—new factories, more people, and higher real-estate prices.

For Lewistonians, the prospect of dam removal or of a river drawdown raised the hateful possibility that history could repeat itself. A window to prosperity, briefly opened, could again be slammed shut. Town boosters did everything in their power to fight back, including grasping at exotic technological fixes such as a Kevlar tube to the sea.

"Now that flex tube is a real interesting theory," F. Ron McMurray, manager of the Port of Lewiston, told me on the afternoon before I got on the barge. Along with the bankers, real-estate agents, store owners, and manufacturers of Lewiston, McMurray predicted disaster if dam removal or the drawdown went ahead.

"There will be a tremendous rippling effect," McMurray said. "There will be no more growth in the tax base. No more new homes. We just got Wal-Mart. We will have to raise our kids to be fishing guides."

McMurray believed Lewiston's real enemies lurked in cities on the West Side of the Cascades.

"There is a philosophy over there among those people, 'Let's lock up Idaho so we can play in the mountains and fish in the rivers. We can pickle it, and then go back to Seattle to work.' Now, why should someone in Seattle or Portland affect the way I make a living? Why should someone from Seattle or Portland tell us what we should do and when we should do it?"

The Port of Lewiston and the city's Chamber of Commerce had joined together in a regional river-users group that staged marches and placed full-page advertisements in newspapers to denounce and discredit salmon-driven changes in the river system. The group's most successful strategy sidestepped the clash between endangered fish and private profits. Instead, it pitted fish species against fish species. Saving migratory salmon, the group said, would wipe out resident river fish, such as bass, which prospered in slackwater. One drawdown experiment killed thousands of bass and other resident fish in the lower Snake. A full-page ad placed in Northwest newspapers by the group showed dead fish lying in the mud. It said, "Some people think drawdowns save fish. Some fish disagree."

McMurray and several Lewiston boosters told me that giving slackwater to Lewiston and then stealing it away would betray everything that America stood for.

"This will destroy the integrity of one of the finest farm-to-market roads in the country. What is our debt to all the businesses who relocated to this area because of slackwater?" McMurray asked me.

"The best time we have had in our history is now. You can't go back in time. We can't allow people to take the pioneer spirit away from Idaho."

I felt right at home talking to McMurray. Like the people I grew up with in irrigation country around Moses Lake, he had a knack for wrapping self-interest in the holy garments of western myth. To deny slackwater to Lewiston would be to tarnish the West's proud legacy of rugged individualism, self-starting courage, and, yes, the pioneer spirit. McMurray effortlessly fuzzed over the fact that the sons of the pioneers in Lewiston owed their slackwater prosperity to a windfall gift from the American taxpayer.

The federal government paid more than $600 million to build dams and locks on the Snake. It spent billions to modify the Columbia for shipping. Northwest grain shippers (whose freight amounts to 80 percent of barge traffic on the Snake), port authorities, and barge companies shouldered none of the construction costs, and they paid less than a quarter of the system's annual operating and maintenance costs. River users had been extraordinarily effective in lobbying Northwest members of Congress to kill proposals that would shift the operating costs of the river system from taxpayers to themselves. A Clinton-era proposal to triple the inland-waterways fuel tax lasted just three days before the river lobby sank it.

Like the bloated Snake River itself, western individualism was reengineered for economic utility in Lewiston, Idaho. It glommed on to federal handouts, defined them as inalienable rights, and fought—with dark warnings of economic chaos and invocations of the pioneer spirit—to defeat those who dared take those rights away.

My first night on the Snake proved bumpy, very bumpy. The *Defiance* shuffled its tow throughout the night. This meant jerking back and forth on the river and goosing the diesel engines beneath my bed, as the tugboat dropped off barges and took on others. When I emerged from my cabin at about 7 A.M., we were only thirty-seven miles downstream from where I had gone to bed.

None of this seemed to trouble McDowell, who had slept soundly for five hours and was back in the wheelhouse, full of the devil, when I climbed the stairs.

"I was wondering if you were ever going to get up," he said, asking if I had had my breakfast and explaining that he never eats breakfast. Just two big suppers, one at noon and one at midnight.

The Snake in the morning looked very much like the Snake at dusk: lazy dark water, puffy bald hills, no human beings. But there was a bit more life. A blue heron tippy-toed in the shoreline mud on the left bank. On the right bank, a herd of mules and horses stood splay-legged in shallows, sipping at the river. Overhead, a freight train rumbled across Lyon's Ferry Bridge. This was the first of more than twenty freight trains I saw along the Snake and Columbia. The tracks, laid before slackwater made river transport so cheap and safe, used to carry almost all the grain and other freight that now creeps west on barges. Rail could do it again, but transport would cost more. When I traveled on the river, it cost just nineteen cents a bushel to send wheat from Idaho to Portland by barge. By train, it cost at least a dime more per bushel. The fight over salmon-driven changes in river operations had a great deal to do with farmers and other users of federally subsidized river transport not wanting to pay that dime.

McDowell, in tour-guide expansiveness, pointed to what appeared to be a small lake, just beyond a gravel levee, on the right side of the river. Beneath the lake, he said, was the cave of "Marmes Man," who lived beside the Snake ten thousand years ago.

"I guess it is better off flooded," McDowell explained. "It keeps people out."

Among those kept out of the ancient rock shelter, which was flooded in 1969 after the completion of Lower Monumental Dam on the Snake, was Dr. Carl Gustafson, an associate professor of anthropology at Washington State University. He told me, after I got off the barge, that the Marmes Man rock shelter was the most important of several hundred archaeological sites flooded by dams on the lower Snake.

"We worked frantically in the winter before the flood, sometimes in 15-below-zero temperatures, to find as much as we could before the waters backed up," said Gustafson, who wrote his doctoral dissertation on Marmes Man. "It is the only site in eastern Washington where we have ten thousand years of cultural history stacked one above the other. It is the basis for understanding almost all the digs in eastern Washington. We managed to excavate only a quarter of the potential of the rock shelter before the flood chased us out."

The Marmes Man site showed archaeologists that Indians along the Snake, when they first appeared in the region about ten thousand years

56 ago, were primarily hunter-gatherers. They depended on big game, elk, pronghorn antelope, and mule deer. Then, about 4,500 years ago, fishing became more important.

The discovery of net sinkers and fish-pounding stones at the Marmes site provided convincing evidence that Indians shifted their diet and remade their culture to take advantage of the easy abundance of fish in the river. Hunting was relegated to the Indians' spare time, as salmon became the center of their existence. A sophisticated barter economy developed, with Indians netting more salmon than they could eat. They dried and pounded the fish so it could be traded for game or edible roots or kept through the winter.

Gustafson said the Marmes site, if not for the flood, might have answered many other questions. It could have, he said, explained annual Indian migration patterns and helped show how ice-age weather changes affected Indian and animal behavior. Arctic foxes were found in the rock shelter, a discovery Gustafson said suggests that eastern Washington, as recently as five thousand years ago, was far colder and wetter than it is now.

Archaeologists were permitted "no input" as to the timing of the Army Corps of Engineers' decision to flood the Marmes site, according to Gustafson. He said it took an appeal to the White House, and a personal order by President Lyndon B. Johnson, before the Corps agreed to build a levee around the site. It was supposed to keep the dig dry after the flood came. But the levee leaked and the rock shelter disappeared under the river.

To perk up his morning, McDowell found the "G. Gordon Liddy Show" on the radio and turned it up. Liddy chatted with callers about the industrial espionage applications of microwave technology, and congratulated his guest, a retired CIA operative, for "patriotic service to our country."

Liddy was a morning fixture in McDowell's wheelhouse. (He would have listened to Rush Limbaugh in the afternoon, but that was the skipper's sleeptime.) McDowell told me that Liddy is "a pretty interesting fella. You know that when he was a kid, he cooked a rat and ate it. He has a lot of humor on the show. He calls himself a 'master debater and cunning linguist.' He talks about guns a lot. A lot of people call him up asking what kind of gun they should buy to protect themselves from criminals."

Cheered by Liddy, McDowell teased me about the most exotic cargo that travels on the Columbia River—worn-out nuclear submarine reactors. The radioactive reactor cores, chopped out of scuttled navy subs, come from the Puget Sound Naval Shipyard, located in Bremerton, Washington, west of Seattle. The reactor cores are hauled up the Columbia for burial in a massive pit at the Hanford site. McDowell's tug, the *Defiance*, was scheduled to pick up one at the mouth of the Columbia, as soon as it had dropped off the peas, lentils, etc., in Portland.

Submarine reactors, which weigh about one-third as much as a barge full of wheat, are babied up the river by two tugs and escorted by a Navy torpedo retriever ship.*

"The only people who come down to the river to see the nuke barges are employees from Hanford and their families," McDowell said, turning his eyes from the river and winking at me. "The three-eyed dogs come out to bark and all the one-armed children wave."

Noon on the river meant lunch and another shift change. McDowell retreated for meat, potatoes, ice cream, and his afternoon snooze. The second pilot on the *Defiance*, Ernest Theriot, heaved into the wheelhouse. Wild-bearded, bald-headed, chain-smoking, wearing baby-blue sweatpants, and weighing in at well over three hundred pounds, "Big Ernie" Theriot groaned the springs in the skipper's chair.

A relative newcomer to the Snake and Columbia, Theriot had been barging on the river system for just four years, not enough time to commit it to memory. Setting up for his six hours in the wheelhouse,

---

*I asked the Department of the Navy for permission to ride on one of the tugs pushing a reactor core up the river for burial. Permission was "respectfully" denied on the obtuse grounds that the reactor shipments "represent less than one tenth of one percent of the commercial cargo that transits the navigational locks of the Columbia River" and "for this reason would not be representative of the much larger interests in the river."

58   he hauled out charts of the shipping channel and studied them as he steered. The river he knows best is the lower Mississippi.

"My wife calls me a coon-ass Cajun," Theriot said, in a soft southern drawl that hinted at a French accent. "I was born in a little place called Cut Off, Louisiana, in the bayou. I didn't speak English until I went to high school. My grandmother died not knowing a word of English. I been on tugs since 1967, on the Amazon and the Yukon, but mostly on the Mississippi."

I asked Theriot to compare the Columbia with the Mississippi.

"The big difference is that the Mississippi is pretty forgiving. If you screw up, you get stuck in the mud. Here, the rocks are pretty unforgiving, they can cut nasty holes, and the wind is so much worse, worse than any river I've ever seen," Theriot said. "There is an advantage to being on this river, though. If it is a little shallow over a sandbar, you can always call ahead to the dams and they will release enough water to cover up your problem."

I did not ask Theriot about salmon, but like every other pilot and deckhand on the river he was obsessed with the fish. The "real problem with salmon," he said, was not dams or slackwater, but "deep-sea gill-netters who cut their lines rather than get arrested by the Coast Guard. Their nets fall to the bottom of the sea full of salmon, and when the fish decompose, the nets float back up and catch more fish and then sink again. That is what is happening to the salmon."

I later bounced this off the Pacific Fisheries Management Council, a Portland-based federal agency that manages offshore fishing in the Northwest. Jim Coon, the agency's salmon staff officer, said Theriot's theory was "a little bit of fact and a lot of embellishment and fiction." He said Japan and other Asian countries had, indeed, used thirty-mile-long monofilament driftnets to catch salmon. But he said the nets were laid far out in the Pacific, outside of the range of most Pacific Northwest salmon. He said the practice ended in 1992, adding that there was no evidence that abandoned nets were endlessly killing salmon. Coon said local utility companies and Northwest politicians have used the driftnet issue as a red herring to divert attention from dams, and to find a "yellow menace" scapegoat.

Muttering about foreigners, Theriot made a U-turn in the Snake and eased the tow against the river's right bank at a place called Sheffler's Elevator. The maneuver, roughly the equivalent of parallel parking in a vehicle that is longer than a city block, was even harder than it looked—water trapped between the riverbank and an incoming tow behaves like a rubber cushion, bouncing the boat back out in the river. "The harder you push, the harder it pushes back," Theriot said, creeping up on the riverbank. Picking up another grain barge brought our total weight to about sixteen thousand tons, the equivalent of a freight train with more than one hundred and sixty boxcars.

Theriot's deft bit of steering seemed to chase away brooding thoughts about fish. He lit up one of his off-brand cigarettes. So I could breathe, he thoughtfully opened up a couple of windows in the wheelhouse. The sweet sawmill smell of freshly cut wood, from a barge heaped with wood chips, drifted in through the open windows.

There are worse ways to while away a cloudless September afternoon than sitting in slanting sunshine forty-two feet above the Snake River. Below us, filling the foreground to the middle distance, the tow spread out as an immensity of green-painted steel (green being the color of Tidewater barges). Like dribbles of gold, spilled wheat burnished some of the barges. It was homey up in the wheelhouse, where standard household light switches turned on many of the motors and pumps in the tug and where, amid the radar screens and the radios, there was a fly swatter, a rack of paper towels, a bottle of Windex, and a battered guitar case.

McDowell emerged from his afternoon nap promptly at six to retake command. Theriot did not rush off to supper, though. He got out his guitar and began to sing in French. His soft, lilting voice was a marvel, coming as it did from a bearded man the size of a sumo wrestler. Theriot sang about a bayou hunter who kills a deer and an alligator with the same bullet.

So began a hootenanny in the wheelhouse, with McDowell and Theriot trading back and forth between steering the tow and strumming the guitar. While Theriot stuck with French bayou songs, McDowell favored ironic country songs. "I don't care if it rains or freezes, long as I

60   have my plastic Jesus." The skipper also played and sang a number that he had written on the river when he turned forty.

> *Ya gotta stop living, if you wanna survive.*
> *Ya gotta stop life to reach sixty-five.*
> *No more beer and pizza pie.*
> *No more drinkin' and gettin' high.*

After an hour of song, Theriot descended to the galley for two plates of beef Stroganoff, two slices of buttered bread, and a heaping bowl of chocolate / vanilla / strawberry ice cream. Up in the wheelhouse, with the sun beginning to set on the river and the guitar back in its case, McDowell directed my attention to the depravity of Native Americans, particularly the ones who live along the Columbia and fish for salmon.

I learned that Indians are always drunk and squirreling around in the river at night in skiffs without running lights, and that, "if you want to know the God's truth," the real problem of endangered salmon is that Indians are usually too drunk to tend their nets, which stink of rotten, uncollected salmon. Particularly galling to McDowell was the power of the Indians in federal courts and the sympathy they get in the West Side press. Newspapers and local TV news often report on disappearing salmon, usually quoting an Indian standing by the Columbia, looking heartbroken.

McDowell was sick and tired, he said, of feeling guilty about Indians and their "poor endangered fish." He said they had trashed their reservations with rusty washing machines and junk cars, and, wherever they congregated along the river, they left behind beer cans.

"They are always giving me this poor-Indian, evil-white-man stuff. You don't see them out on the river very often unless they are drinking beer. They say, 'White man gave me this beer.' I say, 'Don't drink it! Get a job.'"

When I later spoke to Native Americans who fish in the Columbia, they described white men in barges as racists. They claimed barges deliberately steer into Indian gill nets and occasionally try to hit Indian fishing boats. Animosity lingered from the death of three Indian fishermen, who were killed in 1978 when their fishing boat collided with a barge.

"A lot of barge operators feel that Indians should not be out there on the river. These white men feel that since Celilo Falls [the prime Indian fishing site on the mid-Columbia] was flooded by dams, the Native Americans should go do something else. But we eat fish and we always will," Johnny Jackson, a chief of the Klickitat tribe, told me. "Even during the day, when the barge men can clearly see the nets, they won't move to get out of the way and sometimes they go right for them. It is more or less an act of prejudice."

Up ahead in the darkening river, the approaching locks of Ice Harbor Dam, the last dam on the lower Snake, forced McDowell back to work. The tow, as Theriot had configured it, was too wide to get through the locks. McDowell had to take it apart. He steered to the right bank and began backing and filling as his deckhand wrestled cable out on the tow.

The confluence of the Snake and the Columbia lay just beyond Ice Harbor Dam. It was going to take McDowell the better part of three hours to remake the tow so we could fit through the lock. We would not reach the Columbia until about three in the morning. After fifteen hours in the wheelhouse, I decided to call it a night. As I descended the steps of the wheelhouse, McDowell called out after me, "I knew you would get bored."

While I slept we cruised out into the confluence, where the warmish muddy waters of the Snake disappear in the cold, bluish clarity of the Columbia.

Even dammed up, the Columbia lacks the muddy sluggishness, the lazy romance of the Mississippi. Few trees grow near it in eastern Washington. Not many people live beside it. The Columbia has been described as "not a cozy river, not the kind a man can feel belongs to him." The river is an anomaly in a dry country, an ill-tempered ribbon of deep, dangerous water, a resource that is at once fundamental to and distant from the lives that depend on it. As much as it intoxicates engineers, it intimidates those who happen to be born near it.

It began intimidating me when I was eight years old and living for a summer with my father, mother, and little sister in a one-room trailer just a couple hundred feet from its western bank.

The place was called Vantage, an odd name for a town wedged down in the bottom of a canyon that the river had been digging for the better part of eleven million years. Most of the six hundred people in Vantage were construction workers like my father. They worked a few miles downstream, building Wanapum Dam.

There was no shade in the trailer park and no grass. It was hot and dusty and the wind blew nearly all the time, filling my nose and ears with dirt. The wind kicked up terribly at night, whistling and slamming doors. It rocked but never quite managed to topple the camping trailer that my father had bought from a neighbor for four hundred dollars. I had to sleep with my sister in that rig, sharing a Formica kitchen table that after dinner was converted into a bed. To bathe or use a toilet, we walked across the court to a filling station.

We had a normal house in Moses Lake, thirty-five miles east of the river. But my father, who was rotating between day, swing, and graveyard shifts at the dam, was weary of driving back and forth. So when school let out for the summer, my mother packed up my sister and me, and we all camped out by the river. My parents talked sometimes in the evenings about what would happen to the river when the dam was finished. My father said the Columbia would rise up and the town where we lived would disappear underwater.

The idea of a flood—a flood that everyone knew was coming, a flood that would wipe out a place where I personally had slept—thrilled my dirt-nosed, highly suggestible self. I had three imaginary friends in the years before the summer by the river. They were Pops and Pete, and my best friend was Barnes. But as a graduate of the third grade, I was beginning to feel sheepish about them. An honest-to-God flood was something else. It was something you could brag about at school. Since my father was helping to cause it, I could take a measure of credit.

My father fell into the river that summer of 1960, before the dam was finished, before the reach of river behind the dam was made into slackwater. It was late July and the temperature was above 100 degrees. He was perched on a pipe above the river, welding shut a seam, wearing his black hood and leathers, when an overhead crane hit a support cable holding up the pipe. He tumbled sixteen feet into water behind a cofferdam. A rescue boat fished him out within minutes, and he was unhurt. But when I asked him about that fall thirty-four years later, when he was eighty-two, he shuddered to recall how cold a river could be in the desert.

I was not allowed that summer to go near the Columbia. It was too swift, too dimpled with eddies and sinkholes, too cold for a boy. I could only play pictures in my mind of the coming flood, of our trailer vanishing underwater, and of my terrified father, blindfolded by his welding helmet, sweaty in his leathers, somersaulting into ice water.

At the confluence of the Snake and the Columbia, a Tidewater tow sprang a leak. It happened one week after the night I left McDowell in the wheelhouse and slept my way out of the Snake and into the Columbia. An oil barge spilled 3,295 gallons of diesel fuel. As environmental disasters go, it was small potatoes. Much of the diesel was quickly captured by floating booms and sucked up by vacuum skimmers—equipment that Tidewater Barge Lines kept near the river for emergencies. But, as always happens with oil leaks in a river, some got away. Diesel fuel greased the upstream side of a point of land that juts down into the confluence.

I later found my way back to this tiny peninsula, partly because I wanted to stick my fingers in the diesel-slickened mud, but mostly because this finger of land was the precise place where white men first encountered the interior reaches of the Columbia River.

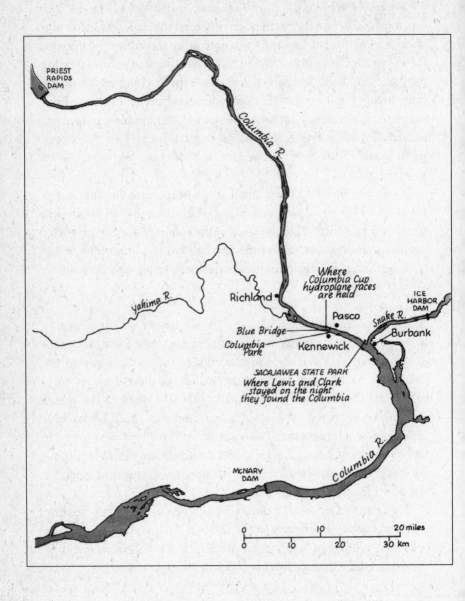

PRIEST RAPIDS DAM

Columbia R.

Yakima R.

Richland

Where Columbia Cup hydroplane races are held

Pasco

ICE HARBOR DAM

Snake R.

Blue Bridge

Columbia Park

Kennewick

Burbank

SACAJAWEA STATE PARK
Where Lewis and Clark stayed on the night they found the Columbia

McNARY DAM

Columbia R.

0   10   20 miles

0   10   20   30 km

 *Machine River*

*We took a pristine river and we turned it into a working
river—a machine. And it is a damn fine machine.*

—AL WRIGHT
**Pacific Northwest Utilities
Conference Committee**

To chart the transformation of the river into a damn fine
machine, you cannot ride in a barge and eat ice cream. You have
to get out and take two soundings: The first, at the confluence of the
Snake and the Columbia in the fall of 1805, when non-Indians discovered and mapped the meeting of the Snake and Columbia. The second,
in the same stretch of water, 182 years later, during the running of the
Water Follies Columbia Cup Unlimited Hydroplane Race.

Captains Meriwether Lewis and William Clark were paddling
dugout cottonwood canoes down the Snake when their party sighted
the Columbia. The explorers had been anticipating such a river since
starting west from St. Louis eighteen months earlier. Their orders from
President Thomas Jefferson, whose Louisiana Purchase of 1803 had
doubled the size of the United States, told them to explore western
rivers that offered "the most direct & practicable water communication
across this continent." The key to their expedition was the Columbia,
even though its existence was barely more than a rumor.

Thirteen years earlier, Captain Robert Gray, a Boston trader looking
for furs to take to China, noticed an outlet of freshwater as he sailed
north along the Pacific Coast. He threaded his ship, the *Columbia Rediviva*, through a narrow channel of breakers and sailed inland for fifteen
miles. Greeted by what he described as "vast numbers of natives," he
traded copper and cloth for one hundred and fifty sea otter pelts, took

66   on board fresh water, named the river after his ship, and took his leave for China.

The river upon which Gray so briefly did business had been deduced, gossiped about, and mythologized for more than a century and a half. At its mythical maximum, it could have been the Northwest Passage, a navigable waterway across western North America, a link between the Great Lakes and the Pacific, a route that explorers had been looking for since Columbus. At its cartographic minimum, it was probably the principal stream draining the mountains of the Northwest.

What was beyond speculation was that Gray had stumbled upon—and established an American claim to—an exceptionally large and important river. Also beyond speculation, as the United States jockeyed with Great Britain in the early nineteenth century for control of the Pacific Northwest, was the urgent need to expand on Gray's discovery and beat the British to the interior of the river. Soon after Gray left for China, the British began poking around in the lower Columbia. But, as of the fall of 1805, when the Lewis and Clark expedition was approaching it from the east, no white man (at least, no white man who kept notes) had been farther inland than the Cascade Mountains.

Both Lewis and Clark were experienced river men not given to overstatement. They had explored and mapped many of America's major rivers. But after encountering the Columbia, they began scratching adjectives into their journals such as "inconceivable" and "incrediable" and "horrid." For the Columbia River, alone among the rivers of the West, they reserved the word "great."

The superlatives, however, did not begin to flow on first encounter with the big river. Lewis and Clark did not even celebrate, in their journals, finding it. Nor did they record any patriotic pride in claiming the Columbia for the United States. It may have been dreary scenery that put them off.

The Columbia meets the Snake in a desolate plain where the wind blows sand in your face and the sun's glare off the water sears your eyes. Clark described it as "open country where the eye has no rest." Another explorer, more than half a century later, described the confluence of the Snake and Columbia as "one of the most uncomfortable, abominable places in America . . . a place of winking, blinking, and tornment." After a full day of making observations at the point where the rivers meet, Lewis wrote, "there is on this plain no tree, and scarcely any shrubs, except a few willow-bushes; even of smaller plants there is not much more than the prickly-pear, which is in great abundance, and is even more thorny and troublesome than any we have yet seen."

Besides squinting into the sun and picking stickers out of their britches, the expedition, on its first day at the confluence, had also to make nice with a large number of Indians who camped and traded on the point of land that lies at the junction. That point, for hundreds of years prior to the arrival of the white explorers, had been one of the major Indian marketplaces in the Northwest. The Indians who lived around the river offered a portable, nutritious, long-shelf-life commodity that tribes from the coast, the Rocky Mountains, and the Great Plains would travel hundreds of miles to trade for. Dried salmon. At the confluence, it was exchanged for horses, elk meat, buffalo robes, smoked sea fish, seashells, blankets, obsidian, jadeite, roots, seeds, baskets, and slaves. The slaves typically were captured members of small nomadic Indian bands that roamed the Great Basin to the south. They were sold by Plains tribes to coastal tribes, with the river Indians usually acting as middlemen.

The mid-Columbia River tribes, among them the Yakima, Walla Walla, Wanapum, Umatilla, John Day, and Wayampam, had no reason, as of 1805, to fear or distrust white explorers. They probably had never seen any. Distance and the Cascades Mountains had insulated them from the white fur trappers who began exploring the Pacific Coast as early as 1775, and whose impact on coastal Indians was catastrophic. By the time Lewis and Clark arrived at the confluence, epidemics of smallpox had reduced the Indian population on the coast by half. It would not take long before disease was everywhere on the river. By the mid-1830s, an imported fever, probably malaria, had killed up to 90 percent of the Indian population on the lower Columbia, in the Willamette Valley in Oregon, and south to the Central Valley of California. It took until the mid-1840s for infections to sweep across the entire Columbia Basin. Missionaries and white settlers introduced scarlet fever, whooping cough, and measles to Indians who had no resistance and who died in droves. The mass death of the Indians was understood by many white settlers to be God's will, a providential clearing of the best farmland for Christian settlement.

Not far from the confluence of the Snake and Columbia, at the Walla Walla mission, Indian rage over a measles epidemic triggered the single most important massacre of white people in Northwest history. A band of Cayuses attacked the mission run by Marcus Whitman, killed him, his wife, and eleven other whites, and kidnapped fifty others. The massacre occasioned white revenge, U.S. Army occupation, and, within thirty years, the confinement of most Indians to reservations. "The history of Indian-white relations in the Columbia Plateau," according to University of Washington anthropologist Eugene S. Hunn, "is first and foremost a history of the ravages of disease."

But on October 16, 1805, when the Lewis and Clark expedition reached the confluence, the mid-Columbia Indians had not yet begun to connect white people with death. They were curious, friendly, and eager to trade.

"We had scarcely fixed the camp and got the fires prepared, when a chief came from the Indian camp about a quarter of a mile up the Columbia, at the head of nearly 200 men," Lewis wrote on the evening after the expedition pitched its first camp at the confluence. "They formed a regular procession, keeping time to the noise, rather the music of their drums, which they accompanied with their voices. As they advanced they formed a semicircle around us, and continued singing for some time. We then smoked with them all and communicated, as well as we could by signs, our friendly intentions toward all nations, and our joy at finding ourselves surrounded by our children."

The expedition presented three chiefs from the Indian delegation with three medals, a shirt, and two handkerchiefs. In return they got seven dogs, a few fish, and twenty pounds of dried fatty horse meat. The day after they sighted the Columbia and traded with the locals, the explorers had their first chance to examine the big river. They had lucked upon the confluence at the height of the fall run of spawning coho salmon. It astonished both Lewis and Clark.

"The number of dead Salmon on the Shores & floating in the river is incredible to say—and at this Season [the Indians] have only to collect the fish Split them open and dry them on their Scaffolds," Clark wrote, after a day trip up the Columbia in a canoe. "This river is remarkably Clear and Crouded with Salmon in maney places, I observe in assending great numbers of Salmon dead on the Shores, floating on the water and in the Bottoms which can be seen at the debth of 20 feet."

As they moved downstream, the explorers found salmon everywhere, leaping up rapids and waterfalls, spawning in gravel shallows, rotting on the shore, drying by the tens of thousands on scaffolds in Indian fishing camps. In just one camp, Clark counted 107 bundles of dried salmon that he estimated weighed ten thousand pounds. Lewis noted that "the multitudes of this fish are almost inconceivable." The explorers quickly got sick of salmon, and varied their diet whenever possible by eating dog. At least six members of the expedition kept journals, and each of them seemed frustrated in their inability to describe adequately the spectacle of "emence quantities" of salmon "jumping verry thick."

The numbers of dead salmon in the river puzzled and slightly alarmed Lewis and Clark. "The cause of the emence numbers of dead salmon I can't account for," Clark wrote. "The fish being out of season and dieing in great numbers in the river, we did not think proper to use them." The explorers did not know that most Pacific salmon, unlike their Atlantic cousins, die after spawning.

The expedition had discovered the world's greatest salmon highway, a commuting route for incomparable numbers of chinook, coho, and steelhead. There were nearly three times as many salmon swimming up the Columbia in 1805 as there were people living in the United States (about sixteen million salmon, about six million people). The fifty thousand Indians who lived along the Columbia before white settlement are estimated to have harvested up to forty-two million pounds of

70 salmon a year from the river. That amounts to a stupefying 2.3 pounds of fish per day per person. The historical Indian catch, however, did nothing to threaten the vigor or sustainability of salmon runs.

Besides being awed by the abundance of its fish, Lewis and Clark were jolted by the Columbia's power. Crossing the Rockies on their journey west, they had become accustomed to swift mountain rivers and chancy rapids. The Columbia was not merely a change in magnitude, it was a change in kind. The big river's rapids and waterfalls showed off the deep churning violence of more water falling more swiftly than any river in North America. The Mississippi, in its seven-hundred-mile journey from St. Louis to the Gulf of Mexico, drops just a hundred feet. The Columbia, in its four-hundred-mile journey across Washington State, falls more than a thousand feet. It was the steepest drop per mile of any major American river. Industrial-strength menace slashed and boiled through jagged black volcanic rock.

Lewis, as he traveled along the Columbia, observed that the Columbia seemed strangely misshapen. He saw whole giant trees poking up amid the worst of the river's rapids. "Certain it is that those large pine trees never grew in that position," he wrote, guessing that the path of the Columbia had frequently been altered by landslides. What he could not have imagined was the degree of violence that cut a pathway for the modern river and sculpted the moonish landscape around it.

The basin that gave birth to the Columbia was formed by North America's two largest floods, one of molten rock, the other of gravel-bearing ice water. The first flood, occurring in stages about thirteen million years ago, was an outpouring of molten lava from north-south fissures in the earth along the present-day border of Washington and Oregon. The great basalt floods, which came in wave after wave for four million years, continued until they had covered most of what is now eastern Washington and northeastern Oregon with a blanket of rock up to five thousand feet thick. The rise of the Columbia Plateau diverted the ancient Columbia River, forcing it to make a massive detour, called the Big Bend, as it flowed south out of what is now Canada. The river was forced west, then south, and then east to meet the Snake, before it finally turned west again for its final run to the Pacific.

Between five million and two million years ago, as the Columbia continued to bend around and eat at the basalt plateau, the Cascade Mountains began to arch up. The river, however, did not give ground to this eruption from the earth. As the Cascades rose, the Columbia cut a deep V-shaped canyon for itself. Erosion and stiff winds during the last ice age (two million to twelve thousand years ago) spread silt and fine sand across the Columbia Plateau. In the Palouse region of southeastern Washington, the silt stacked up 150 feet deep, creating what would become one of the world's richest food-growing areas. The stage was thus set for a two-thousand-year season of the wildest, most catastrophic floods known to have occurred in North America.*

The floods occurred relatively recently, just fourteen thousand to twelve thousand years ago. They started when advancing ice sheets from Canada got stuck in a canyon in what is now northwest Montana. The ice formed a giant dam that stood 2,500 feet high (nearly five times higher than Grand Coulee Dam). Behind the ice dam, a lake formed that contained five hundred cubic miles of water, about half the volume of Lake Michigan. Suddenly, the ice dam broke and the lake exploded into a flood that rampaged across eastern Washington with ten times the combined flow of all the rivers of the world. It traveled at speeds of up to fifty miles an hour. The energy released by the largest of the floods was 225 times greater than the Hiroshima bomb, 75 times greater than the largest nuclear weapon ever tested, and 33 times greater than the largest recorded earthquake.

The floods occurred at least forty times, ripping away silt, blasting through rock, creating a tormented landscape of coulees, dry falls, and barren channels. The worst handiwork of the floods remains uninhab-

---

*The geological detective work that discovered and explained the floods was done in the 1920s by J. Harlen Bretz, a geologist from the University of Chicago. But it took the American geological community more than half a century of scoffing and nit-picking before it accepted Bretz's description of the catastrophic floods. He was awarded the Penrose Medal of the Geological Society of America, the highest honor in his field, in 1979.

72   itable. It is called scabland. In eastern Washington, the value of land for farming varies wildly, depending on where the floods cut. The phenomenal soils of the Palouse, often called the best farmland in the world, lie only a few minutes' drive from the scablands, which struggle to support sagebrush.

The great floods found their way to the Pacific by reaming out the Cascade canyon that the Columbia had been slowly cutting for several million years. Floods changed the steep V-shaped canyon into a magnificent U-shaped gorge. The north side of the gorge was undercut so sharply that for thousands of years after the floods it was subject to massive landslides that dropped as many as fifty square miles of earth. These were the landslides that Lewis deduced while paddling downstream on the Columbia.

"Bad rapid" and "verry bad rapid," Clark wrote again and again as he led the expedition down (and often portaged around) the white water that the Columbia tossed up on its way to the sea.

"A tremendous black rock Presented itself high and Steep appearing to choke up the river," Clark wrote, describing a downstream stretch of the river that came to be known as the Short Narrows. "I could See the dificuelties we had to pass for Several miles below; at this place the water of this great river is compressed into a channel between two rocks not exceeding forty five yards wide . . . it is intersepted by rocks.

"I determined to pass through this place notwithstanding the horrid appearance of this agitated gut swelling, boiling & whorling in every direction."

At the spot where Lewis and Clark first came upon the Columbia, a hard wind still blows, stinging with gritty dust, and glare off the water still tortures the eyes. But the confluence has been encircled, in the last decade of the twentieth century, by agro-industrial sprawl from Pasco, Kennewick, and Richland, the towns in southeastern Washington that call themselves the Tri-Cities. The Chevron Pipeline Company has planted a tank farm at the confluence, where barges unload diesel fuel and gasoline. The Cargill grain company has built a community of giant grain elevators that disgorge into river barges. Just back from the banks of the rivers, there are "sanitary lagoons" with large KEEP OUT signs and bonded warehouse terminals surrounded by chain-link fences. High-voltage power lines swoop over the rivers. The town nearest the confluence is the tiny community of Burbank. Its commercial shopping strip includes the Burbank Laundry Center, the Burbank Video Hut, Burbank Power Trim ("Lose Weight & Gain Energy"), and, most prominently, the Beautiful Downtown Burbank Tavern, where a large outdoor sign says "Only a Rooster can get a better piece of chicken than you can get here." The sum of these developments, if anything, deepens the dreariness that early explorers described on sighting the meeting of the two rivers.

What has changed beyond the imagining of Lewis and Clark is the Columbia itself. It has been raised, fattened, and slowed. By Lewis's measure, the Columbia was 960 yards wide at the confluence. It is twice that wide now. Slackwater has risen to flood out much of the point where Indians traded and Lewis and Clark camped. The river-cum-lake has a new name, McNary Pool, after the hydroelectric dam about twenty miles downstream. The depth and speed of water in the pool, like the depth and speed of water in nearly all of the river, are controlled by power schedulers from the Bonneville Power Administration, the federal agency that markets most electricity in the Pacific Northwest. The schedulers control the river from an underground control room near Portland, about 160 miles west of McNary Dam.

There are no "verry bad" rapids. There are no rapids at all, nor are there waterfalls, riffles, eddies, sinkholes, or a single "agitated gut."

If reservations are made early, the river can be customized for community events.

A member of the Tri-City Water Follies Columbia Cup Unlimited Hydroplane Race Committee writes in early every year to book the river. A letter addressed to the Army Corps of Engineers regional office in Portland requests that the Columbia, just above the point where Lewis and Clark first saw it, be operated in the last week of July at something called "constant full pool."

A constant full pool is, well, a lake. Unless the Columbia behaves like a lake during race week, unlimited hydroplane racing boats cannot safely circle a two-mile oval at speeds approaching 200 miles an hour as 35,000 onlookers bake in the sun, squint into the water, drink cold beer, and celebrate one of the largest spectator events in the Columbia Basin. The Columbia must be groomed to meet the finicky needs of million-dollar racing boats with names like *Miss Budweiser*, *The Winston Eagle*, and *Kellogg's Frosted Flakes*.

"What we can't have is a river that goes up and down," explained Mark Schneider, the Columbia Cup race committee member who books the river. "At 200 miles an hour, our pilots get real upset if the buoys aren't straight. And what happens if *Miss Budweiser* sets a world speed record? It won't count if they pull the plug at McNary Dam, the pool falls, and the buoys are out of place."

The Corps miscalculated in the 1980s, letting too much of the river leak out overnight, stranding sleek hydroplanes in fields of mud. Schneider went down to the boat pits early in the morning during the races to find "there was no river." Since then, planning has been more precise. When I attended the race, the plug was not pulled, the pool held constant, and buoys did not wander. The race went off without a hitch.

There were no hitches, that is, on the river. On the shore, at an event that had become an excuse for widespread public drunkenness in the Tri-Cities, there was the usual trouble. Four cars crashed on the Blue Bridge over the Columbia as drivers rubbernecked the race boats. Police arrested one hundred and two people, mostly for drinking, fighting, driving while drunk, or selling drugs. Among those arrested was Matt Blair, age twenty-two, of nearby Walla Walla. Arriving at midday in the riverside park where spectators watch the races, Blair headed immediately for a "beer garden," where he later testified that he chugged "six or seven" sixteen-ounce draft beers. He ate a burger, some fries, and drove back toward Walla Walla in the late afternoon. Witnesses said his car was traveling at about eighty miles an hour and weaving through traffic when it collided head-on with a pickup truck, killing two people. The family of one of the dead later circulated a petition to ban drinking at the hydroplane races. The managing director of the Columbia Cup objected, telling a local newspaper that attendance already had begun dropping when "we stopped people from bringing in beer. If we take out the beer gardens, attendance is going to drop again."*

But on the river itself, as I said, the race could not have gone smoother. "Every morning during the race, I would call the operator at McNary and get a pool level from him. He would tell me it was at 340 feet over sea level, plus or minus three inches. During ten days of racing, the morning report varied a total of six inches. That is pretty damn phenomenal," said Schneider, intending no pun.

It was a feat typical of river management in the West: an insipid miracle that hardly anyone notices, an intricate series of maneuvers that succeed when nothing much seems to happen. Which is not to say that it is simple to hold the Columbia steady. The river was engineered to rise and fall with the daily appetites of a western power grid that covers half the land area of the United States, serves more than fifty million people, and reaches north to Canada, east to Nebraska, and south to Texas.

McNary Pool usually begins dropping around dawn as gates in the dam open to spill the river through turbines that spin generators that feed electricity to make toast in Seattle and cool air in Tucson. After dinner, as electricity demand falls, turbines back off, and McNary Pool fills throughout the night.

Miss Budweiser, however, could crash (or, more likely, get stuck in the mud) if McNary Pool does its normal daylight drain. So the Bonneville Power Administration fine-tunes the river. It requests extra electricity from other federal dams in the system and allows McNary to back off its turbines and maintain the pool.

So begins a Byzantine series of race-week adjustments. Manipulating the river is like kneading a balloon. A pinch in one place forces a bulge somewhere else. If more water flows into McNary Pool at the top than escapes at the bottom, it can overfill, creating a mess in the

---

*The Columbia Cup was originally called the Atomic Cup in honor of nearby Hanford's contribution to the making of atomic weapons. The name was changed in 1976, with the rise of the anti-nuclear movement, and changed again in 2007 to the Lamb-Weston Columbia Cup, in honor of a corporate sponsor that makes French fries and onion rings.

riverside pits of the hydroplane racers. So just upstream on the Snake, the Bonneville Power Administration orders the Corps of Engineers to throttle down daytime power production at its Ice Harbor Dam.

A different fix is needed to handle excess water coming down the Columbia. The next dam up that river, Priest Rapids, is not owned by the federal government. It belongs to Grant County Public Utility District, a local utility that markets its electricity across the Northwest. Like any business, the Grant County PUD hates to close down when paying customers are eager to buy. So during race week, Priest Rapids Dam usually continues to feed the daytime appetites of the power grid. About twice as much water pours through the dam's turbines while the sun shines as during the night. This creates a daily surge—a mini tidal wave—that rolls downstream toward the hydroplane racecourse. It takes twelve hours for the surge to travel the 105 miles to McNary Dam. By early evening, when it rolls in, operators are ready. They open up McNary's turbines, drain the surge, and feed electricity into the regional grid as power schedulers order other dams to back off production.

If anything goes wrong, if the river feeds the grid more electricity than it can swallow, if a major transmission line topples in a storm, there is a way to keep the system from shorting out. It is called the Toaster. Located in the electrical switching yard near Chief Joseph Dam on the upper Columbia in Washington State, the Toaster is a massive electrical resistor, consisting of three steel towers wrapped hundreds of times with coils of stainless-steel wire. Whenever the need arises (about once a month) the Toaster glows red hot for about half a second, painlessly bleeding surges out of the Northwest grid. The Columbia is, as utility executives like to say, a fine machine.

In the week of the Columbia Cup race, there were at least 487,264 juvenile salmon milling around during daylight hours in front of the closed gates of McNary Dam. They had no choice but to wait for *Miss Budweiser* and eleven other unlimited hydroplanes to finish racing for the day and for operators of the river to lay on mechanized solutions to their transport needs.

These fish, of course, had evolved to swim in a river, not a machine. Before concrete, three-quarters of the Columbia's annual flow raced to the Pacific in the warmest and driest half of the year. This heavy, glacier-fed summer flow was the key to making the Columbia the world's finest salmon expressway. It sped young salmon, called smolts, past predators and poured them into the Pacific at precisely the time when their bodies were undergoing a transformation that allowed them to live in saltwater. The size and swiftness of the river enabled returning adult salmon to scoot safely over flooded rapids and waterfalls. The spring and early summer river, before concrete and slackwater, remained exceptionally cold (usually in the 40s and low 50s) even in the searing temperatures of the Columbia Basin desert. This kept adult and juvenile salmon healthy, vigorous, and on the move.

This all-natural superhighway for salmon, however, squandered hydroelectricity. Had the Columbia been allowed to retain a flow pattern that suited salmon, nearly two-thirds of the river's power potential would have been spent in just three balmy months—May, June, and July. That is exactly the time when the Pacific Northwest, which heats homes with electricity in winter, does not need massive jolts of power.

The river machine, therefore, was built to stand the Columbia on its head, holding back the bulk of the river's annual flow until winter. Salmon, whose annual migration had meshed so elegantly with the rhythms of the summertime river, became engineering glitches. They fouled the power-production schedule. The fish became a mechanical problem to be solved in mechanical ways.

McNary Dam, originally built in 1957 by the Army Corps of Engineers, has been elaborately and expensively modified to offer the latest in high-tech solutions to the technical difficulties that salmon present to the machine river.

The problem with juvenile salmon actually *swimming* to the sea in the dammed-up river is that, sooner or later, they have to go over,

78   around, or through a dam. A Snake River salmon has to pass eight federal dams, four in the lower Snake, four in the middle and lower Columbia. The riskiest passage is through a turbine, which kills between 10 and 20 percent of the fingerling juvenile salmon that get sucked into it. Turbines do not puree these small salmon, rather they kill by creating violent pressure changes that can explode a salmon's swim bladder. Salmon not killed are often stunned, making them easy prey for seagulls and predator fish that hang out behind McNary and other dams.

In recent years, engineers at federal dams have devised surface fish passage and guidance structures that have sharply reduced the number of juveniles going through turbines. This has helped improve survival rates, especially when the Snake and Columbia have plenty of water that can be spilled over dams.

Yet between dams, sluggish and tepid reservoirs disorient juvenile salmon whose instincts lead them to expect a rapid and relatively effortless passage to sea. Juveniles often have to work much harder, swimming through a chain of lakes that is up to 4 degrees warmer and moving at a speed that is up to ten times slower than the natural river. The delay is deadly. For as they swim downstream, juveniles undergo physical changes that allow them to breathe in saltwater. The timing of this transformation is delicate and easily disrupted. Before there were dams, young fish could reach the sea in less than a month. In slackwater, it can take two to three months. In the slowed-down, warmed-up river, many young fish lose their migratory drive. They succumb to predators, disease, or thermal shock.

McNary Dam attempts to cure these unfortunate difficulties by greeting migrating juvenile salmon, at the entrance to each of its fourteen turbines, with a nylon-mesh screen. The screen is supposed to guide them away from turbines, directing the fish out of the river into something called a "juvenile collection, holding, and transportation facility." McNary Dam, like a number of dams in the Snake and Columbia, has been reengineered to become a fish distillery.

Juvenile salmon are sometimes strained out of the Columbia and channeled through a Rube Goldberg maze of stainless-steel pipes, flumes, tanks, and vats. To make the sorting go more smoothly, many of the young salmon swimming around behind McNary have been outfitted with computer signaling devices.

The smolts were captured in hatcheries or seined in streams and then injected with a device called a passive integrated transponder or PIT tag. About the size of a grain of rice, a PIT tag is injected with a hypodermic needle and lodges in a salmon's intervisceral cavity. The device has a fine copper antenna wrapped around a transistor and a computer chip. When a salmon passes through a detector in McNary Dam, its PIT tag transmits a unique seven-digit number that identifies the fish's species, weight, length when tagged, stream or hatchery of origin, and how long it has been trying to get to the sea. (A number of adult salmon swimming upriver to spawn are also outfitted with the latest high-tech communication gear. Radio transmitters the size of a man's forefinger are stuffed down their throats and an eighteen-inch antenna sticks out of their mouths. The transmitters help track how successful adults are in going around dams in fish ladders.)

Based on their size and what their PIT tags broadcast, distilled juvenile salmon are counted, sorted, and sampled for disease. They can be stored in holding tanks. They can be shunted into the river below the dam. But for many years the most likely option for young salmon behind McNary was to be removed from the river altogether and pumped (along with water from the river) into a barge or a truck.

The Army Corps of Engineers offered the fish a crowded but quick ride west (one day by truck, two by barge). The salmon traveled about 150 miles to below Bonneville Dam, the final dam on the Columbia, where they were pumped back into the river. When I attended race week at McNary Pool, 109,505 juvenile salmon boarded trucks, which took Interstate 84 west. Another 225,482 fish were shunted into barges. Only 20,050 were allowed to swim in the river. During the 1990s, McNary and two other federal dams screened, sorted, and transported about fifteen million juvenile salmon a year.

The Corps of Engineers, which began hauling salmon around dams in the late 1970s as an experiment, constantly refined its techniques for sucking fish from the river and putting them aboard mass transport.

80 Still, it was a procedure prone to error. In 1994, after the Corps finished outfitting McNary with yet another upgrade in salmon-distilling technology, something went terribly wrong at the height of the downstream migration of wild chinook salmon. In mid-July of that year, when hot weather had raised the temperature of the river to 73 degrees, a near-lethal environment for juvenile salmon, a mechanical failure in the fish-screening system stranded tens of thousands of fingerlings in a stagnant containment channel. The Corps estimated that thirty thousand fish died, of stress, heat, and overcrowding. A fish-passage specialist for the Idaho Fish and Game Department who stumbled upon the mishap told reporters that he believed up to one hundred thousand salmon died. "The raceways were six to twelve inches deep with dead fish," he told the *Spokesman-Review*. "They had to push them out with squeegees."

Distilling salmon out of the river and bussing them to the sea—a machine fix for a machine river—perfectly suits the operators of the Columbia. It is relatively cheap, costing a few million dollars a year. With the salmon out of the water, dams can generate hundreds of millions of dollars' worth of electricity without the distasteful matter of exploding baby fish. Irrigators can pump water out of the river without worrying that they will be irrigating their fields with salmon. Barging companies do not have to worry about drawdown experiments that might make the river too shallow for giant tows. When the fish-distilling-and-barging fix was in, the Columbia could continue to be turned inside out by dams, with the bulk of the river's water flowing not in summer to suit salmon, but in winter to suit the needs of home-owners, aluminum companies, and potato processors.

The problem with transporting salmon, however, is that it does not work all that well, especially with wild salmon that are on the brink of extinction. For almost twenty years, the Army Corps of Engineers transported ever-larger numbers of juvenile salmon to the lower Columbia. To guarantee that there were lots of juvenile salmon to haul, state and federal fish hatcheries on the Columbia-Snake System seeded the rivers with tens of millions of migrants throughout the spring and summer.

The number of returning adults, however, continued to plummet.

A review of the Corps' barging record by state and federal fisheries experts concluded in the early 1990s that while fish transport seemed to increase returns of certain salmon that migrate late in the summer, it "is not a substitute" for a free-flowing river. The review said that "for some [salmon] stocks transportation may have been detrimental to fish survival." Biologists speculated that distilling salmon from the river and pumping them into barges caused stress that made them more susceptible to disease and predators. It could also interfere with the imprinting process that allowed migrant salmon to remember how to get back to the streams of their birth.

With fish numbers continuing to decline, federal agencies that run the river were pressured in the late 1990s to try a low-tech fix. It did not use the Columbia as a fish distillery or as a staging platform for mass transportation. It simply spilled lots of water (with juvenile salmon swimming around in it) over dams during migration seasons.

And spill worked. Fish counts confirmed that more juveniles swam to the sea, they got there quicker, and they returned a few years later in unexpectedly large numbers as healthy adult salmon. Even so, federal agencies in charge of dams resisted spill, primarily because it was expensive. Water spilled over dams produced no electricity.

That resistance, though, has been crushed by the will of Judge Redden in Portland. Since 2005, he has ordered that spill be maintained. Research has confirmed that spill is by far the best way yet devised to help salmon survive in a machine river.

Those baby salmon waiting around for trucks and barges behind McNary Dam during the hydroplane races became the objects of a debate that rose above hydromechanics and marine biology into the realm of environmental aesthetics.

Environmental groups that opposed the barging of salmon based their objections as much on a predilection for "natural" solutions as on scientific evidence about what helped fish. A Sierra Club flyer described the transport of salmon as "ridiculous," "cockeyed," and an "unnatural charade." Andy Kerr, the outspoken environmentalist from the Oregon

82   Natural Resources Defense Council, told me, "I may be old-fashioned. But I think that fish ought to be in the river, not in barges."

The builders and defenders of the machine river considered questions of naturalness and environmental aesthetics laughably anachronistic. River users said the Columbia River must be viewed as a working river.

"We've got a problem with fish, let's solve it the best we can. If you want increased fish production, what should you care how it happens?" asked Al Wright, the chief lobbyist for the Pacific Northwest Utilities Conference Committee. "If I put them in submarines and I transported them down to the Pacific and then I transported them back, what should you care?

"But if you are telling me that you want the river back in some kind of pristine, pre–white-man condition, then we don't have anything to talk about. I don't have a world to work in that will give you that. Let's not play pretend."

Indeed, it was silly to pretend that the Columbia was a river in the sense that Lewis and Clark understood it. The river was killed more than sixty years ago and was reborn as plumbing. The place where this fateful murder and curious resurrection took place was on up the Columbia at Grand Coulee Dam. My father was up there, trying to make a living.

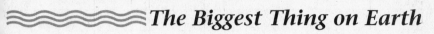

4

The Biggest Thing on Earth

Up at the dam, everybody was young, everybody was crazy.

—ARNO HARDEN

THERE WERE ABOUT four thousand men working at Grand Coulee Dam in early 1936, with hundreds more streaming in every month. A favored few found family housing in carefully planned, all-electric communities down in the mile-wide canyon where the dam was going up. In Engineer's Town and Mason City, the families of government engineers and senior employees of the contractor had indoor toilets and shade trees, flower-growing contests and rules about drinking. The unfavored majority, men without women, pitched up at a distance from the shade, the plumbing, and the rules. The working stiffs, as they called themselves, lived beyond the east lip of the canyon in the municipality of Grand Coulee, a boomtown that had the longest line of brothels the West had seen since the Gold Rush. It was the cesspool of the New Deal, the Sodom and Gomorrah of the engineered West. Dam workers lived in boardinghouses, tents, cars, caves, and the boxes that dance-hall pianos came in.

My father hitched a ride upriver to Grand Coulee in the late spring of that year after losing his apple-loading job in Wenatchee. He and his younger brother, Albert, found jobs as broom-and-bucket men down in the bowels of the emerging dam. They lived in a two-room shack not far from B Street.

Both sides of B Street were oiled with card sharks, moonshiners, pool hustlers, pickpockets, dope peddlers, professional piano players,

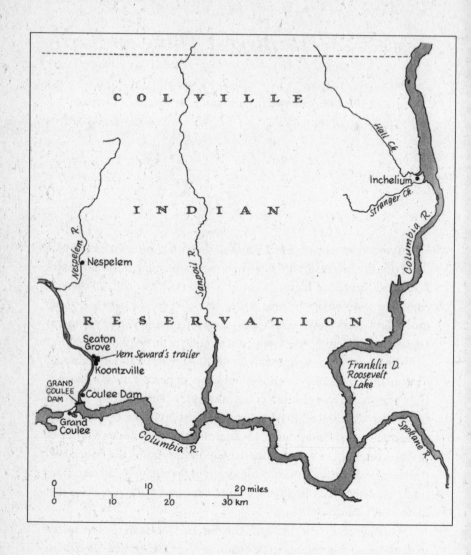

pimps, and a limited number of women who, like everybody else, had come to town for money. B Street was unpaved and had no sidewalks. It was gluey mud in the winter, choking dust in the summer, live music all night long. The town of Grand Coulee was born the year after Prohibition ended. In six loutish years, it was credited with having soaked up more alcohol per square foot than any town in the state of Washington.

My father and his brother frequented the Silver Dollar, an unpainted, false-fronted B Street saloon, where an ex-con named Whitey Shannon employed fifteen dime-a-dance girls. Ill-mannered men who wanted to do more than dance with these girls were tossed out by a bartender named Big Jack. There was a sweet-voiced crooner named Curly who looked and sang like Gene Autry, and between numbers a skinny kid would shovel away the dirt that fell on the dance floor from dam workers' boots.

"At Whitey Shannon's place, the girls stood around like at any other dance. But when you go up and ask if she wanted to dance, she first held out her hand, palm up. If you give her a dime, away you go," my father told me. "These were pretty nice girls, the ones at the Silver Dollar. Hell, they made a fortune. So did ol' Whitey Shannon. The fighting was mostly out in the street. There was quite a lot of fighting. Well, you know, there was bound to be. That many men together and a lot of drinking. It was mostly over women. There weren't many women up there, and what was there didn't always behave. Me and my brother didn't go to B Street very much. It was pretty rough. There was shootings and knifings and all that stuff. There was a guy I saw shot just as you go through town. He run off with someone's wife or some damn thing."

Mary Oaks, chief telephone operator at the dam, took calls from B Street nearly every night: "The owners would say we got a dead man over here and would you call the police. If they weren't dead, of course, they would want a doctor." Trucks with loudspeakers tooled up and down B Street, urging workers to make less noise and refrain from activities that might spread social diseases. Dr. George Sparling, head of the Grand Coulee office of the Washington State Health Department, announced—somewhat desperately—that "everyone found with disease will be sent to the county jail . . . and kept there until cured." State Patrolman Francis McGinn found a number of dam workers unconscious in the alley behind B Street. They told him, when they woke up, that bartenders had laced their drinks with knockout drops and stolen their wallets.

It was not just working stiffs who took their pleasure on B Street. Harvey Slocum, chief foreman for the main contractor at the dam, favored the liquor and the girls at a B Street brothel called Swanee Rooms. The second-floor whorehouse got too hot for Slocum one summer. So he dispatched a government-paid plumbing crew from the dam site to put sprinklers on the brothel's roof. It was Grand Coulee's first air-conditioning system. When Slocum got fired for his assorted sins, the *Wenatchee World* reported the reason as "ill-health." Slocum later dressed down the reporter who wrote the story. "You put in that goddamn paper of yours that I was canned because of ill-health. Now you know damn well I got canned because I was drunk."

Grand Coulee Dam made everyone in the Pacific Northwest a bit drunk. The dam was an intoxicating cocktail of engineering genius, Depression-era chutzpah, and western myth. Larger than any structure ever built in world history, it was a Paul Bunyan story come true. It seemed to prove what westerners had always been taught to believe about themselves. They were a special people who could dream their way out of trouble, who could combine a good idea with elbow grease and overcome calamities as shattering as the Great Depression, as threatening as World War II.

Going into the project, the boosters of Grand Coulee Dam had had no shortage of gall. They proposed building the planet's largest dam, at taxpayers' expense, in a desolate American outback that had more jackrabbits than human beings. It was to be "the biggest thing on earth." What they ended up creating—with the unexpected coming of World War II—was something even bigger, an eye-popping metaphor for Manifest Destiny. It was vaccine for the Great Depression and a club to whip Hitler, a dynamo to power the dawn of the Atomic Age and a fist to smash the monopolistic greed of private utilities, a magnet for industry and a fountainhead for irrigated agriculture. The dam was a mixed metaphor with enough concrete in it to lay a sixteen-foot-wide highway from New York City to Seattle to Los Angeles and back to New York.*

Grand Coulee Dam validated the notion that God made the West so Americans could conquer its natural resources, that He made the Columbia River so they could dam it up, extract electricity, and divert it into concrete ditches.

It was made-to-order for the New Deal, President Roosevelt's grab bag of deficit-spending schemes to rescue America from the Depression. Big enough to make headlines across the country, it quickly created more than seven thousand jobs. For Roosevelt, the dam—with its promise of affordable power for the working classes—had the added political advantage of infuriating private utilities and the Republican Party. The president personally approved the sixty-three-million-dollar emergency grant that jump-started work at the dam in 1933. And Roosevelt himself headed up what became a public-relations extravaganza to justify the dam as a showpiece for the New Deal. Twice the president visited a dust-blown construction site that in the continental United States could hardly have been farther away from the White House or more inconvenient to get to, especially for a man disabled by polio.

Even in Washington State, the dam was not an easy destination. It was stuck out in coulee country, 240 miles east across the Cascades from Seattle, 90 miles west of Spokane. Work had hardly begun when Roosevelt, having traversed Washington State by riverboat, train, and car, first arrived on a hot August day in 1934. He was ridiculously early. There was nothing to see except holes in the ground. No matter. Roosevelt had come not to inspect, but to cheer. Not the dam, but his idea of building it.

"We are going to see with our own eyes electricity made so cheap

---

*Grand Coulee Dam is no longer the largest producer of electricity in the world. Two dams in South America produce more power. The Three Gorges dam in China dwarfs Grand Coulee, producing more than three times as much electricity.

88   that it will become a standard article of use not only for manufacturing but for every home," he said. "I know that this [empty desert] country is going to be filled with the homes not only of a great many people from this state, but by a great many families from other states of the Union—men, women, and children who will be making an honest livelihood and doing their best to live up to the American standard of living and the American standard of citizenship."

Addressing several thousand Washington State residents who followed him out to the middle of nowhere, Roosevelt preached to the converted at the dam site. But his real audience was an army of unbelievers back East who were attacking Grand Coulee as "socialistic, impractical dam-foolishness." Eastern members of Congress, the private power lobby, and the engineering establishment scoffed at the idea of generating record amounts of electricity and building a massive irrigation scheme in a corner of the country that had less than 3 percent of the American population. The president of the American Society of Civil Engineers said the dam was "a grandiose project of no more usefulness than the pyramids of Egypt." *Collier's* magazine wrote in 1935 that the dam's reclamation scheme proposed irrigating a region of "dead land, bitter with alkali," so hell-like that "even snakes and lizards shun it."

After Roosevelt went back to Washington, publicists at the Bureau of Reclamation worked for years to drown out the dam's critics. They did so with a deluge of press releases filled with facts about how fabulously big Grand Coulee was going to be. Its concrete would fill fifty thousand boxcars in a train more than five hundred miles long. It would make a concrete cube two and a half times taller than the Empire State Building. The Bureau of Reclamation built a replica of the dam, one-eightieth actual size, and sent it on a national tour. Hawking what it called the "Eighth Wonder of the World," the Bureau produced films, published picture books, laid on bus tours, and built grandstands overlooking the dam site. They accommodated forty thousand tourists a month.

When Roosevelt returned to Grand Coulee in October of 1937 for another round of presidential cheerleading, he melded all the bigger-than-big Grand Coulee statistics into one all-encompassing American boast: "Superlatives do not count for anything," Roosevelt said, "because [the dam] is so much bigger than anything ever tried before."

While the Roosevelt administration managed to make Grand Coulee Dam a household name across America in the 1930s, it did not succeed in sanctifying the project as part of western mythology until 1941. That is when the federal government came up with the idea of paying a working-class icon $3,200 to write pro-dam propaganda. Woody Guthrie, the Dust Bowl poet and folk balladeer, visited the Columbia Basin for thirty days in a chauffeur-driven government car. Traveling between Bonneville Dam near Portland and Grand Coulee Dam, Guthrie wrote lyrics for twenty-six songs, most of them set to familiar folk melodies. Many of the songs were instantly forgettable, Bureau of Reclamation press releases dressed up in cornpone rhymes. Others were so bad they were hard to forget. In "The Song of the Grand Coulee Dam," Guthrie wrote: "I'll settle this land, boys, and work like a man, I'll water my crops from Grand Coulee Dam. Grand Coulee Dam, boys, Grand Coulee Dam, I wish we had a lot more Grand Coulee Dams."

But the best song, "Roll On Columbia, Roll On," succeeded in ways that the publicists back in Washington could never approach. Blending the power of the river with myths about Manifest Destiny, Guthrie transformed Bureau of Reclamation concrete into proletarian glory.

> *Green Douglas firs where the waters cut through.*
> *Down her wild mountains and canyons she flew.*
> *Canadian Northwest to the ocean so blue.*
> *Roll on, Columbia, roll on!*
>
> *And on up the river is Grand Coulee Dam*
> *The mightiest thing ever built by a man,*
> *To run the great factories for old Uncle Sam;*
> *It's roll on, Columbia, roll on!*

Roll on, Columbia, roll on!
           Your power is turning our darkness to dawn,
           So, roll on, Columbia, roll on!

When the United States entered World War II, the dam became a strategic treasure. Critics went silent. The *Saturday Evening Post*, in an article entitled "White Elephant Comes into Its Own," said that America's need for electricity "transformed the whole costly project of harnessing the latent power of the Columbia . . . from a magnificent day dream . . . into one of the best investments Uncle Sam has ever made."

Electricity from the Columbia River—from Grand Coulee Dam and the much smaller Bonneville Dam—produced about one-third of the nation's aluminum during the war. Grand Coulee generated the power that made half of America's warplanes. B-17 Flying Fortress aircraft rolled off assembly lines at Boeing in Seattle at the rate of sixteen planes every twenty-four hours. In Portland, three shipyards relied on Grand Coulee's power to make nearly 750 big ships. A "mystery load" of electricity (later revealed to be 55,000 kilowatts, more power than all of the electricity civilian consumers in the Northwest used in 1945) flowed from Grand Coulee to a secret tent city along the Columbia called Hanford.

President Harry S. Truman said in 1948 that without Grand Coulee and Bonneville Dams "it would have been almost impossible to win this war." In the same year, Earl Warren, the future chief justice of the Supreme Court and then a Republican running for vice-president against Truman, said Grand Coulee had done nothing less than save America from atomic annihilation.

"Probably Hitler would have beaten us in atom bomb development if it had not been for the hydroelectric development of the Columbia, making possible the big Hanford project which brought forth the bomb."*

---

*Regional historian Paul Pitzer, whose multi-volume history of Grand Coulee Dam is the source of several quotations in these pages, points out that the myth of Grand Coulee

At the beginning of *The Dam,* a popular history of Grand Coulee that was published in 1954, a young philosophy major from the University of Washington explained why he wanted to work at the dam: "There are parts of our culture that stink with phoniness. But we can do some wonderful things too. That dam is one of them. If our generation has anything good to offer history, it's that dam. Why, the thing is going to be completely useful. It's going to be a working pyramid."

The pyramid had begun to rise in the river when my father was handed rubber boots, a rubber jacket, a broom, and a bucket and ordered to work about sixty feet below the surface of the Columbia.

A cofferdam, a temporary dike bulging out from the east bank of the Columbia, had diverted the river so that one edge of its bed could be cleaned of earth and rock. Excavators cut down to granite, 105 feet beneath the surface of the pushed-aside river. Tombstone polishers, using soap and water and hand-held brushes, had been brought in from around the Northwest to clean and buff the granite. When my father reported to work, the east corner of the dam had been built up about forty feet from the polished granite floor.

Dams rise from the bedrock of a river in a series of domino-shaped concrete pours. Before each new pour, laborers pick clean, hose down, and sandblast every surface. Unless hardened concrete is scoured clean, wet concrete might not adhere to it; there could be cracks and structural weakness. For fifty cents an hour, eight hours a day, six days a week, my father cleaned concrete, picking up loose rocks, bits of wire.

"I didn't like that doggone work, down in that hole, pickin' up those little rocks. You could hear the river gurgling on the other side of the cofferdam. It was a helluva thing. It was cool down there and it was wet."

Grand Coulee is a gravity dam, meaning that its sheer weight holds back the river. Tall, graceful arch dams like Hoover or Glen Canyon hold back rivers by transferring their downstream force to the walls

had grown to such a point in the late 1940s that it was getting credit for victories it had not won. "The fact that Germany had been defeated before the advent of the bomb . . . hardly mattered," Pitzer writes. "Grand Coulee provided for the bomb, and the bomb ended the war. Hence Grand Coulee won World War II. The logic became irrefutable."

of high, narrow canyons. But the canyon where Grand Coulee Dam squats was too wide for an arch dam. It demanded a super-heavy gravity dam with lots of concrete, twelve million cubic yards of it, three times more concrete than Hoover Dam, more concrete in one place than ever before in history. It was poured in blocks, about five feet high and varying from thirty to fifty feet square. Block on top of block was poured as the dam climbed up from the bedrock. There was little that was novel about the building methods at Grand Coulee. It simply was much, much bigger.

After three months, my father considered his options in the dam-building profession and quit. He quit because he was bored and because he was uncomfortable down in the hole. He also quit because he did not want to get hurt. Fifteen men had already been killed at the dam. Another sixty or so would be killed as concrete was poured for four more years. They were mangled in conveyor belts, crushed by dropped buckets of concrete, blasted by dynamite, run over by trucks, drowned in the river, and dismembered in long falls. My father found a safer, more lucrative living, one that got him out of the hole and gave him an eye-opening angle on the wicked ways of B Street. He delivered milk.

He began his milk route every morning at 3 A.M., when the brothels on B Street were still accepting customers, the piano players were still playing, and liquored-up workers were still out wrestling in the mud.

"You know what was odd?" my father said. "Those chippy houses used a lot of milk. I guess they made drinks out of it. Maybe they bathed in it. I don't know. I sold two cases a day to Swanee Rooms [where the chief foreman at the dam ordered government-paid plumbers to put sprinklers on the roof]. I sold milk to four of them brothels. But you know those prostitutes never in three years did me out of one dime. No sir, they never did. That is more than you can say about the rest of them up there."

As the dam began to straddle the river, the payroll expanded to nearly eight thousand employees. More housing was built, and thousands of workers began to bring their wives up to the dam site. These young wives, almost none of whom were allowed to work at the dam or anywhere else, had very little to do. Many of them, after their husbands drove off to work at the dam, were stranded without transport in houses perched on barren hills above the dam. According to one memoir, which was written by a man, women were expected to bear their burdens in silence.

"At a gathering at the camp one day the resident wives were asked by the wives who had lived in the cities, 'How can you live here? How can you be happy and get along?'

"'Keep your bowels open and your mouth shut,' was the sage advice."

In his morning milk deliveries, my father found that not very many women lived up to expectations.

"You saw more stuff going on in these homes than you did in the cathouses. You wouldn't believe the stuff that I seen. Some of these homes, these women, their men's workin', see. Hell, I got invited in their homes so many times. You wouldn't believe what goes on in these homes, I'm telling you. They would come to the door, no damn clothes on, yeah they would.

"There was a place outside of town, it was a nice place, too, it was just getting daylight. I set the milk down and I looked up and they had an open porch there. There was a bed there. I just glanced in there. Here she was laying there, not a goddamn stitch on. Just laying there.

"You know the guy who bought the milk route off me. In about three months, he didn't have no customers left. He did what I just would not do. He accommodated these women. His business just went to hell."

While my father was resisting temptation and saving his milk money, his entire family moved up to Grand Coulee to plug into Roosevelt's job-making machine. His brother Albert became a jackhammer foreman, a brother-in-law became a crane operator, and another brother-in-law was a concrete foreman. My grandfather Alfred, assisted by his younger children, opened a very profitable grocery store.

The dam rescued the Hardens from the Depression, allowed them to stick together, and even gave them savings accounts. After my father sold his milk route in 1939, when business was at its peak, he put $2,200 in the bank. His Grand Coulee savings, more money than he had ever seen in his life, paid for welding school in Seattle and gave him a high-wage skill. He also made friends at the dam who later helped him secure a welding foreman's job at the shipyards in Portland during World War II. If not for his Grand Coulee contacts, my father never would have been put in charge of an all-woman welding crew in Portland. He would not have had a chance to meet Betty Thoe, a dark-haired, eighteen-year-old girl from North Dakota who was a member of my dad's welding crew and who became my mother.

On a cloudless Saturday morning in May, my father and I drove the seventy-five miles from Moses Lake up to Grand Coulee Dam. We had made a bargain. He would tell me everything he could remember about the dam in the thirties, about B Street, about his milk route—and I would buy him lunch at the Wild Spot cafe. Like most father-son trans-actions, the deal favored me. But my father welcomed the excuse to look at the dam. He was a month shy of eighty-two years old and had not been up to Grand Coulee in years.

It had been abnormally hot across the Pacific Northwest in the previous week. Snow in the Cascades and Canadian Rockies was melting much faster than normal. The Columbia was rising rapidly. Behind Grand Coulee Dam, Lake Roosevelt was bumping up against its flood-control maximum. It being a weekend, with electricity consumption low across the region, the Bonneville Power Administra-tion had no market for excess power. It could not, therefore, feed the swelling river into Coulee's turbines. For the first time in two years—for one of the very few times since the generating capacity of the dam was tripled in the 1970s—the Columbia River was too big to be corralled or ingested. It had to be spilled. The dam had to become a concrete waterfall. At 5 A.M. that morning, the gates on the spillway opened.*

We had no idea any of this was going on until we drove down into the river canyon on the steep highway that comes in from the south.

---

*For the Bonneville Power Administration, spilling the Columbia is the same as throwing away money. In the twenty-four hours that the Columbia spilled over Grand Coulee Dam that weekend, the BPA lost about $1.17 million in potential electricity sales.

Before we could see the spillway, we heard the dull thunder of falling water. We hurried to the narrow road that runs across the top of the mile-wide dam. Leaving the car unlocked, we rushed to the railed sidewalk that looks down over the dam's spillway. The river seemed to explode as it fell. The dam trembled beneath our feet. We had to shout to talk. At the base of the spillway, 350 feet below us, the Columbia seethed, boiling up a milky spray in the warm May wind, before scuffling downstream and turning a marbled green pocked with sinkholes. The din from the falling river and the vibration from the dam made my father smile. For him, it was like hearing a song from the thirties, a snatch of dance-hall music from B Street.

It triggered memories for me, too, but of a different kind. I had once worked at Grand Coulee. I got fired after less than four weeks.

When I was in college in the early 1970s, my father was again working at the dam. Grand Coulee was expanding, acquiring a new powerhouse, and my father—then in his early sixties—was a welder on the project. He used his contacts at the dam to get me a summer job as a union laborer. It paid the then-princely sum of five dollars an hour. My labor crew cleaned up bits of wire, half-eaten pickles, cigarette butts, gobs of spat-out chewing tobacco, and whatever else might be left behind by craftsmen who were higher up on the wage scale. Iron-workers, men who tie together the steel reinforcing bars that form the skeleton of a concrete dam, were not above blowing their noses and peeing in the places we laborers cleaned. This, of course, was the same job that my father had hated when he worked at the dam in the thirties.

I was nineteen at the time, between my freshman and sophomore years at Gonzaga University in nearby Spokane, and greatly impressed with myself. On the job at the dam, I made a point of telling the guys on my labor crew how unutterably boring our jobs were and how I could not wait to get back to school. Many of the laborers were middle-aged Indians with families. They kept their mouths shut and their eyes averted from me.

Federal inspectors nosed around after our work, sniffing out untidiness. They often spotted un-picked-up wire and other crimes. They complained to a superintendent who complained to some other boss who complained to an unhappy man named Tex, the foreman of our labor crew. Tex then yelled at me, the gabby, self-infatuated college boy. Tex (I never learned his last name) was not much of a talker. When he did speak, he had an almost incomprehensible West Texas twang. Meaning to say "wire," he said something that sounded like "war." Nearly everything else he called "shit."

"Git off yer ass, pick up that war 'n shit," he instructed me, after complaints about our crew's cleaning efforts had trickled down the chain of command.

Our labor crew worked the swing shift, four to midnight, performing custodial duties near the spillway at Grand Coulee. The river, swollen in the summer of 1971 with heavy snowmelt from the Canadian Rockies, rioted over the dam twenty-four hours a day. The cascade had eight times the volume of Niagara Falls and fell twice as far. The base of the dam was a bedlam of white water and ferocious deep-throated noise. Tex would shout "war" in my face, but I barely heard him. Along with the racket, cold spray geysered up, slathering the construction site in a gauzy, slippery haze that was slashed at night by hundreds of spotlights.

Two men were killed the summer I worked at the dam. One was run over by an earthmover as he left the parking lot in a Volkswagen bug after his shift. Another died when someone knocked a bolt off a ledge. It fell a couple of hundred feet before punching a hole through his hardhat. The entire dam site—wrapped in the spray and yowl of the river—struck my sophomoric sensibility as a death trap. At weekly safety meetings I filled out lengthy reports on what I considered to be hazardous work practices on the part of our labor crew.

By my fourth week at the dam, Tex had had enough. He told me at the end of the shift not to come back. He mumbled something about how I spent too much time on my butt when big bosses were around. I slunk away from the river without an argument, driving home alone to Moses Lake after midnight. A stream of Gordon Lightfoot dirges played on a radio station out of Chicago, and I just barely managed not to cry. I was worried about what my father was going to say. His welding job at the dam paid for the Volvo I was driving, for the eight-hundred-dollar initiation fee that got me into the Laborer's Union, for a big slice of my college education. My father had been shrewd enough to work much of his life for men like Tex without getting canned. He had gone to considerable trouble to line me up with the best-paying summer job a college kid could find in eastern Washington. And I had been too much of a smart aleck to keep it.

When I got home at 2 A.M., I left a note for my father on the kitchen table. He would be getting up in three hours to drive back up to work at Grand Coulee. The note said I was sorry for letting him down, which was true. What I did not say was that I was relieved to be away from that river.

Before he went off to work that morning, my father came into my bedroom and woke me up. He was not angry. He said it was not my fault, although he must have known it was. He said I was a good son, and he never again mentioned my firing.

As we stood together on top of the dam twenty-three years later, we did not say a word about any of this. Instead, I told my father that the noise, the vibration, and the height of the dam scared me. He said it did not scare him, that it had never scared him.

My father told me at lunch that he had felt a sense of loss when he left Grand Coulee in the late thirties. Living in the boomtown had been the wildest, most exciting adventure of his life. Unlike many of his friends, he had had the good sense not to blow his money on B Street. The Biggest Thing on Earth put money in his pocket and launched him on a career as a union craftsman—as a home-owning, car-buying, pension-earning family man.

I asked my father if he had ever doubted the wisdom of building the dam. He said no he had not. He did not seem to think my question made any sense.

In the environmental literature of the American West, one federal agency dwells alone in the innermost circle of hell. The late Wallace Stegner, the West's most gifted and authoritative writer on land use, found something redeeming in all the other federal agencies that administer the open spaces beyond the Mississippi, where the federal government owns about half the land. Stegner praised, albeit with reservations, the stewardship of the National Park Service, the National Forest Service, the Fish and Wildlife Service, and the Bureau of Land Management, which oversees grazing land. Stegner believed these agencies had made "western space available to millions. They have been the strongest impediment to the careless ruin of what remains of the Public Domain."

But the Bureau of Reclamation, Stegner wrote, "is something else. From the beginning, its aim has been not the preservation but the remaking—in effect the mining—of the West. . . . It discovered where power was, and allied itself with it: the growers and landowners, private and corporate, whose interests it served. . . ."

Stegner blamed the Bureau for, among other things, failing to protect the family farm, for encouraging westerners to use three times as much water per capita as people back East, for poisoning farmlands with salts from ill-designed irrigation systems, for concentrating power in the hands of a technocratic elite, and for building reservoirs whose constantly changing levels leave dirty bathtub rings in the most splendid canyons of the West.

In the demonic picture of the Bureau that has been painted by Stegner and a growing number of western historians, the foot soldiers of evil are civil engineers: the men (always men, white men) who designed dams and supervised their construction. These engineers have been derided as deracinated henchmen of a centralized state intent on bastardizing nature to make money for a well-heeled elite. The engineer's job in the West, argues Donald Worster in *Rivers of Empire*, "is to tell us how the dominating is to be done. The contemporary engineer is the best exemplar of [the] power of expertise. Though not himself necessarily concerned with profit-making, he reinforces directly and indirectly the rule . . . of unending economic growth."

Bureau engineers stand accused of transforming rivers into purely commercial instruments: acre-feet of water banked in reservoirs and kilowatt-hours to be traded or sold. "In that new language of the market calculation lies an assertion of ultimate power over nature—of a domination that is absolute, total, and free from all restraint," Worster writes. "The behavior that follows making water into a commodity is aggressively manipulative beyond any previous historical experience."

L. Vaughn Downs, eighty-eight years old and living with his wife, Margaret, in a retirement home when I made his acquaintance, did not look or sound like a manipulative agent of the devil.

The retired Bureau engineer had a big bald head, a flat prairie accent, and a firm handshake. He was the son of a Kansas hog farmer. He was courtly, sharp of mind, precise of speech, and hard of hearing. He had read some of the books that vilified the Bureau and its engineers. But they appeared not to have made him bitter. He dismissed the criticism as ill-informed speculation from non-engineers who did not have their numbers straight. The Stegners, the Worsters, and the rest of the environmental bunch had written nothing that tested his faith in the Bureau, nothing that made him doubt the rectitude of Grand Coulee Dam.

Downs devoted his entire professional life to the design, construction, operation, and maintenance of the dam and its irrigation system. He joined the Bureau in 1931, fresh from engineering school at the University of Kansas. For an aspiring builder of dams, his timing could not have been better. Within a year, Roosevelt was elected president and the Bureau was given a blank check to remake the rivers and deserts of the West.

Downs went to work in the Bureau's design office in Denver where blueprints sat on drafting tables for what would become the world's four largest dams—Hoover, Shasta, Bonneville, and Grand Coulee. The young engineer combined good timing with even better social contacts. He married into the Bureau's hierarchy. In a passage from his memoirs that is characteristically short on sentiment but long on engineering detail, Downs explains how he fell in love in the Denver office:

"When the Bureau held an open house to display its new 5,000,000-pound capacity testing machine in the breaking of a mass concrete test cylinder 36 inches in diameter by 72 inches in height, many of the Bureau personnel and their friends and families were present. Such a test had never been performed before. There with my friends . . . was a young woman. We were introduced. She was Margaret Savage going to art school in Denver and residing with her Uncle Jack."

Uncle Jack was John Lucian Savage, an internationally known Bureau engineer, a member of the *Popular Mechanics'* Hall of Fame, and the chief designer of Grand Coulee Dam. With Uncle Jack's blessing, Downs was transferred from a drafting table to a field position as an assistant engineer in quality control at Grand Coulee. He arrived in the Columbia Basin in May of 1934, and he never left. Margaret married him in 1935, and they moved into a tidy yellow house at the base of the dam site in Engineer's Town, which the Bureau built exclusively for its engineers, senior administrators, and their families. The hard-scrabble world of my father—cold-water shacks and B Street's seedy diversions—was just up the hill. But as far as Downs was concerned, it might as well have been on the moon.

The men of the Bureau lived in a separate, subsidized world—physically apart from and socially superior to the workers and the private contractors. The rigid caste system at the dam site stunned newcomers from the East who had assumed that in a western boom-town they would find a classless society. Esther Rice, a schoolteacher from Manchester, New Hampshire, and a graduate of Vassar College, taught school in Grand Coulee in the late 1930s. Nothing surprised her more than the Brahmin status of Bureau men like Vaughn Downs.

"I thought it was fantastic that a government job would bestow such power," Rice told me. "I had met powerful people back home . . . but these Bureau people were different. They exuded the feeling that they had the final power over everything in life. You had to be very careful around the Bureau men about what you said."

When I learned that Downs was living in the Hearthstone Retire-ment Home in Moses Lake, I called him up and proposed the same deal that I had made with my father. I would buy him lunch in Grand Coulee in exchange for his allowing me to see the dam through his eyes. Like my father, he could not resist another look at the dam. After I picked him up on a Saturday morning at the retirement home, he wasted no time in showing me how a Bureau engineer of his generation, a man who came of age in a federal agency where smart young people fell in love at concrete-crushing parties, sees the West's greatest river.

"There are three basic questions in building a dam," Downs explained as we drove north to the dam. "Where? What of? What do you get when you are finished? To all of these questions, Grand Coulee provided excellent answers."

I tried several times to turn the conversation to other questions. What did the Bureau do to Columbia River Indians? What did it do to the salmon in the river? What hijinks do you remember about B Street? Downs seemed uninterested, a bit irritated. He referred me to his memoirs. But *The Mightiest of Them All* says little about B Street and nothing about the effect of the dam on the Colville Indians, whose reservation borders it. As for salmon, the book argues—rather incredibly—that the dam's blocking off of 1,400 miles of salmon spawning grounds on the upper Columbia "did not kill off the salmon resource in the river, but apparently enhanced it."

So we talked about basic dam questions. Where? What of? What do you get? As Downs explained it, there could not have been a more perfect place to build the world's largest dam.

"Nature provided everything but the cement," Downs said.

First, there was the river canyon where the dam was secured to bedrock. Beneath a layer of loose rock and earth, engineers from the Bureau found, to their delight, that the Columbia was cradled in a U-shaped abutment of solid granite. There is, Downs said, no better rock to pour concrete on.

Then, of course, there was the river, incomparably useful for making electricity, and dependably fat in the hottest months when irrigators would want to bleed it for water. Downs was also pleased to point out the massive irrigation storage reservoir, otherwise known as the Grand Coulee, that nature had had the courtesy to dig right next to the dam site.

The Grand Coulee is the largest and most spectacular of all the scars gouged in the Pacific Northwest by the catastrophic floods that came at the end of the last ice age. Fifty miles long, between one mile and six miles wide, with sheer basalt walls nine hundred feet high, it

102 astonished the first white men who saw it. Lieutenant T. W. Simons of the U.S. Cavalry said that "its perpendicular walls form[ed] a vista like some grand old ruined roofless hall." An American fur trader, Alexander Ross, described the coulee as "thickly studded with ranges of columns, pillars, battlements, turrets, and steps above steps, in every variety of shade and colour. . . . Thunder and lightning are known to be more frequent here than in other parts; and a rumbling in the earth is sometimes heard. According to Indian tradition, it is the abode of evil spirits. . . . It is the wonder of Oregon."

The coulee was cut about twelve thousand years ago after a massive sheet of ice, moving southeast out of what is now British Columbia, choked off the flow of the Columbia. The ice dam (located quite close to the spot where the Bureau chose to pour its concrete) backed up the river, creating a giant lake that soon spilled, with savage force, out of the river canyon. The flood washed south, reaming a trench for itself out of volcanic rock—the Grand Coulee.*

When the weather warmed up, the ice plug melted, the ice sheet retreated, and the Columbia returned to its original bed. The Grand Coulee, North America's most splendid runoff ditch, was left high and dry and perched more than five hundred feet above the southeast bank of the undammed river.

It was still dry as a bone, with rattlesnakes, tumbleweeds, and Indian rumors about evil spirits, when Vaughn Downs took a bus to eastern Washington in 1934. He remembers thinking to himself, "My God Almighty, what a desolate country." It took Downs and his Bureau colleagues nearly twenty years to do it, but they filled the big ditch with water. They installed twelve huge pumps behind the dam, which in the summertime can suck a billion gallons of water a day out of the Columbia and spit them up over the lip of the river canyon into the coulee. They named the lake that drowned the Grand Coulee after the late Frank A. Banks, the Bureau's chief construction engineer at the dam.

*A later series of at least forty catastrophic floods, coming from another direction, out of the northeast, deepened and widened the Grand Coulee.

Banks, the dominant personality in the building of the dam and a man who ranks at the top in Downs's pantheon of great Bureau engineers, made no secret about what the Bureau was trying to do in the West. He preached "total use." In a speech to utility executives in 1945, he said: "Our high level of living is chiefly a matter of the intelligent use of power and machinery. If we would have more, we must produce more. We must use more power."

As Downs and I drove along the edge of the Grand Coulee, the engineer took pains to make me appreciate how remarkably suited the coulee is for its government-assigned duty of storing irrigation water. Downs explained that the basalt rock, out of which the Grand Coulee was cut by the long-ago flood, is virtually watertight. The coulee holds water, he said, almost as well as a glass mixing bowl. To prove just how tight the basalt was, he asked me to drive to the southern tip of the twenty-seven-mile-long reservoir.

I stopped my car, as instructed, on a dirt road about a mile south (and downhill) from the end of the reservoir. Downs directed my attention to two eighteen-inch culverts that passed beneath the dirt road. A scant trickle of water flowed in the culverts.

"That's all the water that gets away from Banks Lake," Downs said, quietly triumphant. "The total increase in water in the lower Coulee is on the order of half a cubic foot per second. Like I say, it's tight rock."

When we visited the dam itself, Downs continued to direct my attention to basic questions. He told me more about rock, a special kind of rock called aggregate: a round, river-polished, gravel-like stone that is a key ingredient in making concrete. To build the world's largest concrete structure, the Bureau needed unlimited local access to high-quality aggregate.

Downs explained that nature provided a vast deposit of aggregate, conveniently located on the riverbank, right next to the dam site. It was so convenient that it did not have to be trucked to concrete mixers. The rock arrived by conveyor belt.

"This was really high-quality aggregate. There isn't any better that we know of," Downs said at lunch, allowing himself to use superlatives.

104   Again, I tried to steer the conversation. Why didn't the Bureau build fish ladders at the dam, like at Bonneville Dam on the lower Columbia, which was built at roughly the same time? Did the height of Grand Coulee (350 feet) make fish passage an engineering impossibility?

"It was just money. If you build a dam, you could sure as hell build a fish ladder," Downs said.*

I asked, again, about Indians. What kind of contact did the Bureau have with the nearby Colville tribe? Did Bureau engineers ever attend the Salmon Days festival that the tribe holds each summer and to which it invited everyone in the region? "I never went up to Salmon Days and I never knew anyone who did," Downs said, adding that he had heard that the "sheriffs up there locked up the drunks around tree trunks with handcuffs."

The engineer shifted back to familiar ground, back to rocks and basic questions. As Downs explained it, the construction of the dam was preordained: The aggregate for the concrete was pushed down from Canada by the prehistoric glacier that plugged the river that made the coulee that the Bureau made into the irrigation storage reservoir

---

*The official Bureau position on why Grand Coulee made no provision for fish passage is that the height of the dam made it impossible, given engineering knowledge in the 1930s. As Downs said, however, the Bureau's failure to provide for salmon was more a matter of money and interest.

Milo Bell, professor emeritus in bioengineering at the University of Washington and one of the world's leading authorities on dam design and salmon survival, told me there was no technical reason why a fish ladder could not have been built in the 1930s that would have allowed a very high percentage of salmon to climb around the dam. "The fish don't care how they swim upstream," Bell said.

The more vexing bioengineering problem presented by a high dam like Grand Coulee was safe downstream passage of juveniles over the dam's spillway. But on this, too, the Bureau simply was not interested in conducting tests or spending money to design a dam that would keep salmon alive, according to Bell, a longtime consultant to the federal government in dam design in the Pacific Northwest. Bell said the steep spillway at Grand Coulee forces fish to "fall out of the water on the way down. They strike at 120 feet per second, and they are dead."

This design, Bell said, was chosen by the Bureau because it dissipated most of the river's erosive energy at the base of the dam, where the Bureau built a concrete "bucket" to absorb the impact of the falling river. Bell said the Bureau was worried that a more gradual slope for the spillway, which would have allowed juvenile salmon to survive the fall over the dam, might "cause problems to the [dam's] foundation. Their testing was designed not to dig a hole [under the dam]. They did not test to spill fish. The Bureau did not wish to spend any money on fish."

that hardly leaks. The Bureau, it seemed, was merely finishing up a job on which God had been an early subcontractor.

If God did want the dam built, He did not tell the Bureau, or at least He did not tell the Bureau first. The idea of building the dam originated in a small-town lawyer's office in the Columbia Basin desert in the late spring of 1917. It came up as five young business and professional men from the fly-blown town of Ephrata, Washington, discussed the bleak prospects of raising crops and building a community with less than eight inches of rain a year.

One of them mentioned that he had taken a trip up to the Grand Coulee with a University of Washington geologist who told him how a glacier plugged up the Columbia and diverted the river. Billy Clapp, the young lawyer in whose office the men had gathered, was struck by an idea. If nature could do it with ice, Clapp asked, why couldn't men do it with concrete?

"In their ignorance of the engineering features involved, those present conceded that it might be a good idea," recalled W. Gale Matthews, who attended the meeting. "No one, however, had the courage to go out and say very much about the idea, fearing the kidding which would result."

The idea languished for more than a year until Rufus Woods, a newspaper publisher from nearby Wenatchee, drove his Model T into Ephrata looking for advertisements and news. He got wind of the dam, interviewed Billy Clapp, and adopted the Grand Coulee scheme, first as a circulation gimmick for the *Wenatchee World*, then as a cure-all for the local economy, and finally as the defining cause of his life.

Woods, a failed lawyer and failed Yukon gold miner, devoted almost twenty years of breathless front-page coverage to the dam. "Such a power," Woods wrote, in a typical eruption of boosterism and bombast, "would operate railroads, factories, mines, irrigation pumps, furnish[ing] heat and light in such measure that all in all it would be the most unique, the most interesting, and the most remarkable development. . . . in the age of industrial and scientific miracles." The publisher

106 sent special editions of his paper, which explained the miraculous national benefits of the dam, to every member of Congress. Eastern engineers and local politicians who were less than ecstatic about the dam were scorned in Woods's newspaper. A *World* subscriber, after sixteen years of reading about the dam, complained in a letter that "when a person thinks and talks about the same subject continually, he is mentally unbalanced and headed for the insane asylum."

What Woods wanted from the dam, however, was eminently sensible. It was what every small-town booster across the underpopulated West wanted: to get a rich outside benefactor to subsidize the transformation of his region into an agricultural-industrial hub, while preserving a profitable measure of local control. The trick, as Woods described, was "to get the government to do it" and "at the same time protect the interest of the locality."

When his crusade was won—with the election of Roosevelt and the federal decision to build the dam—Woods learned the humiliating lesson that the Bureau of Reclamation taught local boosters in river basins across the West. Namely, federal funding with local control is an oxymoron. The Bureau runs what it builds. It and the Bonneville Power Administration took over Grand Coulee Dam. They owned its electricity. With the Army Corps of Engineers, they dictated the future of the Columbia River. Federal technocrats exercised power, and locals like Rufus Woods were reduced to exercising their lungs.

Most of Grand Coulee's electricity was piped out of eastern Washington on federally built long-distance power lines to factories on the West Side of the Cascades or to the secret plutonium plant at Hanford. Wenatchee never became an industrial center. North-central Washington State remained a boondock. Woods never got over the loss of local control that was the price of winning the dam. The federal takeover was "just as wrong as it can be," he wrote in a 1943 letter. "This whole section [of eastern Washington] has been treated as though it were a scrub."

The resentment that Woods and his white middle-class business associates felt at the hands of Bureau engineers like Vaughn Downs was largely a matter of bruised pride and lost local business opportunity. It had nothing to do with doubts about damming the river, destroying salmon runs, or flooding land. The Columbia Basin Development League, of which Woods was president, was concerned above all else with squeezing dollars out of the Columbia. Its motto quoted Herbert Hoover: "Every drop of water that runs to the sea without yielding its full commercial return to the nation is an economic waste."

Grand Coulee did generate a purer, less mercantile kind of resentment. On the far side of the dam, it festers on in the collective memory of a people who—before the arrival of the Biggest Thing on Earth—centered their existence on salmon.

5

The Flood

Since the flood, everything is Safeway.
> —MATTIE GRUNLOSE
> *Colville Indian,*
> *born December 17, 1901*

ABOUT SEVENTY MILES northwest of the dam, down near the river on the Colville Reservation, a weather-beaten sign had fallen backwards in the dirt. "DRUGS, ALCOHOL, SUICIDE," it said. Beside the faded words was the silhouette of an Indian brave slumped over a horse. The yard around the sign was littered with wrecked cars, washing machines, and bits of shattered furniture. The place belonged to Martin Louie, Sr., a former forest ranger and sobered-up alcoholic, a teller of Colville tribal legends and professional "informant" to legions of anthropologists.

Louie, at the age of eighty-six, was one of the last remaining Colvilles who, before Grand Coulee Dam, made a living spearing salmon in the upper Columbia River. I found him in bed on a drizzly spring morning in his leaky camping trailer, which was covered against the rain by a blue plastic tarp. The old man had rheumy blue eyes, patrimony from a Welsh grandfather who worked for the Hudson's Bay Company. He wore a blue T-shirt beneath a purple acetate shirt beneath a tattered green cardigan sweater, stained down the front with what looked to be spilled food and slobber.

His trailer had a view of Franklin D. Roosevelt Lake, which is what the federal government calls the bloated remains of the river behind Grand Coulee Dam. It is where Louie used to spear salmon.

"You askin' me what did we do after the flood?" Louie said, looking up at me from his bed.

"We starved. We drank. My daughter-in-law's son committed suicide. He blowed his brains out about three or four years ago with a rifle. I know two or three who committed suicide. Let me show you something."

Louie got up and shuffled into the kitchen of his trailer. He said the federal government sends him food every month. From a shelf he grabbed a can of United States Department of Agriculture food aid labeled "PINK SALMON." Louie shoved the can in my face.

"This is how you replaced our salmon!" he screamed. "You guys took all my food!"

Louie was not screaming at humankind in general. He was screaming at me, the sheepish white man in his trailer. As far as Louie was concerned, I was a member of that arrogant white horde that had castrated his river, killed his fish, and ruined his reservation.

Shortly after Louie shoved the PINK SALMON in my face, a Meals on Wheels van came to take him off to his food-program lunch in nearby Inchelium. The old man left mad. This was not what I had had in mind when I came home from Eastern Europe. Only a few months before I knocked on the door of Louie's trailer, I had been watching and writing about ethnic cleansing in Bosnia. I had compared the Serbs to Nazis. I had been full of indignation, incredulous that humans could be so stupidly cruel to each other. Here, not more than 150 miles from the place where I was born and grew up, an angry old man was accusing me and my tribe of something that a reasonable European might call ethnic cleansing. Instead of artillery and rape and terror, we had used folk songs and concrete. Instead of numbing our collective conscience with plum brandy, as the Serb soldiers did, we had self-medicated with myths about empire.

Louie's anger, I thought, was payback for the undeserved friendship and confidences that the men on the river barge had lavished on me. Because I was white, because I talked the talk of the engineered river, because I was from Moses Lake, the bargers figured I was one of them.

110   The old Indian, for the same reasons, figured I had a hand in making a world where Colvilles had no salmon, drank to excess, and blew their brains out. Stupidly, I had given Louie good reason to be suspicious. In trying to ingratiate myself as his neighbor, I told him my family had lived in the Columbia Basin since the 1930s, that my father helped build Grand Coulee, and that I, too, had worked there.

Left alone in the dirt yard in front of Louie's trailer, I decided to drive back to the dam. I had grown up hearing dark warnings about driving alone on the Indian reservation that lies north of Grand Coulee. Watch your car! Those Indians will steal it. Watch yourself on the roads! They are always drunk. But no one tried to steal my car and no one came close to running me over. My only unscheduled encounter on the reservation occurred on my drive back from Louie's trailer. At a road construction site, the foreman of a Colville highway crew, out on a pothole-patching job, flagged me down and suggested that I not drive so fast.

When Grand Coulee Dam came into view, I tried to see it as the Colvilles have been seeing it for more than half a century: a greasy gray monstrosity surrounded by white people with new cars. At the city limits of Coulee Dam, a town built by the Bureau of Reclamation and still occupied mostly by white dam workers, the blowing dust and rusted junk of the reservation gave way to freshly painted houses, tidy green lawns, and the steady stitching of sprinklers. I stayed on in Coulee Dam for a few days, talking to whites about Indians.

In the town library I asked after a book that had been recommended to me by the Colville Reservation's resident historian. The book explained how the Bureau had been in such a hurry to build the dam that it flooded out anthropologists who were examining Indian artifacts above Grand Coulee.

"Who told you we have that book?" the white librarian asked sharply, clearly doubting her library would harbor such information.

I told her the name of an Indian woman. The librarian, a woman in her late thirties, rolled her eyes and shook her head. Without a word, she indicated that I was a fool to believe that an Indian could know anything about a library. (The book was precisely where the Indian woman said it would be.)

Other whites around the dam volunteered similar views on Indians.

"They are kinda like colored people. They are lazy and they don't want to work," said a retired white telephone operator who has lived near that dam for more than half a century. "They are trying every way in the world to get money for nothing out of our dam."

A retired engineer who worked for the Bureau of Reclamation at Grand Coulee told me that "they [the Indians] are privileged characters. Yeah, they got by pretty easy. You never saw many of them when the real work was going on. Only when it was over did they come sneaking back."

Salmon, in Grand Coulee, seemed tainted by their association with Indians.

"I don't give a good goddamn about salmon," said Dick Taylor, owner of the Four Winds Guest House, a tourist motel with a view of Grand Coulee Dam. "I don't know anybody around here who gives a goddamn about salmon. Salmon are what you see in the cans. Saving salmon, it doesn't make sense. Maybe we should go way back in time to the horse and buggy. Then we could all walk around and step in horseshit."

The Four Winds was full-up with families that came out to coulee country to feast on statistics about the dam. Enough concrete to bury Montana three inches deep. Enough to bury Texas one inch deep. The spectacle that drew most of Taylor's clientele was produced by the Bureau of Reclamation and advertised as the "world's largest laser light show."

I joined Taylor's tourists to watch the show. It began after the sun went down and families had stopped grazing at concession booths that included "Sigfried's Funnel Cakes" and "Custer's First Stand Indian Jewelry." We all gathered in a park beneath the dam to watch needles of colored light dance around on the dam's spillway, a screen that an announcer said was wider than four battleships placed end to end. Just as the show began, operators of the dam released a film of whitish water

112 from the backed-up Columbia. It was just enough to coat the concrete screen, cover it like spilled milk on greasy black linoleum, and make laser lights show up nicely.

Despite the Bureau's professed conversion from dam building to water conservation, the show was an unapologetic throwback. The narrator of the show was a honey-voiced old man who claimed to be the Columbia River.

"You have done what I could not accomplish alone," the river voice said gratefully, thanking the Bureau for the wonder of Grand Coulee Dam. "Through your engineering skills you have diverted part of my course and spread my waters over the land. You have created the missing link in the cycle of life, the rainfall that nature could not provide. You have irrigated the land. You have made the desert bloom."

The voice said, quite misleadingly, that all one million acres of the Columbia Basin Irrigation Project were going to be completed and that the entire project had been an unqualified success. In a bit of Soviet-style revisionism, the voice did not explain that Hanford— with its drifting underground plumes of poison and its secret radiation releases—came to the banks of the river in the 1940s because of abundant electricity generated at Grand Coulee Dam. The voice made no reference whatsoever to the plutonium factory, located just 160 miles south of Grand Coulee. Like a disgraced Kremlin leader, Hanford was erased from memory.*

The voice did mention salmon and Indians, saying that "in stark contrast to the grand scope and vision of the project's benefits came the hard realities of the trade-offs for such aspiring dreams." It said towns were flooded and Indian fishing sites disappeared. But it did not say that Grand Coulee wiped out more salmon than any single structure

*Hanford has not always been politically incorrect. The Department of the Interior produced a movie about the Columbia River in the early 1950s that made glowing reference to Hanford and its role in manufacturing plutonium for the bomb dropped on Nagasaki. The narrator of that film (who did not pretend to speak for the river) said: "In the barren hills below Grand Coulee, the stream grew warmer and almost magically the atomic bomb was born. Thus the power of the Columbia helped bring our boys back from the Pacific two years sooner than they had dared hope."

in American history, nor did it explain that when fishing grounds were flooded and the fish disappeared, the Indians above the dam began a half-century skid into alcoholism, suicide, car wrecks, and death from preventable disease.

The more time I spent around Grand Coulee Dam, the more it seemed a Rosetta stone for the engineered West. It deciphered a history at once glorious and mean, egalitarian and racist, farsighted and blind. The spectacular early success of the dam guaranteed that it would spawn sequels—that the entire Columbia River would be fattened up between concrete. The dam also gave the federal government the strategic toehold it needed to take over the Columbia Basin. If the river was to be thoroughly throttled for the greater good, if the working stiff was to have electricity in his house and food on his table, Grand Coulee Dam proved that federal technocrats had to come in with serious money, elbow aside local boosters, and take control.

The dam's most sobering lesson was personal. I could look at that wedge of concrete and see my tribe of Great Depression runaways as both the builders of a promised land and unrepentant participants in ethnic cleansing. What seemed particularly curious to me about the dam was that no one south of the Colville Reservation—down in irrigation country around Moses Lake, down at Hanford's nuclear site— seemed interested in the whole story the dam had to tell. I asked a history teacher at Big Bend Community College in Moses Lake about local understanding of the dam and its consequences.

"There is a disconnect around here that drives me crazy," said Brenda Teals. "My students grow up in a state of ignorance about what happened with the dam. Teachers have not been taught what to teach. Nobody knows because nobody knows. There is nothing said about what happened to the Indians. There is a feeling that it all happened somewhere else. Of course, the Indians are still around. But everyone tries to ignore them. They don't look like majestic noble savages. They are poor, unattractive people with health problems. The Colville Reservation is another planet."

114   Jeff Korth, a fisheries biologist for the Washington State Fish and Game Department, looked after many of the artificial lakes and reservoirs that were created by Grand Coulee's irrigation system. He told me that the most consistently astounding aspect of his work is that people who live in the Columbia Basin "don't know where they are. They are utterly unfamiliar with why they are able to live in the desert. They don't know where the water comes from."

In *Rivers of Empire*, western historian Donald Worster writes that mass amnesia and apathy about the origins and operations of federally built irrigation schemes are endemic across the arid West. "Power becomes faceless and impersonal," Worster writes, "so much so that many are unaware it exists."

Shortly after my morning with the Indian who accused me of stealing his salmon, I called on the white prosecutor and coroner for Ferry County, which has jurisdiction on part of the Colville Reservation. Allen Nielson described death scenes his work requires him to attend.

"Typically, what I see is a young Indian male with high blood alcohol and perhaps some drugs. He has been suffering from depression and unemployed for some period of time. It is usually a gunshot or a traffic accident. You can take a graduating class at Inchelium High [on the reservation] and in ten years they are all dead. It is absolutely staggering."

Before the dam, each member of the Colville tribe ate, on average, about one and a quarter pounds of salmon a day, according to Verne Ray, an anthropologist who lived among the Colvilles in the 1920s.

The most sacred ceremonies of Colville religious life, along with the most intensive seasons of work and feasting, revolved around the summer salmon harvest. The heart of the catch was the summer chinook, the biggest and finest of Columbia River salmon. Whites called them "June Hogs," and they often weighed sixty to eighty pounds. Most of the salmon were caught in traps or speared in white water around

Kettle Falls, where the river boiled over and around a series of dikes created by giant folds of a hard stone called quartzite.

When the dam was finished and the upstream Columbia became a 150-mile-long lake, Kettle Falls disappeared, along with all the salmon. On the reservations, rates of suicide, fatal car accidents, alcoholism, drug addiction, divorce, and death by house fire soared to levels that stunned the anthropologist who had lived with the Colvilles before the building of the dam. Ray wrote that Grand Coulee Dam was built with "a ruthless disregard for Indians as human beings," creating a dammed-up river that "drowned the culture it had nourished."

The builders of Grand Coulee Dam treated the Colvilles with a disregard that found its way into the Bureau's 1937 annual report on construction progress at the dam. It mentioned Indians only once— in a paragraph that also discussed "rules governing ownership of dogs."

The dam flooded more than 21,000 acres of prime bottom land, where Indians had been living for perhaps as long as ten thousand years. In addition to Kettle Falls, the best hunting, farming, and root-gathering land disappeared. So did most tribal burial grounds. The Bureau of Reclamation decided, only at the last moment, to relocate Indian graveyards. It hired a Spokane funeral home to help the tribe quickly dig up bones and haul them to higher ground. The Bureau belatedly asked University of Washington anthropologists to catalog what was going underwater. They wrote that "the steady rise of the water level back of Grand Coulee Dam put a premium on speed. Many places had necessarily to be slighted or only superficially examined as the water lapped at our heels."

After the flood, drinking water and phone service to some parts of the reservation were cut off for thirty years. None of the irrigation water diverted from the river by Grand Coulee Dam was made available to the Indians. All of the water—pumped daily during the irrigation season in quantities that would more than meet the needs of the entire city of Chicago—went to the non-reservation side of the Columbia. Reservation residents paid more than twice as much for

116   electricity as did their (mostly white) neighbors across the Columbia in Grant County.

As the non-Indian side of the Columbia (the side where I grew up) attracted industry and farmers with its subsidized power and water, the economy of the reservation withered. Unemployment hovered at around 50 percent for decades. A chart of income distribution on the reservation in the early 1990s showed no middle class.

As part of an after-the-fact environmental impact statement that the Bureau of Reclamation prepared on Grand Coulee Dam in 1975 (forty-two years after work began on the project), Colville leaders were asked what the dam had done for them.

"Tribal members paid with their homes, their lifestyle, their food-stuffs, so that others could have jobs, incomes, and wealth," the statement said. "The Indians are treated as non-persons."*

Vern Seward was one-quarter Colville, the minimum "blood quantum" necessary to qualify as a registered member of the tribe. His three children did not qualify because their mother was white. Seward, who was seventy-six years old when I visited his house trailer on the reservation, did not speak the Salish language of the Colvilles, nor did he know much about the tribe's traditional religion, which saw the Creator in the salmon that surged upstream in the Columbia.

What defined Seward as a Colville was resentment. He resented the Bureau for victimizing the Colville tribe. He resented the Colville tribe for living like victims. Feeding his anger was an uncanny memory. With greater precision and with more passion than anyone I came across on the reservation, he described what it was like to spear salmon before Coulee Dam drowned Kettle Falls. He could remember, he told me,

---

*This pattern of treatment has been the same across the irrigated West, with Indian lands being flooded under federal reservoirs as electricity and irrigation water flow away to white people. A National Water Commission, in a comprehensive report to Congress on federal reclamation schemes in the West, said that the federal government consistently ignored Indian water rights guaranteed under federal law. "With few exceptions the projects were planned and built by the Federal Government without any attempt to define, let alone protect, prior rights that Indian tribes might have had. . . . In the history of the United States Government's treatment of Indian tribes, its failure to protect Indian water rights for use on the Reservations it set aside for them is one of the sorrier chapters."

because he had been thinking about it for sixty years. He remembered because the circumstances of his dislocated life allowed him a single season at the falls.

"I only had one summer," he said, "to live like an Indian."

In 1932, the same year my father rode a westbound boxcar, Seward was bumming his way into Washington State aboard a freight train full of migrants. He was escaping an Indian boarding school where he had been learning—since the age of six—how to be a perfect white man.

In a sense, he learned his lessons well. An exception to the rule of want among the Colville, he found work as a teenager at Grand Coulee Dam running a jackhammer, learned blueprint reading in the navy, and spent the bulk of his life off the reservation as a construction boss. For nearly twenty years, he was a superintendent for federal projects that built and repaired houses on Indian reservations across the Northwest. Seward retired with money in the bank and a government pension. He could afford a late-model Buick, an air-conditioned mobile home, and the fanciest satellite dish I saw on Colville land.

His blue single-wide trailer house stood on the bank of the Columbia, about six miles downstream from Grand Coulee Dam. Each morning when he drank his coffee and looked out the kitchen window of his trailer, he saw the river through the black steel mesh of his satellite dish.

Despite his relative prosperity, Seward was not comfortable with what he had made of himself. He drew a federal paycheck most of his life, yet he hated the federal government for damming the Columbia. He lived in the cracks between white and Indian cultures, annoyed by both, completely conversant with neither, a hybrid creation of the engineered West.

When Seward answered my knock on his front door, he reminded me of no one so much as my father. Like my father, he wore a thick flannel shirt, even in hot weather, and he was half deaf. He and my father wore the same make of flesh-colored hearing aids, the ones that fill up ears like gobs of bathtub caulking. They spoke in the same slow rhythms of the blue-collar West: "See, in them days, we. . . ." Seward, like my father, loved Roosevelt above all politicians, living or dead.

118   The youngest of seven children, Seward was sent from the reservation to an orphanage in Spokane when he was two years old. Four years
later, he was dispatched to a federally run Indian boarding school. His
father, a white man from Nebraska, had divorced his mother, a woman
who was one-half Colville, "because she drank too much. My father
couldn't support seven of us. He sent me away. I can remember seeing
him twice in my life and my mother three times."

The school that Seward attended near Salem, in western Oregon,
was part of a national network of federal boarding schools that operated under the guiding philosophy that "the way to 'civilize' the Indian
is to take Indian children, even very young children, as completely as
possible away from home and family life."

At the school, he was drilled like an Army draftee. When he arrived
at age six, he was given a wooden gun, a brown high-collared military
uniform, and ordered to march in formation to meals, church, and his
dormitory. He worked in the school's dairy or the cornfields or the
orchard or in the kitchen, and attended four hours of classes a day.

Along with about 27,000 Indian children across the country, Seward
was an inmate in an educational system that was unique for any group
of American children. According to a scathing 1928 report that led to
wholesale reform in Indian education, "among no other people . . . are
as large a proportion of the total number of children of school age
located in institutions away from their homes."

The report said almost all Indian children were malnourished,
poorly taught, incessantly regimented, and severely overcrowded
in dormitories where tuberculosis and infectious eye disease were
epidemic. Their mail was opened, they were subject to brutal disci-
pline, and there "was a constant violation of the children's personali-
ties." Always, they worked to keep their schools solvent—given that
Congress refused to spend more than eleven cents a day to feed them.
"The labor of children as carried on in Indian boarding schools," the
report said, "would constitute a violation of labor laws in most states."

Seward's best friend at the school, Archie Silverthorn, a member of
the Flathead tribe from western Montana, was gang-raped by a group
of older boys at the school who helped supervise the younger students.

Seward remembers that he joined his terrified friend in reporting the rape to a priest and to the superintendent of the school. Seward said that the older boys denied the assault, and were not punished.

"That night after we told on them, three of the older boys took us to their room, stripped us, and beat us with their belts and buckles. They said, 'If you ever say anything to anyone else, you're going to get it twice as bad.' We learned to keep our mouths shut.

"Archie and me were nine years old at the time, and we wanted to run away. We were always getting beaten, and we were always hungry. But we didn't know just what to do to run away."

It took Seward six years to work up the nerve to run. In the midst of the Depression, he walked six miles to the city of Salem and boarded the first boxcar he saw. He bummed food in rail yard camps in Portland and Seattle. Everyone he met was hungry and looking for a place to live. He had lost all contact with his parents and siblings on the reservation, and he did not know if he would be welcome there. But Seward had nowhere else to go. A freight train dropped him off in Republic, Washington, on the northern edge of the Colville Reservation. A sympathetic train conductor drove him to Kettle Falls and introduced him to an Indian fisherman.

"I had never seen the Columbia River until I came back. I never had the least idea about fishing until I saw all the Indians camped near Kettle Falls. That falls was just a steady roar all the time. It fell about twenty feet. There were awful big salmon jumping up that falls. I couldn't believe they could jump that high. I really couldn't believe my eyes. They were all the way from twenty to sixty pounds. My impression was how can they get that much speed in that current to jump the falls? How can they swim once they landed?"

Joe Adolph, a Colville fisherman, put Seward to work collecting firewood and pulling fish from the J-shaped baskets suspended out over Kettle Falls to catch jumping salmon. Seward was terrified by the river.

"I was afraid of slipping off the wooden scaffold that was built out over the rocks in the falls. If you slipped off that scaffold, you didn't have a chance. It took me quite a number of days before I would take

120   the chance to go out and pick up the salmon. They were hard to pick up because they were so big. I pulled out about four a day. It was a coupla weeks before I went out there with a spear. It was twelve foot long. If the fish jumped close, I would take a shot."

When the run of big chinook salmon in the falls ended in July, Seward traveled downstream with another fisherman, Baptist Louie, to spear smaller salmon in their spawning beds. Seward learned to spear at night by firelight.

"We were in a flat-bottomed boat that had a piece of burning pitch hanging out over the water. Natural fire has no reflection for spearing. We could see the salmon down about twenty feet in the river and they looked white in the firelight. I got so I could spear six to ten of them a night. We dried the fish in the sun, using the smoke of rotten wood to keep away the blowflies and the bees. All that fish was packed away for winter."

The summer by the river was the first time that Seward remembers being happy.

"I never had so much lovin' in my life as from those Indian families. They were really parents to me. They took me into their homes just like I was one of their own. There was nobody to beat on you, to tell you what to do, and force you to do what you didn't want to do. You just live in peace and quiet and with friends. I have never lived that way since."

While Seward was fishing by night with a spear, Roosevelt approved sixty-three million dollars to begin construction on Grand Coulee Dam. Word spread on the reservation that there would be free electricity for all Indians. Seward, like several other Colville Indians who fished in the Columbia in the early 1930s, does not remember hearing that the dam was going to kill all the salmon and flood Kettle Falls.

After wintering with an Indian family, Seward never returned to Kettle Falls to fish. He found a job on Roosevelt's payroll, living in a federal work camp on the reservation, making thirty dollars a month with board and room. He built roads near the dam site. It was the first time he can remember having cash in his pocket.

"God bless old Roosevelt. He took care of the people when there was no work and no money. It was the best thing to ever hit this country."

As the boomtown of Grand Coulee rose from the mud, Seward became a Friday-night regular on B Street. Indians were not allowed to drink in the Silver Dollar Saloon or to dance with the dime-a-dance girls, but Seward said he was white enough to pass.

"I learned how to dance from those girls. It wasn't cheap. In them days a dime was a lot of money. The songs weren't very long. Maybe a minute. By the time you got eight or nine dances, you were broke."

Seward also remembers helping a group of his Indian friends take revenge on white dam workers who were believed to have raped two Indian girls. Thanks to his white skin and an offer of free whiskey, he was able to lure a big redheaded dam worker out of a dance hall in the reservation town of Nespelem. Once outside Seward helped hold the dam worker while his Indian friends cut a big X in the man's back with a pocketknife.

Seward hired on at the dam as a laborer in 1935. He was only seventeen years old. He got the job by lying about his age and failing to mention his Indian blood. With a pick and shovel, he cleaned clay off granite bedrock. Later he became a high-scaler, making seventy-five cents an hour operating a jackhammer, drilling holes for dynamite while hanging from a rope harness on the cliffs above the dam site. He took home $9.80 a week, "the biggest money ever for an Indian."

On a swing-shift night in 1936, a white man who was running a jackhammer next to Seward fell to his death. He fell more than three hundred feet, landing on his back on top of reinforcing steel bars that protruded from the rising concrete foundation of the dam.

"With sixteen jackhammers goin' you couldn't hear nothing. But I seen him fall. There was three of them bars sticking through his body, two through his chest and one through his stomach. There was a steam shovel working down there and they tied ropes around the teeth of the shovel and around his arms and legs, trying to lift him off those bars. They tore him all apart. We was watching from up above. It made me half sick. I have had dreams all my life of people laying there with something sticking through them."

Seward harbors an acid regard for white Bureau engineers like Vaughn Downs.

"I always despised them. They would come around the workingmen and shoot off their mouths, like they knew everything there was to know. They were there to suit themselves. They were there to change this river. They didn't know that the Indian people was depending on salmon for their winter food, and they didn't care."

Keeping his resentments to himself, Seward stayed on at the dam and saved most of his money. Like my father, he used his savings to attend a welding school. When World War II came along, Seward joined the Navy as a submarine mechanic. He did not return to the reservation until 1946. By then, the dam was finished, Kettle Falls was flooded, the salmon were gone, and the reservation was sliding into despair.

"I saw quite a change in the Indians when I came back. I would say that alcohol got a hold of 60 percent of them. Without fishing, they had no interest in what they were doing. Families were breaking apart. Everybody was becoming what I call a 'reservation Indian.' The reservation Indian don't care for nobody or nothin'. I was drinking a lot, too. My best friend, Johnny Reynolds, and his dad Hiram, ran off the road when they were drunk. Killed 'em both. That is what made me get away from here. I went to Alaska and got into the Operating Engineers Union. I was lucky to get out."

Electricity generated by Grand Coulee Dam is worth about five hundred million dollars a year. Although half of the dam sits on reservation property, none of the power earnings was allotted to the Colvilles.

Under the original scheme to build the dam, the Indians were supposed to have received a fair cut. The dam, under the first plan, was to have been constructed by the state of Washington under the Federal Power Act. That 1920 law specifically required that a state must pay Indian tribes annual fees based on the amount of electricity produced on reservation land.

The Federal Power Act, however, was circumvented when the federal government took control of the dam away from Washington State in 1933. Harold Ickes, then both secretary of the Interior and director of Roosevelt's new Public Works Administration, wrote a most unusual letter—from himself to himself. The letter said the dam would be an exclusively federal project and that the Bureau of Reclamation would build it. The Federal Power Act no longer applied. No law required the Bureau to pay anything to the Indians for power revenue that the dam might earn.

For a year or two, however, it seemed that well-intentioned officials in Washington would make sure that the Colvilles would not be shafted by this legal technicality. At a congressional hearing held on the Colville Reservation in 1933, white bureaucrats and white lawmakers listened sympathetically to tribal elders who demanded that the federal government give the Colvilles a share of what Grand Coulee earned.

"This dam comes in here and we are wiped out," Pete Lemry, a Colville fishing chief, told the hearing. "I do not see why . . . we do not hold an equity in that power site that comes in at Grand Coulee. I do not think it is justice. . . ."

"I should say you are entitled to it," replied the chairman of the hearing, Senator Burton K. Wheeler.

"I think we ought to get a ten percent royalty out of the Coulee proposition, if they give the Indian his just dues," Lemry added.

Senator Frazier of North Dakota, in response, said: "That should be looked into by the Indian Department."

It was looked into back in Washington. Memos were written and meetings held. With belated sympathy for the Colvilles, Ickes asked the supervising engineer of the Grand Coulee project to make sure that Indian interests in the dam "be given careful and prompt attention so as to avoid any unnecessary delay."

The delay lasted sixty-one years.

It ended only after a federal appeals court in Washington, D.C., ruled that the government had failed to make "fair and honorable dealings" with the Colvilles. Two years later, in the fall of 1994, after the Justice Department and the Bonneville Power Administration agreed to a negotiated settlement with the Colvilles, Congress approved a lump-sum payment of fifty-three million to the tribe, along with an annual payment of about fifteen million dollars.

124   It was far less than 10 percent of the estimated five billion dollars' worth of electricity the dam had generated since 1942, but it was the largest settlement of its kind in American history. The Colvilles voted overwhelmingly to accept it.

Seward, who moved back onto the reservation in 1982 when he retired from the construction business, voted to take the money. He expected five thousand dollars as his share of the lump sum, along with more than fifteen hundred dollars a year for the rest of his life.

Was it enough?

"If a person wanted money and what-not, he would say it is a fair price. It is the best we were likely to get. But it does not bring back the river or the salmon. It is not a fair price for the torture we went through. No, it is not a fair price."

The Columbia, as it flowed past Seward's mobile home, roiled and curled in dangerous eddies—stirred up from its tumble through the turbines in nearby Grand Coulee Dam. To control erosion, the Bureau of Reclamation lined the bank of the river with a formidable wall of jagged rocks and chunks of concrete. The erosion barrier, called riprap, gave the Columbia, as it passed beside Seward's trailer house, the hemmed-in feel of an irrigation canal.

Seward hated the coming of the riprap. It kept him from going down to the river to fish for the rainbow trout that were planted in the river to replace long-gone salmon.* He slipped on the rocks and hurt his leg. After that, he made peace with the rock barrier by staying off it and staying away from the river.

In compensation, he became acquainted with a family of wood-chucks that settled in the rocks just beyond the window of his mobile home. Seward fed them and watched them play while he drank his morning coffee.

---

*Forty-five miles downstream from Seward's place is Chief Joseph Dam, the second largest hydropower plant in the Northwest. Like Grand Coulee, that federal dam does not have fish ladders. All salmon in the Columbia above Chief Joseph disappeared when it was completed in 1961.

The Bureau spread an herbicide along the bank to control weeds. The woodchucks all disappeared.

"When I look at that river," Seward told me, "there is an awful lot of wicked thoughts go through a person's mind."

The bitterness of the Colville tribe about dams has diminished a bit in recent years. Downstream from Chief Joseph Dam, salmon sometimes returned to the river in fishable numbers. After a 2008 agreement with the Bonneville Power Administration and a local utility that operates two dams on the mid-Columbia, the Colvilles received forty-three million dollars to build a hatchery on the river that was expected to restore chinook salmon to some tribal waters. Colville leaders said that by 2017 or so, they hoped there would be enough of the big salmon in the river for a ceremonial, spiritual, and nutritional rebirth.

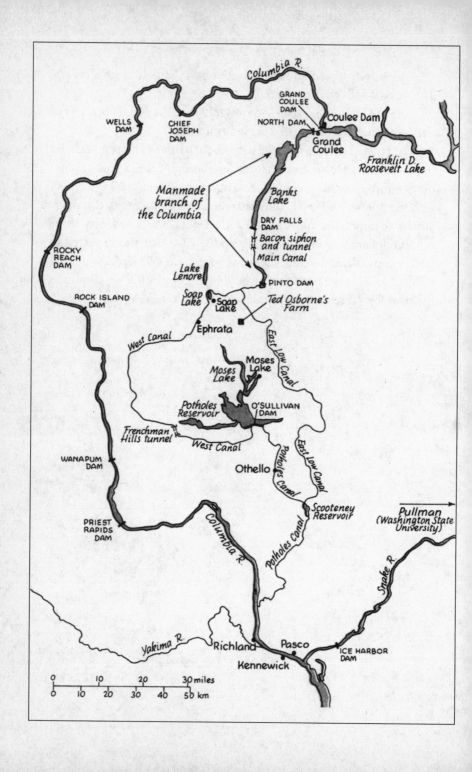

6

Ditches from Heaven

Farmers think those irrigation ditches fell out of the sky.
—BRENDA TEALS,
a teacher at Big Bend Community College
in Moses Lake

I DROVE AWAY FROM the Colville Reservation, crossed the Columbia on a narrow steel bridge just below Grand Coulee Dam, and headed south into the blooming desert where I was born. Suddenly, everything seemed richer. Highways were smoother, farmhouses bigger, pickup trucks shinier. High-voltage power lines loped across farmland where center-pivot sprinkler systems described perfect circles of green. I followed a huge and wholly artificial branch of the Columbia that is pumped out of slackwater behind the dam, poured through six thousand miles of coulees, tunnels, and concrete canals, and then sprinklered on an erstwhile badland that for the past half century has been as consistently coddled by the federal government as the Colville Reservation has been ignored. After the rusted junk and potholed roads, the Columbia Basin Irrigation Project was exceptionally inviting.

It had everything a promised land in the engineered West is supposed to have. The Columbia Basin grows six hundred and thirty million dollars' worth of apples, potatoes, wheat, spearmint, asparagus, and peas a year. It is the French fry and apple capital of the world. If you have eaten fries at McDonald's or bought Red Delicious apples at the Safeway, you have tasted what the sucked-up and ditch-delivered river has done to the sagebrush country around my hometown.

When you add water, the land is fertile and easily worked. In many places, topsoil lies fifteen feet deep. The Columbia Basin has a God-

128 given, gravity-fed gift for circulating and recycling water. It tilts to the southwest like a pool table with one leg sawed short. The top right-hand corner is about one thousand feet above the lower left. Stratified seams of basalt rock beneath the topsoil collect runoff in the north and funnel it into a central reservoir called the Potholes. From there, it feeds into another series of canals for reuse on farms in the south. A single drop of water, as it flows southwest across an arid steppe twice the size of the state of Delaware, can be sprinkled on two or even three separate farms.

The Columbia serves up water that is delightfully pure, rich in nutritive minerals, and low in the poisonous salts that have ruined billion-dollar federal irrigation schemes in the Southwest. "Just beautiful water," exclaimed Jim Cole, local chief of the Bureau of Reclamation. For nearly four decades, farmers in the Columbia Basin Project had all the fine water they need—and more!

The water was so abundant and cheap that farmers cheerfully admitted they had no real incentive to conserve it. They take about three million acre-feet of water a year from the Columbia. An acre-foot, about 326,000 gallons, is approximately the amount of water a family of four uses in a year. About four thousand landowners in the Columbia Basin Project use about a third as much water as the twenty-five million Californians served by the State Water Project.

But best of all, there were subsidies. Many, many subsidies. Subsidies that ran together, cross-pollinated, and subsidized each other. The Bureau of Reclamation calculated that every 960-acre farm in the Columbia Basin Project had been blessed with at least $2.1 million in federal infrastructure subsidies. More than nine of every ten dollars needed for profitable irrigated farming in the Columbia Basin came from federal taxpayers or electricity consumers who lived somewhere else. To lift water out of the river and pump it around the project, Columbia Basin farmers were guaranteed the right to buy electricity from the federal government at a price much cheaper than wholesale.

Farmers around my hometown devised creative schemes to convert their subsidized water into a moneymaking commodity. With rights to more water than they could usefully sprinkle on their land, they sold the excess to other nearby farmers and kept the profits to defray their expenses. They also sold electricity generated by irrigation water as it burbled through canals across the Columbia Basin. The more water they sucked out of the river, the more profits they had.

Water from the Columbia River appeared in irrigation ditches on the edge of my hometown in the first week of April 1952, the same week I was born. A few weeks after the water and I arrived in Moses Lake, the population of the town swelled for one frenzied day from four thousand to fifty thousand. Newsreel, television, and newspaper reporters swarmed in to witness something called "Farm-in-a-Day." Eighty acres of scrubland on the north edge of town were to be transformed in twenty-four hours into a modern irrigation farm, complete with crops, cows, sprinklers, and drapes in the living room.

A thirty-year-old World War II tank driver named Donald D. Dunn, who had lost his farm a year earlier to a Kansas flood, had been chosen by the Veterans of Foreign Wars as the nation's "most deserving" veteran. Dunn, his extremely pregnant wife, Vernetta Jean, and their two small daughters, Deanna and Sally Ann, were to take possession of a farm that would be free from start to finish.

It was a public-relations stunt dreamed up by the Bureau of Reclamation and local boosters to whip up national interest in the Columbia Basin Irrigation Project, which, after nearly two decades of meticulous preparation, was supposed to create a "planned promised land." Veterans and other deserving Americans from across the nation were invited to find out if they qualified for guaranteed cheap water on small family farms.

Like everybody in town, my family was delighted that Moses Lake had hit the big time. Absent water from the river, the town was a windblown hellhole, disparaged by even its own residents as Moses Hole. But the federal government, in its beneficent wisdom, had given us water. So, in a shiny new 1952 brown Chevrolet Bel Air coupe, the first new car my father ever owned, we drove out to join the crowds on a hill overlooking Farm-in-a-Day. My father remembered the ungodly racket generated by legions of men with hammers. My mother remembered having to deal with fifty-four-day-old me. My older sister, Mary,

130 then eight, remembered being thrilled by the concept of Farm-in-a-Day. But her delight, along with her face, was sullied by blowing dirt. Water trucks had been dousing the work site for a week prior to the big day. Yet, when a stiff westerly wind picked up, spectators began to gag on the dust of one hundred and fifty farm machines digging up the fields.

Poor visibility did not stop three hundred volunteers from planting crops, erecting a seven-room ranch house, a workshop, a chicken house, a pump house, and a two-stall milking parlor. They also unpacked dishes, made beds, and filled the fridge with groceries. Dunn told the press he especially liked the "climate-controlling plywood butterfly roof" on his house. His wife said the plywood built-in storage units were "just perfect."

In the late afternoon, with the dust still blowing, the commissioner of the Bureau of Reclamation turned a valve-control wheel, releasing frothy white water into Dunn's freshly dug ditches.

"Here this afternoon we celebrate the addition of the equivalent of a new state to the union," intoned Michael W. Strauss, the gawky, homely commissioner who tirelessly promoted dam construction and river diversion across the West. "For out of the wisdom and the effort which have gone into this project our country is now about to reap harvest from the desert. . . . Here the world sees a project which means food for the hungry, food from farms which will never know drought, from land which guarantees abundance to those who work it wisely. . . ."

Six days after the Dunn family moved in, Vernetta Jean gave birth to a girl and the Bureau of Reclamation claimed the child as a symbol of irrigation in the West. In a proclamation from Washington, D.C., Strauss announced that the baby was "born with a gold-plated irrigation shovel ready to be placed in her hands. . . . The Reclamation program must be pushed forward with utmost speed so the Dunn child and all the other kiddies born this year will have a happier and more secure life on the land. . . ."

Life on irrigated land proved less than happy and secure for the Dunn child. After three years, her father went broke. The "most deserving" farmer sold his free farm for $75,000 and fled with his family for Colorado. The Bureau of Reclamation quickly explained that Dunn was a poor manager. Yet the farmer who bought out Dunn also went bust and moved on, after just two seasons. Over the next four decades, that model farm changed hands five times.

To make sense of the plumbing system that is the Columbia River, to make sense of any major western river that is bled for irrigation, you have to get away from the river itself. You have to turn your back on Native Americans who stand beside the river and speak with pain about what used to be. Most important, you have to wangle an invitation for coffee in the farmhouse kitchen of an irrigator like Ted Osborne and his wife, Barbara.

To get my invitation, I told the story that worked so well with the river bargers, that worked so badly with the Indians. I called up the Osbornes and introduced myself as born into the Columbia Basin Project in the year that their farm got water from the river. Yes, Ted and Barbara would be pleased to talk to the likes of me.

When I entered their kitchen, the smell of freshly perked coffee was mixed with the aroma of a spice cake baked in my honor. Barbara was a thin, gray-haired, welcoming woman in her sixties. She told me she knew all about me, that she had seen me at the Sons of Norway potluck dinner, where I had given a little talk about the trouble in Bosnia. Ted Osborne, tall and fit for a man of seventy-four, had a Jimmy Durante nose and a shy smile. He herded me to the kitchen table and asked what I wanted to know.

The Osborne farm was about ten miles north of Moses Lake, about seventy miles south of Grand Coulee Dam, and about three miles from the periodically bankrupt Farm-in-a-Day. Like many family-owned irrigation operations across the arid West, the Osborne spread was not picturesque. Its 350 acres were blemished with scabby outcroppings of black volcanic basalt rock. There were high-voltage power lines on the horizon; concrete ditches lined dusty gravel roads. Japan Airlines 747 jumbo jets performed flight-training exercises over the farm, circling like great silver buzzards, rattling windows and casting huge skittering

132   shadows over fields of alfalfa and wheat and pastures of beef cattle. (Japanese flight training, a daily ritual that began in 1968 and ended in 2008, was easier on the nerves than its American predecessor. When Moses Lake airfield was occupied by the U.S. Air Force, an occupation that ended with base closure in 1966, sonic booms triggered nervous fits in Osborne's cattle and dogs.) Surrounding the Osborne farmhouse there was a patch of suburban-style lawn, a big steel barn for tractors and farm machinery, a couple of dogs that licked a stranger's hand, and towering shade trees—Chinese elms, mountain ash, and hybrid poplars. Ted Osborne planted the trees in the early 1950s.

The farm connected to the outside world via a freshly paved, arrow-straight highway. But the Osbornes' fundamental lifeline was the EL-18 lateral canal, which connects to the East Low Canal, which connects to the Main Canal, which connects to Banks Lake equalizing reservoir, which connects to the twelve pumps that slurp water out of the Columbia River.

The Osbornes were among the first farmers to receive water from the pumps behind Grand Coulee Dam. They had since built their lives around the irrigation scheme, and they spoke of it in a measured and respectful tone. They called it, simply, the Project, much as devout Roman Catholics speak of the Church. For them, as for federally subsidized irrigators across the West, the Project was far more than a mechanism for extracting river water and distributing it on dry land. It was a framework for raising a family, a way of seeing the world.

The Osbornes raised three sons on the Project. The boys grew up suntanned and strong, moving sprinklers, bucking hay, and playing baseball in irrigated pastures, using cowpies for bases and old bed springs for a backstop. Ted allowed the boys to build a motorcycle track on his fields, an attraction that lured swarms of neighbor kids for a decade of weekend races. One of the Osborne boys, Donald, stayed home to take over the farm. He lived in a brown double-wide trailer near his folks' farmhouse.

In their lifelong devotion to the Project, the Osbornes belonged to a sprawling congregation of western irrigators who have received more than nineteen billion dollars in federal subsidies to farm more than ten million acres of land in seventeen states. These farmers have fashioned a religion unique to the arid American West. Its fundamental precept is that the only godly work a man can do is grow food. From that precept comes the corollary notion that the American taxpayer has an obligation—economic, patriotic, and religious—to deliver cheap water to farmers so they can continue to do God's work.

A voluminous Dogma of Irrigation springs from these revealed truths. It blends traditional western water rights (the notion of "first in time, first in right") with hoary myths about noble cowboys and rugged individualism. It pays nitpicky attention to contractual law, to the latest sprinkler technology, and warns, at all times, about a coming catastrophic food shortage. The rites of irrigation theology include constant and aggressive litigation, intense lobbying, and large donations to sympathetic local, state, and federal politicians, as well as vituperative attacks on the jobs, values, and patriotism of those who doubt that giving large subsidies to irrigators makes economic or environmental sense. Environmentalists, Native Americans, urban salmon advocates, and other defenders of free-flowing rivers are viewed—through the lens of Project doctrine—as socialist troublemakers who would like nothing better than to sabotage one of the few things in America that still works. The orthodoxy of the Project teaches that subsidies are freedom, salmon are frivolous, Indians are suspect, and rivers are fuel for sprinklers. Finally, the Dogma of Irrigation seems designed to be inscrutable to the non-irrigator.

I am not suggesting that the Osbornes and other irrigators were not friendly, honest, and likable people. It is just that the Project, in a semi-desert that gets less than eight inches of rain a year, casts an irresistible spell. An irrigator would have to be out of his mind to believe that water is more valuable in the public's wild river than in his concrete ditch. A farmer cannot help but believe that anyone who thinks otherwise—who celebrates salmon over human beings, who prefers a free-flowing river to a well-managed farm—is a troublemaker or a fool.

A useful way to see what the Project can do to a farmer, to see what

134   it can do to a river, to see what it has done to the West, is to watch how it percolated over time in the life of a respected farmer and an honest family man like Ted Osborne.

He was born in 1919 in a shack just a few hundred yards from where we had coffee. The rain-shadow desert of eastern Washington then had no precise circles of sprinklered green. Ropes were strung from farmhouse to outhouse so homestead children would not get lost in weeklong summer dust storms. Ted Osborne's father, who came to the Columbia Basin at the turn of the century to wrangle wild horses, raised potatoes by building a dike on Crab Creek, which was the only stream in the desert and which usually ran dry by mid-summer. Osborne's father supplemented his family's income by trapping coyotes for a five-dollar bounty. The land was good—with loamy topsoil six to eight feet deep—but rains nearly always failed by early summer.

The first decade of Ted Osborne's life ended in a blur of failed crops and dust storms, collapsed commodity prices and farm bankruptcies. Unable to pay taxes as the Depression deepened, Ted's father abandoned the homestead in 1932. The family sold off its four hundred sheep and twelve milk cows, loaded furniture onto a flatbed truck, and moved to the nearby town of Ephrata.

There, Ted Osborne, at age thirteen, started mowing the lawn of Billy Clapp, the lawyer who first proposed damming the Columbia River and diverting its water south through the Grand Coulee for farmers.

"The first thing I remember in Ephrata is Billy Clapp playing pinochle and talking to my dad about the Project. They talked and talked and talked. It seemed fantastic to me that we could have water on our farm. I questioned ol' Billy Clapp. I said, What are you going to do with the water? How is it gonna get to the farms? How do you keep it from disappearing down some badger hole? He assured me that everything would be great, if we only had water from the river. He said we could go back to the homestead, and I believed him."

Before he graduated from high school, Osborne began building a life on the back of Billy Clapp's daydream. He found a job at Grand Coulee Dam, pushing a wheelbarrow, shoveling concrete, making ninety cents an hour.

"Ever since we lost our farm to taxes, I had it in the back of my mind that we should go back and reclaim it. I never had any other plan for my life. I really didn't. I always had confidence that we would make it. Maybe it was just stubbornness."

To reclaim the farm, Osborne needed money for taxes and he needed water. He saved enough at Grand Coulee to begin paying off eight hundred dollars in back taxes. But water for the farm had to wait until both the Germans and the Japanese had lost the war. Making electricity for airplanes, ships, and atom bombs became an overriding national priority, and all construction work on the irrigation aspects of the Grand Coulee project halted for the duration. Osborne joined the Marines and spent most of the war fighting in the Philippines. He sent checks home regularly to the Grant County tax assessor to pay taxes on the dried-up farm about which he kept dreaming.

In the meantime, the most comprehensive federal study ever proposed for a single irrigation scheme was under way. Teams of mapmakers, hydrologists, soil experts, and engineers fanned out across the Columbia Basin desert, taking nearly a decade to categorize soil quality and figure out how best to deliver water to more than one million acres of potential farmland. Roosevelt said the Project should be reserved for small family farms, and his government went to unprecedented lengths to try to limit farm size and head off speculation that would jack up land prices beyond the means of working-class people. The Columbia Basin Project was designed to showcase the principles of the New Deal. It was to be a precise mixture of science and compassion.

Ever since the federal government became involved in irrigating the American West in 1902, its professed motives have been pure. Reclamation was intended to infuse the arid, empty West with the sturdy values of Thomas Jefferson's yeoman farmer, that mythical American who lived in a close-knit rural community, paid his taxes, and breathed

136 life into participatory democracy. The purpose of the Reclamation Act, according to its author, Senator Francis G. Newlands of Nevada, was to "prevent monopoly and concentration of ownership . . . [and preserve] small tracts for actual settlers and home builders."

The Columbia Basin Project was supposed to exemplify the noblest of these motives. It imposed the tightest land ownership regulations in the history of federal reclamation. The government limited the size of a Project farm to eighty acres for a married farmer. New Deal planners figured that was enough land, given the fertility of Columbia Basin soil and the purity of Columbia River water, to provide a decent living for a family of four. Farmers had to divest themselves of excess land if they wanted access to federal water. To prevent speculators from cashing in on the federal investment in irrigation, farmers could not, in the first five years after water arrived, sell their land for more than its appraised value *before* irrigation.*

For a young Marine struggling to hang on to his father's small homestead, these restrictions sounded fine. Osborne was still in the Philippines when he received an invitation by mail to join the Project. He immediately signed the papers that locked his eighty acres into a forty-year commitment to repay the Bureau for his share of building the irrigation scheme. After returning home in 1946, Osborne had to live in Moses Lake for five years, waiting for the Bureau to finish canal and ditch construction. When the water finally did arrive, Osborne admits that he and most of the farmers in the Project did not know what to do with it.

"As a whole, we didn't know much about irrigation. We didn't know weeds. We didn't know insecticides. A lot of us were returning veterans and irrigation sounded good, but it turned out to be more complicated than we anticipated."

Osborne and his new wife, Barbara, who grew up in Spokane,

*The on-the-ground record of federal reclamation across the West is rather different from its intentions. While encouraging some of the worst water-conservation practices in the world, it has been a tool of agribusiness, has ignored Native Americans and Hispanics, and has failed to protect small farms.

eastern Washington's biggest city, moved out to the farm in 1953. They set up housekeeping in a prefabricated one-room office building that they bought for a hundred dollars from a company that dug canals for the Bureau. Out in the fields, Osborne soon found he did not know how to control his water. He had not yet poured his own concrete ditches, and the ditches he dug by hand were routinely breached. Gophers tormented Osborne, burrowing holes in his ditches, causing them to collapse. It took more than ten years of failed crops, weed infestations, grasshopper invasions, and hard-knocks learning in the craft of irrigation before Osborne felt confident enough to give up his day job driving a school bus.

Over the decades, the farm expanded (with several changes in federal rules on land ownership) more than threefold. Osborne said that on paper, with his land and his equipment, "we are probably millionaires."

It does not show.

Although the Osborne farmhouse was refurbished and enlarged (and is spectacularly clean), it is still, at its homely heart, a converted construction office. Ted and Barbara Osborne were far from wealthy, clearing a profit of only about thirty thousand dollars a year from their wheat, alfalfa, and cattle.

By this one measure—actual disposable income—there was something peculiar about the economics of the farm that the Osbornes devoted their lives to building. The federal government spent roughly three-quarters of a million dollars to build the irrigation canals and other infrastructure that delivered water to the farm.* Had the Bureau of Reclamation simply *given* the cash to the Osbornes, and had they kept it in a conservative mutual fund paying an unspectacular 5 percent a year, they could have had a disposable income of about thirty-eight thousand dollars a year.

---

*The Bureau of Reclamation calculated, in a 1988 letter to a House subcommittee, that it had spent $2,164.40 on each acre in the Project. Multiplied by the 350 acres that the Osbornes own, the subsidy for their farm comes to $757,540.

*

When Columbia River water first reached Osborne's farm in 1952, it was no great secret that irrigating the arid West was a hugely expensive shell game.

The official policy of the United States government explicitly declared that all irrigation costs should be repaid in full. But from Nebraska to California, Montana to New Mexico, every major federal reclamation scheme taught the same dismal lesson. Farmers never could come close to paying back the government for the real cost of their water. Again and again, reclamation engineers and farmers were too optimistic in assessing the capacity of irrigated land to pay for itself. To compensate for this optimism, to keep farmers from defaulting on their repayment obligations, and to make sure that farmers voted for incumbent members of Congress, the federal government, as decades rolled by, kept fudging the rules.

The rules were generous in the first place. Under the Reclamation Act of 1902, money spent on irrigation projects was to be repaid within ten years—without any interest. Not having to pay the interest rates of 1902 gave the farmers a healthy 14 percent subsidy on project costs.

But farmers could not come close to paying off their debts in ten years. So in 1914, Congress stretched the repayment period to twenty years, again interest free. This increased the interest subsidy to 42 percent of construction costs. But farmers could not come close to paying off their debts in twenty years, so the repayment period was stretched to forty years, again interest free, which increased the subsidy to more than 50 percent at prevailing interest rates. But farmers still could not pay what they owed. So a ten-year payment-free "development period" was tacked on to reclamation law in 1939, which gave farmers a tidy half century of interest-free money.

In addition, in a move that would prove a godsend to Ted Osborne and his neighbors in the Columbia Basin, a provision was added to the law saying that all reclamation costs that exceeded a farmer's "ability to pay" could be borne by other water users, such as consumers of hydroelectricity.

As interest rates rose in the second half of the twentieth century, so did the value of interest-free money committed to irrigation farmers. To get a grip on how subsidies had mushroomed in the West, the Bureau of Reclamation studied eighteen major irrigation projects in the early 1980s. On twelve of the projects 80 percent of construction costs were free to farmers, paid for by city folks. The highest percentage subsidy for any single project was a hefty 96.7 percent. This generous gift from the taxpayers of the United States went to none other than the farmers around my hometown, to Ted Osborne and his fellow irrigators in the Project.

Farmers in the Project seemed to have everything going for them. The world's biggest dam fed fertile land with pristine water from the West's greatest river. The Project was expected to become the largest single irrigation scheme in the history of the Bureau of Reclamation. It had been the most thoroughly planned, the most exhaustively surveyed, and it had the West's tightest rules against land speculation. It operated according to sweetheart regulations written by a Congress that was loathe to offend farmers and consistently willing to forgive and forget whatever debts they said they could not pay. And since Grand Coulee Dam churned out more marketable electricity than any hunk of concrete on the planet, the federal government could afford to be exceedingly generous in its assessment of the farmers' "ability to pay." The farmers, under their contract with the Bureau, had fifty interest-free years to pay back just 18 percent of the cost of the Project.

But it was not nearly enough.

As elsewhere in the engineered West, both federal engineers and local farmers grossly underestimated the cost and difficulty of making a living by pouring water into a desert. One of every four farmers went broke in the first four years of the Project. Washington State University economists calculated that more than half of the first generation of Project farmers failed to make money, became disillusioned, and sold out. The Project never came close to creating the thirty thousand small farms or attracting to the Columbia Basin the one million new settlers that were predicted by the Bureau in the 1930s. Planned for one million

140 irrigated acres, the Project stalled at about half that size. Its population never got much higher than eighty thousand people.

After the war, returning veterans (half the farmers on the Project were vets) simply did not want to eke out a living on a subsistence farm. They wanted farms that were big and profitable enough to give them a middle-class living.

Ted Osborne and his fellow irrigators, if they were to survive on the land in a middle-class manner, believed they had only one choice. They had to fight for more federal subsidies and fewer federal rules on farm size. As Columbia Basin historian Paul Pitzer explains, the farmers felt "no price is too high to pay for their water so long as someone else is paying the bill."

To defend the farm that he had dreamed about since boyhood, Osborne became a director of the East Columbia Basin Irrigation District, one of three farmer-controlled districts in the Project. In his thirty-three years as an irrigation director, Osborne acknowledged that he never paid much attention to the Columbia River or to its salmon. The river was about forty-five miles from his farm, but it may as well have been in Kansas.

Osborne was under the mistaken impression, when I had coffee and cake with him, that Grand Coulee Dam had fish ladders. He was not aware that the dam had wiped out one of the world's greatest runs of salmon. He did not know that the Project's early-summer diversion of water from the Columbia limited downstream river flows at precisely the time that millions of juvenile salmon were migrating downstream.

"Most folks who came here in the early years didn't eat salmon," he told me, echoing what I had heard for years from my father. "They could not keep them [from rotting in the heat]. I am not that much of a fisherman and I don't know much about fish."

Osborne has had virtually no personal contact with the Colville Indians or any of the Native American tribes that built their lives around Columbia River salmon. Yet, like many irrigators, he was deeply suspicious of Indians. He accused them of illegal overfishing and of being a major cause of the salmon crisis.

"My neighbor told me that he seen Indians on the Columbia working at night loading up trucks with salmon and heading for California."

Osborne was also under the impression that the Colville Indians profited handsomely from the construction of Grand Coulee Dam and that they have always lived comfortably on the federal dole.

"There is no [state sales] tax on their food. It costs half of what we pay for it. They bought a lot of whiskey, bootleg, that creates crime and everything. Indians is different from a white man. They drink whiskey and they go nuts. They buy cars and just wreck them."

Indians and salmon and rivers were not subjects about which Osborne pretended to have any great expertise. He only discussed them with me because I kept asking questions. What he knew was irrigation. As an irrigation director, he developed a lawyer-like understanding of western water law. He learned the bureaucratic ways of the Bureau of Reclamation. He befriended state and federal lawmakers. He helped write the irrigation contracts that farmers signed with the Bureau. These contracts, under Osborne's vigilant eye, were revised again and again to make life easier for Project farmers.

The first significant victory came when farmers ducked the cost of fixing a major technical glitch. The problem was drainage. In some parts of the Columbia Basin, water was not draining away from irrigated fields. It puddled up, swamping crops, flooding basements, fouling septic tanks, and raising the water table. It bubbled into a resort lake, threatening the lakeside town. The cost of fixing the glitch would come to $171 million, which farmers were obligated to pay under their contract with the Bureau.

"The farmers could not stand that kind of obligation," Osborne told me. "Now the Bureau was kind of reluctant to pay for it, but we had a coupla good senators who put on the pressure."

The senators, Henry Jackson and Warren Magnuson, were the best friends a Washington State irrigator could have hoped for. They were perhaps the most successful pair of irrigation boosters in American history. They held major committee chairmanships and they both had more seniority in the Senate than any members outside the Deep

142 South. They remained in Congress for nearly four decades by paying close attention to their constituents' needs. On their watch, the Bureau was pressured to subsidize a higher percentage of the irrigated land in Washington State (54 percent) than in any other state.

Osborne never lost a major battle with the Bureau when Magnuson and Jackson were in the Senate.* They were the ones who sponsored the law that in 1956 lifted the strict limits on land ownership in the Project.† In the drainage imbroglio, the senators won their farmers an exceptionally attractive deal. In return for accepting a small increase in their interest-free construction debt, the farmers in 1961 shifted complete financial responsibility for the drainage mess to the Bureau.

So began what for Osborne and his fellow irrigators was a golden age of federal concessions. With Jackson and Magnuson massaging the Senate, and Congressman Tom Foley (an eastern Washington native who was chairman of the House Agriculture Committee before moving up to Democratic majority leader and then Speaker of the House) working the House of Representatives, the irrigators bullied the Bureau.

The percentage of construction costs that Basin farmers had to pay back to the federal government was cut in 1963 by a third, from 18 to 12 percent. The interest-free repayment period for Project farmers was stretched once again, from fifty to sixty years. Farmers took over management of the Project from the Bureau in 1969, and immediately reduced the annual operating and maintenance fees they paid for delivery of water from thirty dollars per acre to twenty dollars.

Irrigators won the right to sell water from the Columbia and use the profits to defray their expenses. Being able to sell water gave

---

*Jackson died unexpectedly in office in 1983, after thirty years in the Senate and twelve years in the House. Magnuson was defeated in 1980, after thirty-six years in the Senate and seven years in the House.

†The 1956 law allowed an unmarried farmer to own 160 acres of land in the Project and a married couple to own 320 acres. These limits, however, were a fiction because farmers were allowed to lease as much land as they wanted. In 1981, in a major overhaul of reclamation law, the ownership limit in Bureau projects across the West was raised to 960 acres. In an attempt to prevent wealthy farmers from unfair use of subsidized water, leasing inside Bureau projects was banned. This limit, however, was widely ignored by farmers who enlisted their family and friends to hold legal title to Bureau land that they farm.

them a strong economic incentive not to reduce the amount of water they extracted from the river. Even though new sprinkler technology sharply reduced the amount of water they needed to grow healthy crops, Project farmers left none of the conserved water in the river. They sold it to their non-Project neighbors.

In the victory for which Osborne deserved personal credit, farmers gained exclusive rights to sell electricity generated from water flowing through turbines installed on Project canals.

"The Bureau wanted half of that power money," Osborne told me. "It felt that since the federal government owned and built the Project, it should have some of the revenue. But the amended contract we have with the Bureau clearly states that we have the right to reclaim and reuse water and to generate power. I know that it is true because I am the one who put that language in there."

After farmers began generating electricity with Bureau water in 1985, the amount of water the Project diverted from the Columbia River increased substantially. Although Osborne and other farmers heatedly denied it, citing drought and expansion of irrigated acreage, they were accused by a congressional subcommittee and international agricultural experts of diverting water from the Columbia River so they could make money selling electricity.

"That is a bunch of crap," Osborne said.

What farmers could not deny was that the inbreeding of subsidies on the Project rewarded them for every gallon of water they took from the Columbia. Under the terms of their original 1939 agreement with the Bureau, the farmers were guaranteed a deeply subsidized price for the electricity that pumped water up out of the river and into their canals. Yet once that water got into Project canals and spilled through their hydroelectric generators, farmers could sell the resulting power at market rates. They put a twenty-seven-fold markup on the power they sold as compared to the power they bought. A study of the Project by the International Food Policy Research Institute concluded that it would be "quite rational for [farmers] to increase their water orders to increase revenues from the sale of power while simultaneously holding down [their] water rates. . . ."

144   The concessions that Osborne helped win made farming on the Project more profitable and more secure. Gross returns to Project irrigators rose steadily for thirty years. Farm profits also seemed to rise. Farmers juggled their subsidies, cut operating costs, and manipulated their water-marketing schemes in such a way as to reduce by one-third the price per acre they paid for water from the Columbia. They paid less for water and took more of it out of the river.

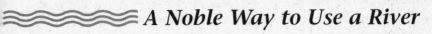

7

A Noble Way to Use a River

FOR NEARLY HALF a century, Osborne and his fellow irrigators had no important enemies. Every year the Bureau compiled reports about the Project that trumpeted impressive numbers about tons of wheat and bushels of apples and millions upon millions of dollars of gross farm revenues. Regional newspapers gave prominent display to the figures, confirming that irrigation subsidies were a sound and patriotic investment. It was painless to believe in irrigation because nearly all the benefits of the Project stayed within the state while 98 percent of its costs were paid by taxpayers who lived somewhere else.

The screw started to turn, however, when irrigators attempted in the 1980s to double the size of the Project. They wanted to expand it to the one million acres that was envisioned during the early years of the New Deal. They hit a snag back in Washington. For the first time in the Project's history, both the executive and legislative branches of the federal government were balking at giving Columbia Basin farmers all the money they wanted. Jackson and Magnuson were gone, replaced by senators with less clout and more doubts about subsidizing un-poor farmers. The Bureau was coming under intense environmental criticism for ruining too many western rivers with too many dams; its construction budget was shrinking. No longer willing or able to foot the entire bill for expanding the Project—a bill estimated at more than two billion dollars—the Bureau instructed Columbia Basin farmers to

146 look closer to home for expansion money. They turned to the Washington State legislature.

The man who ended up turning the screw on Osborne and his neighbors was, by background and manner, an unlikely enemy. Norm Whittlesey grew up on an irrigated cattle farm near Aspen, Colorado. He talked the slow talk and walked the bowlegged walk of a cowboy. A small, wiry man in his early sixties, he favored string ties, cowboy boots, and turquoise belt buckles. He taught agriculture economics at Washington State University, a land-grant school in eastern Washington with a long tradition of indulging the interests of local irrigators.

When Whittlesey first moved out to Washington State in the mid-1960s, he worked for the Project as a researcher. Like most westerners who grow up on farms, his natural inclination was to believe that irrigation was a noble way to use a river.

That natural inkling, Whittlesey told me, did not change until he hired on in the mid-seventies as a consultant to a state legislator from eastern Washington whose constituents were farmers in the southern part of the Project. The legislator wanted the professor to prepare a report showing how it made good sense to expand the Project and get somebody else to pay for it.

"The conventional wisdom was that we should go ahead and irrigate more ground. No one anticipated that I would not be favorable to that idea."

To his surprise and dismay, the more Whittlesey studied the numbers, the more he became convinced that any expansion of the Project would be a net loss to the economy and environment of the Pacific Northwest. He found that water had a much greater regional value if it was kept out of irrigation ditches and left in the Columbia River, where it could generate electricity and transport fish. Expansion of the project, Whittlesey calculated, would benefit only a few thousand farmers, fertilizer dealers, and equipment suppliers while taking cash out of the pockets of millions of Pacific Northwest electricity consumers. Many of the likely winners already were well-off, Whittlesey concluded, while many of the likely losers were poor.

Testifying before the state legislature in 1984, Whittlesey ambushed

Osborne and other Columbia Basin farmers. What they had expected to be another easy seduction of friendly lawmakers turned into a surprise massacre. Whittlesey calculated that each one-thousand-acre farm added to the Project would cost the Northwest about $200,000 a year in higher utility bills. That was the cost of replacing the electricity lost when farmers took water from the river. The $200,000-a-year per-farm price tag, Whittlesey said, would continue and perhaps increase for as long as the Project existed. And that was only for replacement energy costs.

As for construction costs, Whittlesey calculated that any expansion of the Project would cost $5,000 an acre, with farmers paying just $115. Somebody else would foot the rest of the bill. Washington State residents would pay about $1,000, Northwest electricity consumers about $192, and federal taxpayers the remaining $3,693.

The professor further concluded that expanding the Project would increase the country's surplus of grain, take water away from migrating salmon, and penalize the vast majority of Northwest farmers, who lived outside of the Project and yet would have to pay higher taxes and electricity bills to support a scheme that only benefited their competitors. Most curiously, Whittlesey's figures showed that after the public ponied up nearly $5,000 an acre for new land in the Project, its resale value would be about $1,500 an acre. "If you took that $5,000 and gave it to the farmer, hopefully he would invest it in something more useful," Whittlesey said.

Osborne and his fellow farmers hired economic consultants to discredit Whittlesey. His numbers, however, were solid. No one of his academic stature was inclined to challenge them. Beaten on the facts, farmers tried to appeal to the state legislature's sense of honor. They said that a solemn promise had been made in the 1930s to complete the entire one-million-acre scheme. When that did not work, the farmers argued regional rivalry. They said that if Washington State did not quickly give its own irrigators more water from the Columbia, then the state of California would come up with some sneaky plan to come north and steal the river for its own water-starved irrigators. When that did not work, farmers predicted mass bankruptcy. Some irrigators on the uncompleted part of the Project (who used well-water in their sprinklers) had exhausted nearly all the groundwater beneath their land. They did so in anticipation of being bailed out by water pumped in from the Columbia. They complained that they faced ruin. But the lawmakers were unmoved. They refused to spend any state money on expanding the Project.

Helen Sommers, a legislator from Seattle, later wrote that Whittlesey's work "helped state decision-makers avoid a significant misallocation of resources." Predictably, legislators from around my hometown were spitting mad.

"It's hard for me to understand how the work that went into this Project by people like Franklin Roosevelt, Scoop Jackson, Warren Magnuson, and [former Washington governor] Dan Evans over the past fifty years can all go down the drain based on three hours of testimony by one man," said Curt Smith, a state legislator from the Columbia Basin.

Whittlesey insisted that he had nothing against farmers.

"I was not anti-irrigation, and I was not saying the Project should never be expanded," Whittlesey told me. "I was merely trying to inform the public of what we were buying."

Ted Osborne and his fellow farmers did not see it that way. They believed that anyone against expansion of the Project was against the American tradition of family farms. Furthermore, they believed it was unethical for a professor from a land-grant university that they supported with their tax dollars to betray the interests of local farmers. Never before had Project farmers been so convincingly rebuffed in their search for subsidies. Never before had they felt so humiliated. They took it personal.

"We tried to get rid of Norm Whittlesey," Osborne told me as we ate his wife's spice cake. "I don't think Whittlesey knew the value of food. He thought electricity was more important than food. We called up our state senator [Frank "Tub" Hansen], and we badgered Tub to get something done, to get rid of that guy. Tub was with us all the way. Tub felt Whittlesey was giving out misinformation that was harmful to the Project. 'Ol Tub said he'd be damned if he was gonna appropriate money for the kind of stuff that was coming out of Washington State University. He went over to WSU and tried to get Whittlesey fired. We nudged Tub right along."*

Tub Hansen, a New Deal Democrat with a lifelong commitment to the Project, met with the president of Washington State University and with the dean of its College of Agriculture. He complained to them that Whittlesey was biting the hand that fed him, that the professor had no business receiving a paycheck from the agriculture department while "putting out data that did not reflect solid support of agriculture." Jim Ozbun, then dean of the College of Agriculture, does not recall that Hansen explicitly demanded Whittlesey's firing. But Ozbun added, "Whittlesey's firing would have pleased Hansen. . . . Norm could have lost his job had he not had tenure. That was the only situation I can recall where a professor was that irksome to the agriculture community."

The state senator attempted to single out Whittlesey's salary as a line item in the state budget. Whittlesey's personnel records were subpoenaed by the state Senate Agriculture Committee, of which Hansen was the ranking Democrat. The subpoena was part of an investigation that Hansen launched of state university professors who did outside consulting.

"It was a fishing attempt," Whittlesey told me. "What he [Hansen] was looking for was anything he could find to discredit me. The university, being fearful of budget cuts, stepped aside and said there is Whittlesey, do what you want to him."

After several months, Tub Hansen's fishing trip failed. The tenured professor kept his job and went on to win national recognition for having risked his career for the public interest. He received the annual prize of the American Agriculture Economics Association in 1987, a peer award that in his academic specialty is the equivalent of a Pulitzer Prize.

"Whittlesey almost single-handedly transformed the public sector's

*Washington State Senator Frank "Tub" Hansen, a Moses Lake cattle rancher and member of the state legislature for nineteen years, died in 1991 at age seventy-eight.

150   understanding of irrigation-hydropower trade-offs, and in the process
       forestalled the tragic misallocation of billions of dollars in public
       funds," Ralph Cavanagh, director of the Northwest Energy and Water
       Project for the National Resources Defense Council, wrote in a letter
       supporting Whittlesey's nomination for the award. "Absent Professor
       Whittlesey's findings, I am convinced that the Pacific Northwest would
       now be committed to new irrigation diversions in the Columbia Basin
       exceeding two million acre-feet per year, three times the city of Los
       Angeles' annual consumption."

       After surviving the ire of the farmers, Whittlesey began paying
       more and more attention to what had happened to the Columbia
       River and its salmon. He became increasingly annoyed at the way that
       irrigators—along with other users of the Columbia, such as barging
       companies and utilities—calculated the river's value.

       "They feel the current status quo is sacred. It does not matter
       to them how that status quo came about. They assume the value of
       what they destroyed—the river and its salmon—was zero. It is only
       their present use of the river that has monetary value. It has somehow
       become a God-given right from which all costs are to be measured,"
       Whittlesey said.

       The professor, who became persona non grata in the Columbia
       Basin and was skittish about attending meetings there, said that neither
       farmers nor other river users were willing to concede that their middle-
       class prosperity had come at the expense of the river, its fish, and the
       Native Americans who depended on both. Defenders of the sacred
       status quo, he suggested, were deadbeat debtors, unable to pay the bills
       they have run up, unwilling to acknowledge that debts even exist.

       Whittlesey started what became an avalanche of criticism of the
       Project. For a few years, it was confined to unread academic reports.
       A doctoral dissertation at Washington State University concluded in
       1985 that the only people who benefited more than they lost from the
       Project were farmers living in it. It said the Project's annual cost to
       Washington State exceeded its direct benefits by sixty-three million

dollars. Earlier, another Washington State University researcher found that the Project, which was supposed to have been a national showcase of government assistance to small family farmers, had been far friendlier to rich farmers than poor ones. "Program benefits are shared in a very unequal fashion," Craig Lynn Infanger concluded, citing figures showing that the richest 5 percent of Project farmers enjoyed 20 percent of its subsidized benefits. The poorest 10 percent received only 0.7 percent of the benefits.

As the salmon crisis deepened, with the invocation of the Endangered Species Act and with fish advocates demanding that more and more water be made available to migrating fish, Osborne and his fellow farmers lost support from their one reliable benefactor, the Bureau.

After nearly a half century of winking at flagrant violations of reclamation law, the Bureau moved for the first time in 1992 to prosecute a Basin farmer for conspiring to exceed limits on the size of an irrigated farm inside the Project. A millionaire farmer from Royal City, Washington, pleaded guilty to falsely understating the number of acres he sprinkled. He lied so he could have access to river water at the subsidized price of $2.63 an acre, rather than the full price of $85 an acre.*

Back in Washington, D.C., the Bureau announced it would never again be a builder of dams or big water projects. It would be a water manager with an environmental mission. The transformation did not take long to be felt in the Columbia Basin Project. Under mounting pressure to help save salmon, the Bureau ordered a moratorium on all new sales of river water to farms on the fringes of the Project. The order halted expansion of the water-selling scheme that Project farmers had used for more than two decades to cut their costs.

The Department of the Interior, a year later, singled out eastern Washington irrigators as the most egregious water outlaws in the West. The farmers were accused of "water spreading," the illegal irrigation of

---

*Under the law, farmers may receive project water at subsidized prices on up to 960 acres of owned or leased land. If they lease land in excess of 960 acres, they are required to pay full cost. Despite the guilty plea of the Royal City farmer, widespread violations of federal limits on farm size continue in the Columbia Basin, according to a number of farmers and irrigation experts.

152   unauthorized land. Interior charged that "water from the Columbia Basin Project was delivered to an estimated forty-two thousand to fifty-three thousand acres of ineligible lands that could have been used to provide increased stream flows for migrating salmon." The government threatened that it would demand up to twenty-nine million dollars in compensation.

Hardly had the farmers swallowed that accusation when the Bureau formally announced that, in light of the salmon crisis and the Bureau's new role as a water manager, it was giving up on the expansion of the Project to the full one million acres envisioned in 1933.

Congress, too, turned on the farmers. Searching for ways to save salmon and staunch the flow of red ink at the Bonneville Power Administration, which supplies half the power consumed in the Northwest, the House Committee on Natural Resources zeroed in on the ultra-cheap electricity that is reserved for Project farmers. If farmers paid normal wholesale rates for their electricity, a committee report said, Northwest consumers would suddenly save thirty-two million dollars a year. More important, the report said that "the extremely low price" farmers pay for electricity encourages them to waste water that could be used for salmon or power generation.

Another damning report from the same House committee, entitled "Taking from the Taxpayer," singled out Project farmers for enriching themselves by selling electricity generated by subsidized water. "Every drop of water added to the canals provides more profit" to the farmers, the report said.

Finally, farmers in the Project were bombarded by attacks from a regional think tank that delighted in making them look greedy and environmentally blind. Bill Bean, director of the Portland-based Columbia Basin Institute, which attracted money from the Ford Foundation and the Aspen Institute, was obsessed by the short-sighted acquisitiveness of farmers and other users of the Columbia River. The best way to understand the Columbia Basin scam, Bean told me, is to compare it to welfare cheating in New York City.

"I used to work for the New York City welfare department on the Lower East Side, investigating welfare fraud. Mrs. Rodriguez would say she had six kids, when she only had four kids. Why does that happen? She gets more money if she says she has six kids. I don't think there is much difference between Mrs. Rodriguez and farmers in the Columbia Basin Project. In this country everyone takes what he can get."

Bean's institute charged that some farmers worked hand-in-glove with giant fast-food corporations, such as McDonald's. About 80 percent of America's French fries were grown and processed in the Columbia Basin. The processors set up shop inside the Project to take advantage of its subsidized water and electricity. Even as they profited from subsidies, Bean's report said, potato-processing companies refused to pay their fair share of cleanup costs for polluting local groundwater. The multinational potato processors also failed, according to the report, to shoulder the social costs of a large and impoverished Latino workforce in the Basin.

"A regional system of federal subsidy, expanded during the New Deal to provide a better life for a distressed class of small farmers and rural residents, has evolved into a mechanism for creating a new rural underclass, impoverished communities, and degradation of the very water and public power developments upon which the entire system depends," Bean's study said.

Less than a year after the French-fry attack, Bean and his associates lobbed another grenade at Project farmers. The Columbia Basin Institute accused them of scheming to "convert federally subsidized water into an economic commodity." It said farmers, by selling subsidized water and generating power with subsidized water, were thumbing their noses at national water-conservation goals and emergency efforts to save salmon. Bean took his report to Washington, D.C., and presented it at a House hearing to which Columbia Basin irrigators had been called to defend their irrigation practices.

As Bean had hoped, he and his institute succeeded in making farmers look bad.

"An uncharitable person would say that since you are making money off hydropower, you don't have any incentive to conserve water, even if you could," Representative Peter DeFazio, a Democrat from Oregon, told the irrigators. "They [Bill Bean and his institute] have

154 aimed a dagger at your heart. You have to do a more effective job of defending yourselves."

As seen from Ted and Barbara Osborne's kitchen, the Project's fall from honor was nothing less than treachery. Interrupting her husband and getting genuinely mad, Barbara Osborne said, "We feel we are being betrayed by our own country.

"You can't expect a narrow segment of society [irrigators] to pay all their costs to grow the country's food. How much are those environmentalists willing to pay for their food? People won't understand the need for us until there are no Wheaties on the table."

"What's this latest damn fish?" Ted Osborne said, warming to the argument. He was referring to environmentalist petitions to list summer chinook in the mid-Columbia as an endangered species. "They are not on the endangered list yet, but I'm sure they will be. The fish people have the power now. Rush Limbaugh calls them wackos."*

Ted and Barbara both repeated the word "wackos," laughing bitterly.

"We have water rights for the rest of the Project," Ted said, referring to a 1939 agreement that, in theory, gives farmers the right to extract more than twice as much water from the Columbia as they are taking now. "But it don't mean a thing anymore. The fish are going to take that. I think people are going to have to get a little bit hungry before they realize that fish ain't that important."

The irrigators' remaining self-justification was hunger. They claimed they were a bulwark against hunger. The claim did not make much sense until food shortages became an urgent global concern in 2008, as crop failures dovetailed with sharply increased food consumption in developing nations.

Still, more than 60 percent of the Columbia River water consumed

---

*As it turned out, the petition to list mid-Columbia summer chinook salmon as an endangered species was turned down by the federal government. Federal fish agencies concluded in 1994 that the salmon's numbers were declining, but it was not facing extinction. After a long losing streak, the decision was a major victory for irrigators and other users of the river.

in the Project, and nearly half of the land under cultivation, did not produce food for human consumption. It produced forage and pasture crops, primarily alfalfa. Much of the hay was cut, compacted into cubes, and barged down to Portland for export to Asia, where it was fed to cattle. And more water pumped from the river for irrigation would mean less water for hydropower, which was relatively cheap and did not warm the planet.

A number of cost-benefit analyses of reclamation projects showed that, as far as national economic development was concerned, most federal irrigation schemes devoured rather than created wealth. The schemes were found to represent an inefficient use of land, water, capital, labor, and materials.

Ted Osborne, who died in 2009 at the age of eighty-nine, was not so quick to anger as younger farmers and irrigation managers in the Project. Though he did not want to lose water for fish, for him it was more a matter of principle than need.

"Nobody wants to give up anything. If the farmers really wanted to conserve water, and they knew that was all they were gonna get, they could do it. The new technology allows it. Farmers around here could get by with a third less water. A lot of water is being wasted.

"Yeah, we could get by on less, but don't spread that around too much."

Younger irrigators did not share Osborne's resigned view that "the fish" were going to take their water.

"We are going to use the courts and the political arena to fight back," Dick Erickson, manager of the East Columbia Basin Irrigation District, told me after he had been humiliated in a hearing room on Capitol Hill. "We are not going to apologize for what we do. This Project grows a lot of food, creates a lot of jobs. We keep getting characterized for doing something that is evil because of politics.

"This whole thing is being driven by urban centers. This idea of saving all the wild runs of salmon has gotten to be such a priority that people are not looking at how they are damaging rural areas. There is a lot of environment other than salmon. But the votes are in the city. The money is in the cities. Elected officials are catering to cities.

156   "In the cities they don't understand where food comes from. The guy from Microsoft in Seattle, as soon as he drives east over the mountains, he does not want to see dams or farms or people making a living. He wants to see pristine wilderness, and he wants a nice four-lane to get there and get back home."

Erickson and his fellow farmers were far from helpless. As evil as they said political games had become in the New West, they still played them. Farmers and their lawyers were resourceful in court. Their lawyers stopped the Bureau from collecting a penny of the millions earned by hydroelectric generators on government-owned canals. Erickson warned that any attempt by environmentalists to reduce the amount of water the Project extracted from the river would be met by a lawsuit.

By 2008, global food shortages, climate change, and relentless lobbying from irrigators combined to give a glimmer of new life to the Project. Washington State approved a limited plan to use more water from Columbia River reservoirs for irrigation. It would replace groundwater from an aquifer that had been depleted by the wells of potato growers. In 2010, the federal government proposed a number of alternatives that would further expand the Project and use more water from the Columbia to grow food. It was not clear how much water the irrigators would get, but it seemed likely they would get more.

8

Wild and Scenic Atomic River

As they seek to become the world's leading experts in solving waste problems, the men and women at Hanford will help make a cleaner, safe environment for everyone everywhere.
—THE HANFORD STORY
a children's coloring book printed for the fiftieth anniversary of the Hanford nuclear site

THE RIVER THAT arcs around the edges of the plutonium factory is not the bathtub Columbia that we have come to expect, all fat and listless and stoppered up behind concrete. On the contrary, this stretch of river is swift, undammed, exuberantly wild. Shallow water scuds over gravel bars where chinook salmon spawn by the tens of thousands. Bald eagles swoop to capture spawned-out fish. Pregnant deer fight the current as they swim out to islands in the river to fawn at a safe distance from coyotes. Great blue herons nest in apricot trees along the shore. A dun-colored desert plain rises gradually from the right bank of the river, climbing three thousand feet to a distant basalt spine called Rattlesnake Mountain, where river Indians once sent their sons to pray alone to the Creator. Between the fast river and the sacred mountain, amid a covering of sagebrush and bluebunch wheatgrass, about fifty species of wildlife take refuge. From pygmy rabbits to Rocky Mountain elk, the plain is one of the last sanctuaries in the Pacific Northwest for endangered and threatened wildlife. On the river's left bank, a sheer bluff of creamy white clay juts up six hundred feet, containing within its sun-bleached verticality the fossilized remains of rhinoceros and camel, mastodon and bear. Prairie hawks, peregrine falcons, and other raptors rifle down out of the mausoleum bluffs to prey on migrating ducks and geese.

The Hanford Reach of the Columbia is not unlike the "incredible"

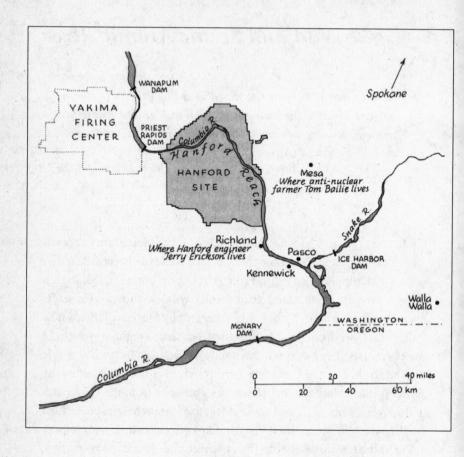

river that awed Lewis and Clark in 1805. For fifty-one miles, it surges through an arrestingly uncivilized landscape, cantankerous as its ancient self. It cuts through the only extant shrub-steppe ecosystem in eastern Washington and is the only free-flowing, non-tidal segment of the river in the United States. It also offers salmon the finest spawning habitat on the Columbia and is the best reason to believe that wild salmon will never be completely engineered out of the river. In 2000, President Bill Clinton proclaimed this stretch of the river to be the Hanford Reach National Monument. It is the only national monument managed by the U.S. Fish and Wildlife Service.

This curiously undead fragment of the Columbia, of course, is an accident. The Hanford Reach eluded dam builders not because it was exceptionally scenic but because it was eminently expendable. The Manhattan Project, the U.S. effort to develop an atomic bomb during World War II, knew little and cared less about rivers or salmon. Frantic to beat Hitler to the bomb, the government needed a substantial factory site for the production of weapons-grade plutonium, a process that demanded huge quantities of cold water and electricity. After a nationwide search, the bomb-makers settled on the tiny riverside village of Hanford because the surroundings offered access to the nation's coldest big river and power from the world's biggest dam. But even more important, in the words of Franklin T. Matthias, the Army lieutenant colonel who in 1942 scouted locations for a plutonium plant, Hanford was "an area with almost no people." There would be few victims—or witnesses—in case the biggest secret of World War II happened to blow up.*

The army ordered the few hundred farmers and fruit growers who lived in and around Hanford to get out within thirty days. It bought up about six hundred square miles of what it considered to be wasteland and sealed it off behind barbed wire and machine-gun-toting men. Federal authorities in later years vetoed a proposed dam for the

---

*The U.S. Army ruled out Oak Ridge, Tennessee, as a site for the huge plutonium factory because, as General Leslie R. Groves, head of the U.S. effort to develop an atomic bomb, put it, if a "reactor were to explode and throw great quantities of highly radioactive materials into the atmosphere when the wind was blowing toward Knoxville, the loss of life and the damage to health in the area might be catastrophic."

160   Hanford Reach, it being poor public policy for the river to back up over America's largest depository of radioactive crud.*

As the decades went by, an astonishing thing happened behind the high-security fence at Hanford Engineering Works. While the plutonium makers were spilling 440 billion gallons of contaminated liquid into the sandy soil (enough to flood Manhattan to a depth of eighty feet) and sowing the seeds for what the Energy Department calls "the single largest environmental and health risk in the nation," they inadvertently invented a post-nuclear paradise.

The Hanford Reach emerged from the cold war as a wild and scenic nuclear dump, a sanctuary for endangered species and toxic waste, a spawning ground for healthy wild salmon and a burial ground for hydrogen-belching plutonium sludge that can kill on touch. It is a fine place to see an eagle hunt, deer graze, or fish spawn. But best not drink the groundwater for a quarter million years.†

The character of this aberrant Eden was neatly packaged when a hell-raiser by the name of Norm Buske paddled a rubber boat along the Hanford Reach. Buske positioned himself just downstream from N Reactor, a giant decommissioned nuclear plant that for twenty years had pumped about a billion gallons of radioactive waste into two open trenches, one of which lies less than the length of a football field from the Columbia. An underground spring, affectionately called N Springs by plant workers, ran beneath the two trenches and dribbled into the river. Among the many unappetizing pollutants that were measurable

---

*Radioactive or not, dam builders from the U.S. Army Corps of Engineers were eager to seize and squeeze electricity out of this last wild stretch of the river. As recently as 1979, after Hanford had been in the plutonium business for more than three decades, the Corps organized a tour of the Hanford Reach to show how useful the proposed Ben Franklin Dam could be. "The unimpounded Hanford Reach represents a break in the total Columbia River hydropower system," tour literature said. "A dam and a reservoir on the Reach could provide an additional energy supply and improve the hydraulic efficiency of the entire Columbia River hydropower system." Ben Franklin Dam is now considered a dead idea.

†That is the half-life for the longest lived of the radionuclides known to be shifting around in the uncontained aquifer beneath Hanford. The aquifer discharges to the Columbia.

in N Springs was strontium-90, a highly carcinogenic radionuclide
with a half-life of three hundred years and a penchant for seeking out
and lodging in human bone. The concentration of strontium-90 in N
Springs was, at the time of Buske's rubber-boat adventure, about nine
hundred times higher than the federal standard for safe drinking water.

In the rubber boat that day, Buske, by training a physicist and
by avocation an anti-nuclear troublemaker, knew where N Springs
was and what it contained. What he had not expected to find, on the
shoreline and washed in the nightshade seepage of N Springs, was a
crop of perfectly ripe mulberries. Inspired by their juicy pulchritude,
he paddled up to the west bank of the river, picked a quart of berries
without getting out of his boat (which would have been a violation of
federal law), and rushed home to make jam. He mailed his jam, along
with a letter, to the governor of the state of Washington and to the
secretary of energy. The letter said: "This mulberry jam is a token of
the future hazard of unidentified, uncontained, and unmanaged radio-
activity at Hanford."

So it was that two jars of ruby-red preserves triggered the mulberry
syndrome.

Alarmed consumers swamped the Washington State Department of
Health with questions about the safety of the state's celebrated apples
and peaches. Agribusiness got angry. Politicians demanded action.
The mulberries, in fact, were a very low-level risk. Buske told me he
would have had to eat an entire jar of mulberry jam every day for a year
before he would begin to worry about his health. But in the politics of
nuclear fear, where paranoia is a given and distrust of the government
runs deep, a nicely turned media perception usually outweighs scientific risk. Hanford workers, therefore, were ordered down to the river.
Wearing blazing white radiation suits and armed with chainsaws, they
mowed down every mulberry bush in sight, stuffing severed limbs and
mashed berries into concrete coffins.

After three years of policy-option papers and mid-level bureaucratic
waffling, the mulberry coffins were sent out on the road. They were
trucked to Oak Ridge, Tennessee, to the nation's only certified incin-
erator for low-level radioactive waste. There, the bushes and berries

162   were mashed, analyzed, cremated, placed in an urn, and shipped back to Hanford for burial in a special pit designed for low-level waste.

The price tag for the hysteria that Buske so shrewdly ignited—for cutting, boxing, storing, shipping, burning, compacting, testing, reshipping, and burying the mulberries—exceeded two hundred thousand dollars. The price tag for stanching all radioactive dribbles at N Springs will be much, much higher. As part of an "Expedited Response Action," the government has hatched several multimillion-dollar schemes to prevent hot jam from ever again reaching the desks of higher-ups. One plan under high-level review would insulate the west bank of the Columbia from radiation by inserting refrigerant tubes in the sandy soil and freezing it solid.

The Hanford stretch of the river, ever since the federal government saved it by deciding it was expendable, has been a reliable source of astonishment.

The first surprise came on August 6, 1945, the day the first combat atomic bomb fell from an airplane. Called Little Boy, it exploded over the Japanese city of Hiroshima. Birds incinerated in flight. Telephone poles burst into flame. Human beings within a half mile of the bomb's hypocenter shriveled into smoking piles of ashes. "The corpse lying on its back on the road had been killed immediately. Its hand was lifted to the sky and the fingers were burning with blue flames," said a woman who lived to describe the work of Little Boy. The bomb killed about sixty-four thousand people, a quarter of the population of Hiroshima.

"IT'S ATOMIC BOMBS," screamed a banner headline in an extra edition of a Hanford newspaper on the day the bomb exploded. The Manhattan Project was out of the bag. President Harry Truman explained what nearly 150,000 workers had been building for thirty months at the "big war project" in the desert beside the Columbia. Except for a handful of physicists, engineers, and army officers, those workers had been as ignorant about the bomb as the Japanese.

It turned out that the Hiroshima bomb was armed with enriched uranium from Oak Ridge, not plutonium from Hanford. But just three days later, Hanford's handiwork hit the headlines and lit up Nagasaki. That bomb, called Fat Man, killed about thirty-nine thousand people, some quickly, many others over time. Within two days, Japan began talking surrender. "PEACE! Our Bomb Cinched It," proclaimed a newspaper in Richland, the federally managed town that housed Hanford's engineers and technicians.

With World War II won, Hanford churned out the coinage of the cold war. It manufactured fifty-three metric tons of weapons-grade plutonium, which armed most of the U.S. nuclear arsenal.* The arms race with the Soviet Union spelled a long, lucrative boom for the Tri-Cities of Pasco, Kennewick, and Richland, towns clustered just downstream from the plutonium factory. Richland, with one of the highest rates of Ph.D.s per capita of any municipality in America, evolved into a wondrous company town, a prosperous mix of normalcy, secrecy, paranoia, and pride. Each Cold War morning, teams of health scientists collected urine samples from the front porches of Hanford technicians. The FBI made yearly rounds, asking neighbor about neighbor. The main hospital in Richland was built with a nuclear-incident wing, where a monorail whisked patients exposed to radiation through a sort of car wash, hosing them down before doctors worked on them behind lead shields.

Richland sprouted Atomic Bowling Lanes, an Atomic Body Shop, Atomic TV Repair, even an "Atomic Man." He was Harold McCloskey, a technician who survived a 1976 accident at Hanford that sprayed his

---

*Plutonium, first identified in 1940 at the University of California in Berkeley, was named after the planet Pluto, which was named for the Greek god of the underworld, the lord of the dead. The synthetic element is the preferred fuel for bombs because it is highly fissionable; that is, easy to explode. Weapons-grade plutonium is made inside an atomic reactor, from natural uranium. After being separated from uranium by chemical means, it is molded into hockey-puck-sized "buttons" for use in bombs. While plutonium itself is one of the most poisonous substances known to man (a microscopic speck in the lungs can cause cancer), a nickel-plated plutonium button can be oddly comforting to touch. "When you hold a lump of it in your hand," wrote physicist Leona Marshall Libby, "it feels warm, like a live rabbit." Storing the live rabbit can be treacherous. Too much plutonium kept too close together can create a spontaneous "criticality," a deadly flash of radiation and heat.

164 face with the largest human dose of radiation ever recorded. He became the most thoroughly studied nuclear victim in America. Baggies of his feces and urine (labeled "Caution Radioactive") were stored for years in laboratory refrigerators and freezers across the Hanford site. After the accident, McCloskey was almost blind and his face could set off Geiger counters fifty feet away. But he was pro-Hanford until the end (of a heart attack in 1987). "Just forget about me being anti-nuclear, because I'm not," he said a decade after the accident. "We need nuclear energy."

Football players from Richland High wore a mushroom cloud on their helmets and called themselves the Bombers. The symbol of the atom was carved atop stone columns at the entrance to the cemetery. When liberated from federal ownership and allowed self-government in 1958, Richland's residents staged a simulated atomic explosion in a vacant lot on the edge of town. And when the Cold War began to wind down, announcement of the closure of N Reactor brought mournful Tri-Citians into the streets by the thousands. They held candles and sang "Kumbaya."

Though Hanford lost its original reason to exist, it did not lose its capacity to astonish. In 1986 when an environmental group in Spokane forced the release of classified documents from Hanford, the public learned that the plutonium factory had made a practice of poisoning its downwind and downstream neighbors. Huge atmospheric releases of radiation, all of them secret and some of them intentional, occurred throughout the second half of the forties and early fifties. Radiation drifted east with the prevailing winds across eastern Washington, Oregon, and northern Idaho. An alarmed army of "down-winders"— farmers and housewives, many of them irrigators from the Columbia Basin Project—queued up to sue, claiming thyroid disease, cancer, still-births, and birth defects.

Hot water from Hanford made the Columbia the most radioactive river on earth. River water was piped into eight reactors as a coolant, stored in basins for a few minutes or a few hours, and then pumped back into the river. The temperature of the Columbia went up by as much as 2 degrees as the river swallowed highly toxic radio-nuclides that found their way all the way out to the mouth of the river (more than 350 miles) to lodge in oysters and clams. Hanford documents show that biologists secretly discussed the "advisability of closing" a downstream stretch of the river to public fishing and hunting in the late 1950s when plutonium production was at its peak and resident fish and ducks showed dangerously high concentrations of radioactive phosphorus. But no warnings were issued. The last of the primitive-technology "single-pass" reactors was shut down in 1971. To the immense relief of federal and state health authorities, the river diluted and swept away nearly all the contamination. The most susceptible victims of the "river pathway" turned out to have been the same people who were most susceptible to dams on the Columbia—Indians who ate a lot of fish.

Hanford's final astonishment (barring a catastrophic environmental accident) is the cost of cleaning up the mess. It has become one of the most expensive environmental cleanup projects in history. The bill was initially pegged at $50 billion over thirty years. But that may jump to more than $100 billion over nearly fifty years, according to a 2009 report by the U.S. Government Accountability Office.

Hanford is home to two-thirds of the country's high-level radio-active waste, some of it in tanks and some of it in the soil. The federal Agency for Toxic Substances and Disease Registry ranked Hanford as its top health hazard among more than a hundred major cleanup sites across the country. Because of the threat of explosion and the threat to groundwater, Hanford was the only site on the "most urgent" list.

Even though the last reactor was shut down in 1987, none of the fifty-three million gallons of highly toxic waste in aging and leaky underground tanks has been mopped up. That will have to wait until at least 2019. If all goes well, that's when a unique waste-treatment plant will begin turning radioactive sludge into radioactive logs suitable for long-term storage.

Hanford's cleanup has rarely gone well. The cost of the plant that would convert gunk to glass, a process known as vitrification, keeps going up. It rose from $5.5 billion in 2003 to about $13 billion in 2011. The safety of the waste-treatment process itself was questioned by the

166 Defense Nuclear Facilities Safety Board, which monitors how the U.S. Department of Energy cleans up nuclear weapons sites. The questions were almost certain to cause more delays and drive up the price of the cleanup.

This is music to the ears of people who live in the Tri-Cities. Since the early 1990s, they have been feasting on their "environmental mission." The Great Recession that began in 2008 skipped Richland, Kennewick, and Pasco. House values rose amid a national housing crisis. Job growth in the area was, amazingly, the highest in the country in 2010. Environmental scientists earned higher salaries in Richland than in Seattle. Business publications included the Tri-Cities on their lists of the best places in America to live and work. At the Columbia Mall, where it was often difficult to find a place to park, a Hallmark shop selling greeting cards was replaced in 2010 by a Coach shop selling $800 handbags. In the first decade of the cleanup, Sam Volpentest, head of the Tri-City Industrial Council, told the *Wall Street Journal* that "the green stuff is just raining down from heaven." That rain was expected to keep falling until the middle of the twenty-first century.

For travelers on the Columbia, the Hanford Reach is an anomaly, a skinny irradiated thumb sticking out of the bloated continuum of the dammed-up river. Barges and irrigators and utility companies have been kept out. The politically volatile trade-off between salmon and commerce does not pertain. The reach was never fattened up by a dam, so there was no fight over dam removal or a reservoir drawdown. In its sick quarantine way, the Hanford Reach was too healthy to be part of the engineered West, too isolated to be muddied by the politics of the working river. Although I found myself spending more time around Hanford than any other part of the river, I did not quite know what to make of it.

Then one warm July night in Richland, at a crowded public hearing during which nuclear technocrats were floating a scheme to process more plutonium, the Hanford Reach snapped into focus.

What sharpened up the picture, amid the plastic chairs and fluorescent lighting of the windowless meeting room in the Hanford House Red Lion Inn, was a fog of intolerance. The crowd was choking on it. Most of the people attending the hearing that night worked at Hanford, and they welcomed the proposed restart of the aging plutonium finishing plant. It would be a hundred million dollars more gravy for the Tri-Cities, money that would trickle down to the assembled technicians, enabling them to redo their kitchens, take trips to the Columbia Mall, save for college tuition. The locals nodded their heads approvingly as Hanford officials explained that an eighty-week "stabilization run" at the plant was needed to convert volatile plutonium scraps left over from the Cold War into talcum-like powder that could be stored safely.

Along with these locals at the meeting, there were a few outsiders—anti-nuclear activists from Seattle, downwinders from the East Side of the river—who had come to ask thorny questions. They seemed convinced that Hanford was again conniving to drizzle carcinogens into the air, the river, and the groundwater. Their manner suggested that everyone at Hanford was a war criminal. While the outsiders asked their questions, the locals stared in stony, resentful silence. Finally, when a long-winded Seattle environmentalist pressed for detailed answers about the disposal of the "waste stream" from the plutonium plant, a middle-aged Hanford worker in the audience could take it no longer.

"Shut up, you pup!" the man yelled, and the locals applauded.

It occurred to me, as I watched these westerners who detested each other, that the Hanford Reach, rather than being an aberration in the making of the engineered river, was its culmination.

The plutonium factory was the endgame for the New Deal on the Columbia. Federal domination that began in the 1930s with a well-meaning effort to create jobs at Grand Coulee had mutated into an interminable and ludicrously costly struggle to mop up lethal waste. There had been an inexorable slide from public-works projects that saved the common man to clandestine schemes that contaminated him.

168 The final irony of federal domination was the river itself. The Columbia was at its free-flowing, salmon-choked best only when flowing past the Western world's largest and leakiest nuclear dump.*

Now that most of the secrets were out at Hanford and the cleanup was under way, the most enduring consequence of federal control in my home country was not pollution, but intolerance. It had taken firm root during a half century of lies and secrets. Nobody had known anything about what was going on out at Hanford, nobody had a right to know, and nobody was inclined to complain because, as the head of the Tri-City Industrial Council so aptly put it, the green stuff was just raining down from heaven. In the democratic vacuum, Hanford created another accidental and pernicious byproduct: a binary society. Technicians versus hayseeds. Believers versus victims. Separated by the river, they had come to see each other as nothing less than murderers and fools.

My little epiphany in the Red Lion Inn came after I had made the acquaintance of two men, a believer and a victim, who live on opposite sides of Hanford Reach. They had never met, yet they loathed the very idea of each other. Each man showed me his version of Hanford and warned me not to believe what I might hear from the mendacious simpletons on the other side of the Columbia. They were both likable and open and noisily good-natured in the way that westerners are so proud of. Except, of course, when they talked about the enemy across the river.

"Did you ever see the movie *Deliverance?*" Tom Bailie, the down-wind victim, asked me at our first meeting. "You know, those Appalachian squirrel hunters, those retarded in-bred guys with funny looks

---

*The relative health of the Hanford Reach, as far as fish and wildlife are concerned, is a function of a half century of isolation from farming, suburban sprawl, slackwater, and other development. Wildlife on the site has, on occasion, been measured with dangerously high levels of radiation. But, in general, all species of fish and game have prospered. Radiation in the river, which is diluted by the enormous flow of the Columbia, does not appear to have had any deleterious effect on salmon. The fish, of course, spend the bulk of their lives in the Pacific Ocean, far from N Springs and Hanford's other riverside delights.

on their faces. Well, the cast of *Deliverance* is living in Richland and working at Hanford to this day."

In Richland, Jerry Erickson, an electrical engineer who has devoted most of his professional life to N Reactor, told me that the downwinders are a sad symptom of a poorly educated nation.

"It is just a matter of ignorance," said Erickson, whose three sons all work in the nuclear industry, two of them at Hanford. "I think our society is technologically in the dark ages. These people think Hanford is like some kind of science-fiction movie. I don't understand a public that can be led down such strange alleys."

The gulf between believers and victims showed up clearly in public-opinion surveys. Three-quarters of eastern Washington residents did not believe the government had been honest about Hanford's dangers, according to a survey by Washington State University. Two-thirds of those surveyed believe Hanford would damage the health of their grandchildren. Residents of eastern Washington were as skeptical about Hanford, the study found, as Russians are about Chelyabinsk-65, that nation's dirtiest nuclear site.

Across eastern Washington, the exception to this opinion was in the Tri-Cities. The closer people lived to Hanford's paychecks, the less skeptical they were of the government. A reader's poll in the *Tri-City Herald*, the region's dominant daily newspaper, suggested that Hanford's believers were upset not at the federal government but at the downwinders who claimed to be Hanford's victims. Asked if the government should pay compensation to downwinders affected by radiation from the plutonium factory, nearly 60 percent of respondents said no.

Jerry Erickson, the engineer at Hanford, arranged to take me on a tour of his life's work. He had come to Hanford in 1959 because he liked to "build stuff." He now has seven patents on instruments he invented for N Reactor.

"For a technical person, when you build stuff, it is candy," Erickson told me. "From a technical point of view, Hanford has been a candy

170 shop. I have put bread on the table and raised my kids in a very healthy environment and I am proud to say that I have had a wonderful technical time."

Erickson, sixty-four years old when we met, was a tall, skinny, hyper-energetic man who wore horn-rim glasses and whose left shirt pocket bulged with pens and scribbled drawings of projects in progress. He bore a passing resemblance to what Jerry Lewis might have looked like had he, like Erickson, been a lifelong jogger. The engineer's youngest son, Tim, also an engineer, told me that his father "can't sit still. If you give him a present, he will take it apart before he uses it." When Jerry Erickson installed an underground sprinkler system around his Richland house, he made drawings and a plastic mockup to gauge sprinkler overlap at different wind velocities in his yard. He made a paper mockup to determine if his wife's piano would fit in the basement. (It would, but it remains in the living room.)

Erickson was a fourth-generation northwesterner, whose forebears came West on the Oregon Trail. His great-grandfather, James Longmeyer, led a wagon train that briefly lost its way in what became the Hanford site. In his memoirs, he recalled camping on the empty desert in 1853 beside the Columbia River, just opposite the soaring White Bluffs and not far from the nuclear reactor his great-grandson would help build. Longmeyer was searching for a well-watered place to settle, worried about Indians who kept tagging after the wagon train. "We placed a couple guards out, as we supposed they had led us into this trap in order to massacre our whole party," Longmeyer wrote. The Indians did not attack and Longmeyer's party wandered off to the southwest toward a less arid settlement on the Yakima River, a tributary of the Columbia.

Jerry Erickson grew up on a farm not far from the Yakima. A poor student, he excelled only in machine shop. His most vivid boyhood memory was of assembling, from a bucket of parts and without instructions or adult help, a 1929 Harley-Davidson motorcycle. A neighbor had taken the bike apart for an overhaul, but could not figure out how to put it back together.

"I don't have any idea how I knew. I just knew, that's all. I was just inquisitive enough and I had enough ego."

After high school and apprenticeship as a tool-and-die maker, Erickson went into the Navy. He considered electronics "a sissy kind of a thing," but was pushed into becoming a specialist in flight simulators and other electronic training equipment. To his surprise and delight, he found he could compete with college-trained electrical engineers. After leaving the Navy, he enrolled in engineering school at the University of Washington. Once he had his degree, he was recruited by Philco in Palo Alto, California, where he helped develop a receiver for one of the first military satellites. However, he hated California.

"I came up to Yakima in 1959 to visit my family, and decided to drive over to Hanford [a distance of about fifty miles] to see what was going on. I stopped at the five-and-dime in Richland, called up the employment office at Hanford, and asked them if they needed an electrical engineer. They said, right on the phone, 'Don't move!' They rushed down and brought me back to the employment office. I didn't have a résumé with me, so they got me a secretary to take dictation. She typed it up right there. Boy, they were solicitous."

Erickson went to work designing instruments for N Reactor, then under construction as the largest of Hanford's nine riverside reactors. It was commissioned in 1963 as the country's first and only "dual-purpose" nuclear plant, capable of turning out both plutonium for bombs and electricity for a half-million people. President John F. Kennedy visited Hanford to dedicate the reactor and made a speech about how it marked a turning point for the peaceful use of atomic energy. Erickson, his wife, Peggy, and their boys, along with thirty-seven thousand other Tri-Citians, trooped out to the reactor site to hear Kennedy describe Hanford as "a great national asset and I can assure you it will be maintained."

N Reactor, unfortunately, bore more than a passing resemblance to an unlucky nuclear plant in the Ukraine. It was called Chernobyl

172   Number Four. When Chernobyl blew in 1986—in the world's worst nuclear accident—N Reactor became a public-relations embarrassment to the federal government.

The Hanford reactor resembled Chernobyl in that it was built out of graphite blocks, produced both power and plutonium, and lacked a containment dome to seal in contaminants in case of accident. Erickson and other Hanford engineers insisted that these similarities were cosmetic, and that N Reactor had a fundamentally safer design.

"We tried to explain why our plant was never going to have the same problems as Chernobyl, but nobody wanted to listen," Erickson told me.

N Reactor plant shut down in 1987 for a safety overhaul. The collapse of the Soviet Union in 1991 turned the overhaul into a mothball job.

In the cutbacks that followed, Erickson accepted what he calls a "very attractive retirement plan." It was so attractive, in fact, that N Reactor lost many of the senior engineers who understood the plant well enough to preside over its cleanup and dismemberment. The government had to go begging for expertise from old-timers. When I met Erickson, he was back working at N Reactor as a consultant, driving out to the Hanford site two or three days a week.

Security at the old plutonium factory had been sharply reduced since the collapse of the Soviet Union. The site was open to just about anybody who requested a guided tour. Delegations of journalists, anti-nuclear activists, even Russian physicists had been squired through nearly every building on the site, including the plutonium finishing plant, once a sanctum sanctorum of American national security. But Hanford remains closed to unescorted gawkers. Besides the potentially explosive underground waste tanks that are larger than the Capitol dome and the 1,400 or so radiation hot spots spread around the site, vaults at Hanford house several tons of weapons-grade plutonium, perfect for terrorist bomb assembly.

To get past the security gate, I needed—in addition to Erickson's invitation—a security badge, a radiation-exposure badge, and an official guide from Westinghouse, then the lead contractor on the site. We all met on a cloudless July morning in the parking lot of Westinghouse offices in Richland. Don Brauer, our garrulous Westinghouse tour guide, suggested that we go in his company car. Erickson insisted on sitting in the backseat.

We started the tour in Richland, a fastidiously tidy riverside town of thirty-two thousand people who live just beyond the southern tip of the Hanford reservation. Many of Richland's inhabitants are either managers or technicians. Nine out of ten residents are white. As we tooled through Richland's quiet, tree-lined residential streets, Brauer and Erickson competed with each other to praise the town as a comfortable and safe place to bring up children.

"Richland has more parks per capita than any city in this state," said Brauer. He pointed to Chief Joseph Junior High School, a gray concrete structure that he said was "the only junior high school in the world built to look exactly like a nuclear reactor."

"There is a mint F!" exclaimed Erickson from the backseat, pointing to a handsome two-story, three-bedroom house. All the houses in the older parts of Richland were built by the government in 1943–44 as homes for Hanford technicians. The "F" to which Erickson pointed would have been reserved for a senior manager, since it was close to the Columbia. Erickson lives farther from the river in a more modest "E," a one-story saltbox. Far larger than any room in his house is his garage, which the engineer designed and built and which he describes as "the best workshop in the neighborhood, the place where I keep all my toys and tools."

Beyond the security gates, where armed guards scrutinized my badge, my driver's license, and my face, Hanford opened up before us as a big spread of sun-drenched nothing. About 96 percent of the site, according to the federal government, has been untouched by plutonium production or any other kind of development for a half century.

"You know, I would move out here in a minute and build a house," Erickson said, leaning forward from the backseat and directing my attention to the encircling emptiness. "Of all this area, darn little is contaminated. It is a beautiful place. But I would be careful about where I sank a well."

174   To address that point, our Westinghouse guide pulled off the asphalt highway that runs through the Hanford site. Brauer, who used to make videos for Westinghouse Hanford before he semiretired to teach media courses at the community college, wanted to show off an experimental way of neutralizing some of the toxic chemicals and radioactive waste that Hanford's workers had a habit of dumping in long trenches and burying. Throughout most of the Cold War, only the most dangerous of Hanford's waste—concentrated plutonium syrup and other very toxic nucleotides—was stored in underground tanks. There are 177 of the tanks, more than a third of which are known to leak. The vast bulk of the waste was poured or pumped directly into the soil. This included ninety-three thousand tons of volatile organics and other chemicals, half a million pounds of uranium, and four hundred pounds of plutonium. At least 1.2 million cubic yards of soil at Hanford is radioactive, according to the Department of Energy, enough dirt to cover a football field to a depth of seven hundred feet.

"It's called in-situ vitrification," Brauer said proudly, as we got out of the car to see the antidote to hot dirt. It works, Brauer explained, when electrodes are jabbed into the ground and enough electricity is pumped through them to power a fifty-story hotel. Intense heat (2,000 degrees centigrade) cooks the soil into disks of black, obsidian-like glass, destroying some dangerous chemicals and immobilizing radioactive waste so it will not leach into groundwater. Brauer said tests have been promising.

What he did not say was that cleanup experts are having a devil of a time figuring out where to jab the electrodes. A lot of contaminated soil at Hanford has been "lost." Technicians kept careful records of how much plutonium they produced, but not of where they stashed its toxic by-products. Not long after my tour, Thomas Grumbly, the Department of Energy's assistant secretary for environmental restoration and waste management, complained that at Hanford "it's as though you had a party every night for forty-five years, and you never cleaned it up." Retired workers have been interviewed to see if they happen to remember what they may have buried and where. One landfill, discovered to contain barrels of toxic solvent, was dated to the mid-1960s, primarily because bulldozers unearthed aluminum trays from Swanson's TV dinners.

As we drove north along the river toward the reactors and chemical plants that are the toxic heart of Hanford, Brauer and Erickson explained that outside criticism of this place had gotten out of hand. They said the original designers of Hanford had the good sense to locate its giant chemical plants, which produced massive volumes of liquid waste while extracting plutonium from irradiated uranium fuel, several miles from the Columbia. They noted that the chemical plants sit atop 250 feet of sandy soil, gravel, and rock, which they said provides a natural barrier between dangerous waste liquid and the groundwater.

"It turns out that the soil loves this [radioactive] stuff. It just grabs it," Erickson told me, explaining that many of the most dangerous radionuclides that were dumped into the soil, such as plutonium, have bonded chemically with the soil and cannot move into groundwater aquifers that flow into the Columbia River.

What Erickson told me was true, to a point, but too rosy. The original builders at Hanford had guessed it would take up to 180 years for contaminated groundwater to reach the river. But just eleven years after plutonium production began, radioactive groundwater was detected near the Columbia. One underground plume of radioactive tritium penetrated the soil beneath the chemical plants and traveled nine miles to the river in just seven years.

So far, though, the threat of these plumes to people or the environment is minimal, according to a hydrogeologist who did not collect his paycheck at Hanford. Ralph Patt, who worked for the Oregon Water Resource Department as that state's expert on figuring out what Hanford might be doing to the Columbia, told me that "there is nothing at the moment in the river downstream from Hanford that even comes close to being above drinking water standards."

Patt said that the Columbia, by pushing one hundred thousand cubic feet of water per second past Hanford, easily dilutes and defangs Hanford's groundwater.

"The good news is the enormous flow of the Columbia, but the bad news is that there is more contamination on its way. The open question is: How long will it take for it to reach the river? There is a lot of cesium and strontium in the ground at Hanford. It sits in soil about one hundred feet above the groundwater. It will decay away in three hundred years. Will it move down into the groundwater before then? Nobody knows for sure.

"But it is not just radioactive materials that worry Oregon. Just about every chemical known to man has been used at Hanford. This stuff will not decay away. Will some of it get to the river? The answer is absolutely yes. But we can't say how much and how soon."

As we drove farther north toward the reactors, Brauer and Erickson agreed that it would be a good idea for me to see the old Hanford town site. Its original inhabitants, farmers and fruit growers, had all been ordered out in 1942, when the Army Corps of Engineers swarmed in to erect barracks to house fifty-one thousand workers for the Manhattan Project. Hanford sprouted in less than six months into the fourth-largest city in Washington State. Everything about the place was supposed to be a secret. Rules prohibited the publication of statistics about how much ice cream was consumed on the site. Workers arrived from around the country with no idea of what they were in for. They had read DuPont recruiting pamphlets that said "you'll find a lot of conveniences you wouldn't expect in a construction camp." As promised, there was no wartime meat rationing. The government, desperate to overcome a severe wartime labor shortage, used meat as a recruiting lure. What most workers remember finding at Hanford were Sahara-style sandstorms. They darkened the sky for days at a time. Construction excavation had torn up thousands of acres of sagebrush, allowing the sandy dirt to blow. It turned workers' faces and underwear black. The meat served at Hanford's eight mess halls, which could seat more than five thousand workers at a sitting, was often seasoned with gritty dirt.

"We'd been taught in school that Washington was the Evergreen State," said Larry Forby, of Topeka, Kansas, who was persuaded to come to Hanford by a recruiter from DuPont. "If I could have caught that joker three days after I got here, I would have killed him."

Hanford was a rough place to live. Recruiting pamphlets advised that the most essential thing to bring to the site was a padlock. Men were segregated from women. Whites were segregated from blacks. "There was nothing to do after work except fight, with the result that occasionally bodies were found in garbage cans the next morning," wrote Leona Marshall Libby, a Hanford physicist. DuPont designed taverns with hinged windows that could be opened from the outside, allowing security guards to toss in brawl-ending canisters of tear gas. Nearly a quarter of the nonprofessional workforce quit within a month. The list of quitters usually doubled during dust storms, which came to be known as "termination winds."

Sagebrush had grown back when I toured what was left of the wartime boomtown. The workers' barracks had all been demolished. But the old Hanford High School building, a concrete structure built in 1916, still stood. It was a telling artifact of the action-movie subculture that blossomed inside Hanford during its decades of isolation. The school's roof had been blown off, Brauer explained, for the sheer hell of it. A munitions expert from Battelle Laboratories, one of the lead contractors at Hanford, "blew the roof off without hurting the walls. It was a nice job. The roof went up about six hundred feet," said Brauer, who watched the explosion. Besides its blown-away roof, the walls of the old high school were notable for a wide-ranging exhibition of machine-gun pockmarks. It reminded me of Serbian handiwork in Bosnia. Brauer explained that the Hanford Patrol, an exceptionally well-armed security force that for decades was subject to no local governmental control, "used to play a lot of cops and robbers out here."

We repaired to the riverside where a few apricot trees remained from pre-war fruit orchards. The apricots happened to be ripe, but— remembering the mulberry syndrome—I was afraid to eat them. (A couple of weeks later, on another tour of Hanford, I threw caution to the winds and ate two apricots. They were misshapen, but pleasantly tart.) Besides apricots we saw white-tailed deer, a blue heron, a couple of coyotes, and one of the hundreds of towers that are part of Hanford's emergency evacuation system. The towers sample windborne radiation. In case of a major accident at Hanford—the most likely cause of which would be an explosion in an underground waste tank—the towers would assess the direction and intensity of the radiation release

178   and provide information about how to get the hell away from Hanford. Erickson told me that he takes the possibility of a waste-tank accident quite seriously.

"If one of them blew up, I would move out of town for a while, depending, of course, on which way the wind was blowing at the time of the explosion."

"Look out for rattlesnakes," Erickson warned me, quickly changing subjects as we wandered around the riverbank. He remembered rattlesnakes from the regular noontime jogs he and a pack of N Reactor engineers used to take along the river. "Some of those fellahs would take a dip in the Columbia. They weren't supposed to, because we were downstream from the reactors, but they did and it never caused them any problems. I personally was never too keen about swimming in the river. I still don't. Being of a conservative nature, I would advise against it."

Back in the car, we drove north along the Columbia toward N Reactor, following a narrow dirt track along which early Hanford scientists had conducted radiation experiments with assorted animals and plants. Brauer explained that "they did serious studies. For example, they put plutonium in the soil to see if flowers would grow. They kept the birds away from the flowers with screens, so they would not fly off the site and shit plutonium."

Back away from the river, in the eastern distance, we could see the hulking buildings and smokestacks of Hanford's "200 Area," where plutonium was chemically separated from uranium. The most imposing of the structures is the clean-sounding PUREX (an acronym for "plutonium uranium extraction") plant, the world's largest plutonium reprocessing facility. It was anything but clean. For every kilogram of plutonium product, it generated 2.5 million gallons of wastewater for evaporation ponds, 55,000 gallons of low- to mid-level radioactive waste for dumping in dirt trenches, and 340 gallons of high-level waste for pumping into underground steel tanks. The plant was closed in 1989 because of steam leaks and has not reopened.

"There's where all the fuel was processed for all those years," said Erickson, pointing east. "I've driven through this area twice a day for thirty years. You know those iodine-131 releases that the downwinders are worried about? [He was referring to massive releases of radiation from unfiltered smokestacks at Hanford in the 1940s and 1950s. These releases amounted to the nation's largest and potentially most dangerous pattern of leaks from a nuclear plant.] Well, I think that very little of that reached the population. None of the workers out here got any thyroid cancers."

This casual statement, more than anything that Erickson told me, was hard to swallow. The secretary of energy formally acknowledged in 1990 that Hanford's releases of iodine-131 (a short-lived radioactive element that collects in the human thyroid, where it can cause thyroid malfunction, benign tumors, and cancer) were high enough to cause illness among people living downwind. Seven years of federal research on the size and spread of the releases have found that about eighty thousand people, including sixteen thousand children, were exposed to more than 10 rads of radiation.* Some children, who drank milk from cows that grazed on irradiated grass, were exposed to a lifetime dose of as much as 870 rads to their thyroid. The head of Hanford's dose reconstruction project has said that some eastern Washington downwinders were exposed to twice as much radiation as civilians who lived downwind of atomic testing in Nevada and who have higher than normal rates of thyroid disease and cancer.

As for workers at Hanford, they have a long history of being misled about the risk of radiation in their workplace. The Atomic Energy Commission knew in 1947 that Hanford workers were exposed to "significant quantities" of radioactive particles. But it chose not to inform them, even as it secretly characterized the exposures as "a very serious health problem." Access to the health records of thirty-five thousand Hanford workers was, until 1990, strictly limited by the federal government to friendly scientists of its own choosing. Since then, a study by British epidemiologist Alice Stewart, an unfriendly

---

*A rad is a measure of absorbed radiation. It is roughly the equivalent of a dozen chest X-rays. The current federal limit for an annual safe dose of man-made radiation is 0.025 rad. Federal guidelines call for evacuation if the dose to the thyroid reaches 5–25 rads.

180   scientist who established her reputation by showing a link between prenatal X-rays and cancer deaths in children, has found a correlation between cancer deaths and worker exposure to low levels of radiation at Hanford. Stewart concluded that two hundred workers have lost or will lose years of their lives because of radiation-induced cancer.

Erickson knew about all of this, of course. But he did not believe that it added up to much. Since he struck me as an honest, intelligent, and good-hearted person, I pressed him to explain why he and so many others in the Tri-Cities were convinced that the risk of radiation from Hanford has been exaggerated. The engineer told me, first of all, that he personally had never seen, after three decades of looking very carefully, how workplace exposure to radiation had done him or anybody that he knew any harm.

Second, Erickson, who felt confident designing anything from a home sprinkler system to zirconium cladding for highly enriched uranium rods, said that he and the other smart fellows at Hanford could manage all the plant's safety problems, if only "technical people were not losing out to non-technical people." He complained of meddling on the part of people "who do not understand isotopes." These meddlers included the media, know-it-alls from the West Side of the Cascades, frightened farmers from the East Side of the Columbia, and bureaucrats in Washington.

"You have people who are technically limited reviewing data that they don't understand," Erickson said.

Hanford engineers have never had a problem with self-confidence. They began to swagger in the 1940s, when they "saved" the site's first atomic reactor by intuiting that physicists had screwed up its design. Acting on their own authority, engineers built the B Reactor with extra fuel-loading tubes. Those extra tubes turned out to be the key to fixing a reactor glitch and sustaining a nuclear chain reaction. Seat-of-the-pants guesswork allowed the Manhattan Project to meet its wartime deadline. That, in any case, is the myth among engineers and technicians at Hanford. Whether their job was making plutonium or cleaning up its mess, they were convinced that they could handle it—if only the non-technical types would get out of the way.

"We used to run nine reactors with seven thousand people and we weren't leaking. Now we aren't running any reactors and we have nearly seventeen thousand people. Paranoia is forcing gridlock," Erickson told me.

It all made perfect sense, except, of course, for the facts. When engineers ran nine reactors with seven thousand people, they were indeed leaking into the air and into the river. And their supervisors were lying about it, while refusing to warn civilians about possible dangers.

Erickson tried to convince me that Hanford's technicians were pioneers and their work was a high form of patriotism. Hanford's myth of the cowboy engineer was a local variant on the riverside myth of the western individualist. Like irrigators with their cheap water and bargers with their bloated river, Hanford's technicians had come to be totally dependent on federal cash and deeply resentful of federal control.

"If they just turned us loose," Erickson said, "we could clean this place up at a quarter of the two billion a year they are spending now. But the way it is now, if you know anything about the nuclear industry, you are disqualified. The public is going to get tired of pouring money down a rat hole."

We drove on to N Reactor, a complex of hulking yellow block-shaped buildings, silvery water tanks, high-voltage transformers, and a labyrinth of steam pipes. Like all the dormant reactors at Hanford, N sits close to the river. That made it and its waste a cleanup priority.

In the N lunchroom with Erickson and Brauer, the conversation turned to nearby K East Reactor, which had sprung a chronic leak in its concrete fuel basin. The basin was designed as a temporary container for enriched uranium fuel rods. They were supposed to be suspended in water for only a few weeks or months before being transported to the PUREX plant for processing. The closure of PUREX, however, meant that Hanford had no place to process and no place to store the intensely radioactive fuel rods. K East basin held 1,250 tons of them, many of which were broken and corroding. The rods had contaminated the sixteen feet of water in which they were submerged with a vicious stew of plutonium, strontium, cesium, and tritium. In the 1970s, about fifteen million gallons leaked out of the basin and into the soil. Some got to the river, about four hundred yards away. In 1992, the basin leaked again, ninety-four thousand gallons, and Hanford officials announced that they would be giving the basin their "utmost attention." Hanford cleanup officials say that, so far, the consequences of the leaks are not serious. The volume of water in the river, they say, dilutes radiation leaks into insignificance.

"Hey, Lil," Erickson yelled across the lunchroom, speaking to a woman familiar with K East's problems, "you know that basin leak we have over at K? Has that sort of gone away?"

"The leak is running at twenty-four gallons a day," the woman replied. "That is unofficial."

Both Erickson and Brauer blamed the K basin leak on outside meddling in Hanford's business. Had the PUREX plant been allowed to operate, there would be no hot water to leak.

"What they should have done is process all the fuel and then shut down PUREX," Brauer maintained. "The *Seattle Times* will make hay out of this until hell freezes over."

Erickson nodded sympathetically. "It's a very difficult environment to work in," he said.

In 2007, fifteen years after that lunchroom conversation, Hanford announced that the cleanup of spent fuel and radioactive sludge at K East basin was complete.

While we were eating our lunch, about 150,000 fall chinook finger-lings were swimming healthily in another concrete basin at K East Reactor. That storage basin had been an intake facility. It had always contained river water that was on its way into the reactor. The basin had been filled with fish as part of an experiment to beef up fish runs in the Hanford Reach and dispel Hanford's public image as a factory of death. And it worked. The young salmon prospered in the basin before being hauled off to a hatchery and released to migrate downriver.

After lunch, Erickson showed me around the out-of-service N Reactor. We entered the central reactor building through a security gate surrounded by razor wire. After passing through a bewildering maze of instrument panels, we arrived in a large room in which we could see the reactor's towering face. Uranium fuel rods were (until 1987) inserted into a huge wall of graphite.

"It was a wonderful reactor," Erickson said wistfully. "We set all kinds of records for steam production. But it is all gone now."

We drove back away from the river toward the dirtiest part of Hanford, the 200 Area, with its chemical plants and waste tanks. To get there we had to skirt Gable Mountain, a basalt butte. Deep tunnels were dug into the mountain in the 1980s when Hanford boosters were lobbying Congress to choose the site as America's main burial ground for high-level radioactive waste. The plan was to put the waste—once it was encapsulated in glass logs—into tunnels in Gable Mountain.

"We lost that deal because the West Side of the state was against us," Brauer complained. "Those who understood the technology were disappointed."

Erickson joined Brauer in a sigh of regret.

Digging the tunnels, Brauer noted parenthetically, violated a U.S. Army promise not to disturb the mountain. The promise was made to the Wanapums, a small band of river Indians who were ordered off the Hanford site in 1942. They considered Gable Mountain to be a particularly sacred place and, as I later discovered, were furious with the government for desecrating it.

Beyond the mountain, we caught sight of the plutonium finishing plant, where Erickson's youngest son, Tim, worked as a maintenance supervisor. There were few buildings in North America where maintenance was such a critical issue. Deep inside the plutonium plant, which Hanfordites call the PFP, plutonium scraps grew more radioactive with each passing day, as plutonium-241 decayed into an element called americium. The scraps presented an inexorably increasing health risk to the plant's cleanup workers.

Brauer said that we could not drive up to the plant for a closer look. As befits its status as a factory that made "buttons" for nuclear warheads, the PFP was set back from the main highway and encircled by a double row of razor wire. There are television cameras on the fence. Inside, guards in black shirts patrol with machine guns.

184   About two months later, with a handful of reporters from around the Pacific Northwest, I toured PFP. Each of us had to wear five separate badges. We were not allowed to photograph the black-shirted guards because, as a Westinghouse public-relations person explained it, "they are equipped with certain things we don't want the not-so-nice part of the public to know about." The tour was part of a charm offensive by Hanford to show that the plutonium plant had a problem that could best be solved by starting up the plant and processing volatile scraps into more stable powder.

To get to the heart of the factory, we first had to put on yellow radiation shirts, pants, booties, and hats. Then we filed through two airlocks. Finally, we were allowed a few minutes to gaze through thick windows into greasy chambers where plutonium junk—rags, jars, discarded crescent wrenches—was invisibly festering. "The stuff is off-gassing. We have no other place to put it. All the nooks and crannies are full," we were told.

Inside the plant, I spotted Tim Erickson and waved hello. He nodded nervously and avoided eye contact. Journalists had never before been allowed in the building.

I managed to talk to Tim Erickson one evening at his house, which is an "E," just like the one his parents live in. Tim, a thirty-two-year-old mechanical engineer who earns fifty-eight thousand dollars a year, told me that he always wanted to become an engineer at Hanford. He started at the plutonium finishing plant during the Reagan arms buildup and stayed on for the cleanup.

"I pretty much cut my teeth and grew up at PFP. When you grow up in Richland, you fall back to your roots. My dad is an engineer. All my friends' dads are engineers. As a kid, our teacher told us to write letters to President Nixon, begging him not to shut down N Reactor.

"Richland is proud of itself. I think you could say it is egotistical about itself. In school, we thought, 'We are the Bombers. We are the scientific elite.' People used to say, 'Oh, you're from Richland. You must be stuck-up.' And we were kind of insensitive. We gave plaques to Japanese foreign exchange students that had, you know, the mushroom cloud on them."

Tim expects never to have to leave Hanford.

"There is enough work in the cleanup for a career. The idea of moving does not make me happy."

By 2011, the cleanup of the plutonium finishing plant was still going on. The deadline for getting all the weapons-grade plutonium out of the plant was 2016.

Outside the gates of the plutonium finishing plant lies Hanford's most intractable cleanup mess—the "tank farm." Because of its potential for explosion and groundwater pollution, it was the primary focus of the government cleanup. On the day I drove around Hanford with Jerry Erickson, access to the tanks was even more restricted than usual. Technicians were installing a giant circulation pump in Tank 101-SY, which habitually burped hydrogen and was considered the single most explosive item at Hanford.

"All the tanks make hydrogen as they decay," Brauer explained matter-of-factly, as if talking about cows passing wind in a barn. "But on the surface of some of the biggest tanks the liquid has developed a crust that is kind of like peanut brittle. This keeps the tanks, particularly 101-SY, from venting the hydrogen slowly and safely. Every eleven weeks or so it farts and that could be a problem."

Hanford then had one known and three potential farters. Since hydrogen is highly flammable, sudden puffs of it have the potential of setting off a catastrophic explosion that could spray radioactive sludge high into the atmosphere.

It took technicians nearly a week to finish installing the pump. When it was turned on, it stirred up the peanut brittle in 101-SY so that it stopped abruptly passing hydrogen. Good news at the tank farm, however, did not hold. Two glaring safety violations a month later forced Hanford officials to order more than three hundred tank-farm workers into remedial safety classes. In one goof, a worker accidentally turned on the new mixer pump inside 101-SY. In the second, a worker tried to unplug a pipe inside a waste tank by tying a rock to a string and lowering it down. He pulled the wet rock up, held it in his hands, and

186 contaminated himself with radiation. At the Department of Energy in Washington, an assistant secretary for waste management characterized the rock incident as "one of the more stupid activities I've heard about on a [nuclear] reservation."

My day at Hanford ended at a respectful distance from the tank farm. Brauer wanted to get home for dinner. I did not particularly want to catch a closer look at high-level waste. As we drove back to Richland in the late afternoon, Erickson leaned forward from the backseat and explained what it is like for an engineer to watch Hanford die.

"My most productive years are sitting out there in a factory that is being shut down. Do I regret it? No, not really. It was really challenging working there. It was fun. I took care of my family and sent my boys through college. If a man can do that, he has done enough. The rest is just ego. It was a good place to live and die and whatever."

9

≈≈≈≈≈≈≈≈≈≈ *Born with No Hips*

ABOUT TEN MILES east of the river and downwind from the pluto-nium factory, Tom Bailie, my farmer acquaintance, had figured out what Hanford was really about. He explained it in detail on a sunny Sunday morning in his pickup truck while taking me on his famous "death mile" tour. We rode through the southern district of the Columbia Basin Project, where water from the river nourishes lush fields of alfalfa and lima beans, potatoes and corn. Bailie showed me twenty-eight farmhouses where he said that members of twenty-seven families, including his own, have had cancer or thyroid disease or birth defects. As he drove, he delivered a frightful accounting of the dead and the deformed. He has been giving this tour for years, and he talks fast, like a bright Sunday-school student rattling off the books of the Bible.

"My mother and father had cancer. Both my sisters had cancer. And my uncle who lived here with us for twenty years had cancer. In fact all of my father's brothers and sisters had cancer and they lived here in this house at one time or another and they worked on the farm in the summer with us."

Pointing at various houses as he drove, Bailie told me about a baby born with no head, another born with no eyes, two others born with no hips. He told me about a farm wife who committed suicide in her bathtub after drowning her "really deformed" baby. As for Bailie

188 himself, his best description of his downwind ailments appeared in an op-ed piece that he wrote for the *New York Times*:

"I was born a year after my stillborn brother. I struggled to breathe through underdeveloped lungs, and suffered to overcome numerous birth defects. I underwent multiple surgeries, endured paralysis, endured thyroid medication, a stint in an iron lung, loss of hair, sores all over my body, fevers, dizziness, poor hearing, asthma, teeth rotting out and, at age 18, a diagnosis of sterility."

After giving me what seemed to be his standard tour, Bailie pulled his pickup truck off the road. He needed to move a few siphons in the irrigation ditches of a cornfield. For all his childhood ills, Bailie, in middle age, appeared healthy and fit. He had thick gray close-cropped hair, bright blue eyes, and an athlete's trim waist. He is a successful irrigator with a middle-class income. He cooperates with other members of the Bailie clan, an extended farm family that owns thousands of acres. The biggest building in his hometown is the Bailie grain elevator. Tom Bailie ran for the state legislature a few years back, but lost badly. He is a Democrat and most of the local farmers are Republicans.

When he finished moving his siphons, Bailie apologized for not inviting me over to his house. He explained that his wife, Linda, was fed up with hearing talk about Hanford. Bailie then launched into a meticulously detailed (and wholly unsubstantiated) theory about what scientists at Hanford were trying to accomplish with their secret releases of radiation. This, too, had a well-rehearsed quality.

"I call the Columbia Basin a laboratory project, not a reclamation project," Bailie began. "The people who settled around here were truly a test group. For the government to give you land in the reclamation project, you had to be young and of childbearing age. . . . If I was looking for a place to do radiation research, I would think that an area like this, with low-education skills, with honest, hard-working, fiercely patriotic people, would make a wonderful place to test.

"I think we had a group of scientists who were researching an iodine-131 bomb. Its purpose would be to affect human fetuses in the womb so future soldiers [in an enemy country] would be lazy and dumb and not be a force to be reckoned with."

There was a "self-cleansing" element in the secret radiation experiments in the Columbia Basin, Bailie said. He said the federal government lured veterans into the irrigation project in the 1950s with low-interest loans that were foreclosed if farmers or their families got sick from radiation-induced disease. The government chose eastern Washington for its experiment, Bailie said, because of its Western European blood stock.

"Our enemies were expected to be European people. After our bombs dropped on Japan we had all this information on what radiation does. But that was a different gene pool. Those people's genes may not be as strong as the Russians and the Germans.

"It was a neat operation, what they did here. It was really neat. Jesus, these [government] people were smart. The reason nobody noticed what was going on was because whenever there was a serious life-threatening illness, farmers would have to sell their crops or animals to pay off medical bills. They would end up violating Farmer's Home Administration regulations, they'd have their loans called in, and they'd move out. Then what I call the 'vulture effect' occurred. Tougher farmers, we call them the land-gobblers, would buy up the land, and knock down the old farmhouse. All the evidence would be gone. There is always a stigma of shame that goes with failing in a farm operation, so people left quietly."

As Bailie explained it, the Bureau of Reclamation was in on the conspiracy. He said that the Bureau arranged, in the early years of the irrigation project, to flood land, rinse radiation out of the soil, and wash it down the Columbia River. The Mormon Church also was in on it. Bailie said the church directed the Utah & Idaho Sugar Company to build a granulated-sugar processing factory in Moses Lake to encourage Basin farmers to grow sugar beets, a crop that Bailie said is particularly effective in sucking pernicious radionuclides from the soil. And local hospitals were in on it. Bailie said that it was impossible to get treated for thyroid problems in the Tri-Cities and that all radiation-sick people were spirited away to hospitals in Portland or Seattle.

But the conspiracy went higher, much higher.

"If I tell you what I really think happened, it is not very pretty. I think

190   a small elite group of bitter, angry, arrogant, highly intelligent men got together and took control of what we now know as the Atomic Age.

"They proceeded to slice up the atomic money pie. Ignorant Congress and the president accepted them because of their awesome power. There was no oversight, no accountability. These men created the Cold War by helping arm Russia so it could continue the arms race and allow the military-industrial complex to continue feasting on our nation's resources. The number of loyal, trusting American citizens who are victims of this nuclear gang is truly uncountable."

Tom Bailie's hometown of Mesa, Washington (population 252), lies on the state highway that connects Moses Lake with Hanford. On my trips back and forth to the nuclear reservation, I occasionally stopped off in Mesa to talk to him. He could be found in the late afternoons in the town's one restaurant, the Country Kitchen, where he was the loudest and most exuberantly opinionated of the sunburned irrigators who gathered for coffee and gossip.

In his neighbors' eyes, Bailie was part celebrity, part pain-in-the-butt. He had got himself on national television talking to Connie Chung. His picture had appeared at the top of the front page of the *New York Times*. He had been featured as a heroic rural American in a book called *Atomic Harvest*. He was a member of the Hanford Downwinders Coalition and the most vocal of the 1,400 plaintiffs in a lawsuit against Department of Energy contractors at Hanford.

Some of his neighbors said Bailie was in love with the sound of his own voice and never knew when to shut up. They called him the "glow-in-the-dark" farmer. I heard one of his neighbors sneer, under his breath, "I wonder who is out to get him now?" His own cousin, a potato farmer named Matt Bailie, told me that after he talks to Tom he gets so anxious that "I find it hard to concentrate on my potatoes."

Scientists studying the effects of radiation releases on civilians living downwind of Hanford find Bailie entertaining but sensationally ill informed. "He provides the media with very interesting stuff. But I would discount what he is saying," said Genevieve Roessler, a specialist in radiation dosimetry and a member of a federal panel studying downwind doses from Hanford. "I don't want to discount the doses [of radioactive iodine] that he may have received. They are high enough to warrant study. But I don't believe the effects he is talking about. Those sort of effects [headless, eyeless, hipless babies] have not been observed in the children of people who have been exposed to even very high doses of radiation in Hiroshima or Nagasaki. What he is saying is sort of off the wall."

Talking with Bailie was like trying to catch your breath at the business end of a fire hose. I often drove away from Mesa with a headache and an upset stomach, after struggling to get him to sort out fact from fantasy. I could not decide what to make of him. He was one of the most shameless blowhards I had ever met. But he was also an intelligent, angry, overwhelmed victim. Bailie himself seemed comfortable with both characterizations.

"The reason I can espouse this crap without someone shooting me," he told me, "is because it is too far out."

Bailie grew up in a Columbia River farm community where soldiers with Geiger counters came around regularly to test the wheat and the cows. They never explained what they were looking for or what they found, except to assure farmers that everything was okay.

When Bailie was two years old, the Atomic Energy Commission publicly guaranteed the complete safety of the air around Hanford, saying that "discharge standards . . . are at a rate so low that no damage to plants, animals or humans has resulted. . . . The methods of safe handling used to date have successfully protected workers and the public." That same year the government staged the single largest release of atmospheric contamination in the history of Hanford. It was a secret military experiment called the Green Run.

It came about, in part, because the Pentagon was curious about what the Soviets were up to. By measuring the dispersal pattern of a known amount of radioactive material from Hanford's smokestacks, the Pentagon hoped to come up with a rough gauge for guessing how much plutonium the Soviets were making. To that end, a huge cloud of radioactive iodine was spat out of Hanford's smokestacks. It spread

192 across most of eastern Washington and eastern Oregon. Vegetation samples taken not far from Mesa in the week of the experiment showed radiation counts as high as one thousand times the then-tolerable limit. The amount of radiation pumped into the air during the Green Run was more than seven hundred times greater than what was released during the 1979 partial core meltdown at the Three Mile Island nuclear plant near Harrisburg, Pennsylvania.

Three Mile Island, America's worst civilian nuclear accident, released about 15 curies of radiation, causing alarm across much of the East Coast and forcing the confiscation of milk and vegetables. The Green Run released at least 11,000 curies of radiation and remained secret for thirty-seven years.

When Bailie was between five and seven years old, a Hanford chemical plant called REDOX repeatedly spewed carcinogenic particles of ruthenium into the wind. The risk was considered serious enough behind the fences on the Hanford site to restrict travel to main highways. But in nearby Mesa, where farms were showered with ruthenium, no warnings were given or restrictions imposed. "Nothing is to be gained by informing the public," Herbert M. Parker, the head of health and safety at Hanford, wrote in 1954. "Not all residents will be as relaxed as the one who was recently quoted as saying, 'Living in Richland is ideal because we breathe only tested air.'"

In Bailie's less-than-ideal neighborhood, the government knowingly risked the health of thousands of civilians, lied about it for nearly forty years, and only reluctantly began to disclose some of the facts in 1986 when forced to do so by Freedom of Information lawsuits. The doses of radiation and deceit that set off Bailie's imagination have affected most other downwinders in ways more predictable, less quotable, more piteous. Numbed by betrayal, they live out their lives on the East Side of the Columbia in a murk of anger, fear, and cynicism.

I attended a midweek meeting of downwinders in the Blue Mountain Mall in Walla Walla, Washington, about sixty miles east of the Hanford Reach of the Columbia. Just off the mall's food court, a dozen late-middle-aged and elderly people congregated in a windowless community room. They breathed the greasy smells of the mall's fast-food emporiums, sipped coffee from Styrofoam cups, and listened intently as a stocky woman in a tent-sized purple flower blouse explained why the federal government is evil.

"They have spent five million for this Hanford Health Information Network, which is money that is supposed to help each and every one of us understand what Hanford did," said Kay Sutherland. "Tragically, it has gone for denial and downplaying the damage to our health."

Sutherland, like the members of her sad, small audience, was a physical wreck. She reeled off her maladies like a bailiff reading an indictment. The fifty-four-year-old housewife-activist blamed them all on Hanford. She grew up on the rural edge of Walla Walla, a town in the middle of Hanford's downwind path. Throughout the late 1940s, when surrounding pastureland was laced with Hanford's radioactive iodine, she drank milk from local cows and ate locally grown produce.

"I am as round as I am tall from a lifetime of thyroid problems. I have cysts and nodules all over my body. I have had four miscarriages, and two of my children died after birth. I have an autoimmune syndrome called Sjogren disease. I have had kidney cancer. They removed a four-and-a-half-pound tumor."

As Sutherland ticked off her diseases, members of the audience nodded. They, too, blamed Hanford for all manner of misery. In the front row, for example, Mary Pengelly, age sixty-two, who lived in downwind parts of Oregon and Washington in the 1940s and 1950s, had hypothyroidism, digestive problems, ulcers, chronic fatigue syndrome, and chronic weight problems. Pengelly stood up and told the meeting that she has eight brothers and sisters, all with hypothyroidism.* She and her siblings have together tallied forty miscarriages, stillbirths, or birth defects. Her four children, she said, have been cursed by rare diseases. The oldest had a brain tumor removed

---

*Hypothyroidism is caused by an inadequate production of thyroid hormone. Its early symptoms read like a shopping list of the ills of middle-aged America. They include fatigue, forgetfulness, unexplained weight gain, and constipation.

194   at age seven. The second-oldest weighed two pounds, eleven ounces at birth. There was a large tumor attached to his placenta. The third child started passing out at age three and has been diagnosed with Raynaud's disease, a circulatory problem. The fourth child has had three operations for degenerative spinal disease.

"Something has happened to the genetic system of my family," Pengelly said. "I will be dead in a few years and I have got to know exactly what Hanford did."

The federal government attempted to find out and tell Pengelly and other downwinders what Hanford had done. In response to the public alarm that followed disclosures about radiation releases, Congress funded two massive long-term health studies, as well as the Hanford Health Information Network. A dose reconstruction survey that took seven years to complete and cost twenty-six million dollars plotted the spread of all the radiation released to the air and the river from Hanford between 1945 and 1992. It allowed downwinders to calculate their probable radiation dose depending on where they lived, how much milk they drank from a backyard cow, and how much time they spent out of doors. A thyroid disease study tracked down three thousand randomly selected downwinders and examined them for thyroid ailments. It found "no association" between Hanford's releases of radioactive iodine and thyroid disease. It also concluded that rates of thyroid disease among downwinders were "generally consistent" with rates of the disease found in other populations.

But in the community room of the Blue Mountain Mall, the assembled downwinders called the studies an elaborate cover-up. They said they could never again trust anything paid for by the government.

"People are getting harder to fool," said Barbara Howard, a forty-six-year-old downwinder from eastern Oregon. "You will never get my generation to fight in another war. There are enough things about Hanford that concern me that I can never not be cynical."

Sutherland and Howard later resigned as members of the advisory board for the Hanford Health Information Network, which was set up to inform and comfort downwinders. In a letter to the Department of Energy, they said the network withheld information from the public and harassed Hanford's victims as "troublemakers." The letter said that the department remains "unable to shake off a fifty-year tradition . . . of making light of citizens' worries about radiation exposure."

Downwinders showed up to sneer at the results of the dose reconstruction survey and mock the specialists who put it together. Their necks bearing the scars of thyroid surgery, they told the demographers, meteorologists, epidemiologists, and physicians that it was a waste of time to draw up maps charting how many rads of radiation fell where. The experts should have listed how many patriotic Americans were killed by their own government.

"I didn't expect this level of anger. We perhaps didn't handle this very well," Genevieve Roessler, of the dose reconstruction survey, told reporters after a meeting in Spokane.

The unsatisfying truth about radiation releases from Hanford is that the health effects are not nearly as clear, as extensive, or as diabolical as one might believe from hanging out in the community room in the Blue Mountain Mall.

As for downwinders' complaints about ills ranging from arthritis to heart attacks to Hodgkin's disease, Dr. Glyn Caldwell, a leader of the dose reconstruction panel, told me that the cause may be as much political as radiological.

"These people don't like Hanford. Anything that happens to them is blamed on Hanford. There is no population in this country that never dies and is free of disease. Cancer occurs everywhere. There is no reported bunching of cancer deaths in eastern Washington.

"I would not suggest that nothing is happening to these people. They felt they were more patriotic than most Americans because they tolerated Hanford. They were reassured it was safe. Now they don't seem to believe anything. We have accepted that they are not going to believe us, at least not for a long time," Caldwell said.

As for the birth defects that Tom Bailie describes so vividly and the genetic damage that Mary Pengelly insists has afflicted her family, studies so far have found no evidence around Hanford of radiation-related problems. Dr. Lowell Sever, an epidemiologist in Seattle who works for Battelle Laboratories and is one of the country's leading

196   researchers on the relationship between environment and birth defects,
said there are no solid studies anywhere in the world that suggest an
association between birth defects and low-level radiation exposure of
the kind that occurred downwind of Hanford. Sever participated in
a study that did find elevated rates of birth defects around Hanford
between 1968 and 1980, a period when atmospheric leaks from the
plutonium factory were all but nonexistent. But he and his colleagues
attributed the cluster of birth defects to intensive use of pesticides by
farmers.

   Tom Bailie told me that "so-called experts" like Glyn Caldwell and
Lowell Sever are not to be trusted. Dose surveys, thyroid studies, and
the multibillion-dollar Hanford cleanup are all, in his words, "a joke."

   "The reason they are putting in the money—hush money I call
it—is to confuse everybody. Studies and the cleanup are cheaper than
settling lawsuits and taking care of sick people for the rest of their lives,"
Bailie told me.

   We were sitting in his pickup after the "death mile" tour. For some
reason, I had mentioned to Bailie that I had had a tour on the Hanford
side of the river. I said I had gotten to know an engineer from N Reactor
and that Jerry Erickson struck me as a decent, intelligent guy. I said that
since I met Erickson and his family, Hanford made a lot more sense to
me. It was bizarre, I told the farmer, but at least it was human. Bailie
did not want to hear it.

   "Oh, sure they may dress normally, but their eyes look strange.
They are robotic, almost like followers of a cult." Bailie warmed to his
harangue. "When we were kids growing up, those people didn't want us
dating their daughters. We farm boys would go to Richland and they'd
have the cops waiting for us.

   "You know those Hanfordites wear security tags around their necks
wherever they go. Oh, boy, they remind me of registered cattle."

   Hanfordites and downwinders, even though they disdain each
other, shared a common sentiment toward the river that separates
them. Apathy.

   Tom Bailie has lived his entire life within ten miles of the Columbia.
But he told me he had no idea when salmon migrated in the river that

he relies on for water for his crops. He was puzzled and annoyed by the possibility that he, as an irrigator and downwind victim, might be implicated in the extinction of salmon.

Across the river, I asked Jerry Erickson's son, Tim, the bright young engineer at the plutonium finishing plant, if he had any ideas about what should be done to revive the Columbia and its famous salmon runs. The question stumped him. It was not his department.

"I sort of always felt that if you throw enough money at the river, if you build more hatcheries, then you could solve the problem. As far as the salmon and the river were concerned, I didn't hear anything about the dams being a problem. I had heard around here that it was the Indians' fault."

The massive federal presence that had alienated Hanford's believers and victims from each other had also alienated them from the one natural resource that kept their fractured desert community from drying up. The Columbia, for most of the people I met around the Tri-Cities, was merely an object, not unlike an irrigation ditch, a dam, or a tank farm. Talking with them about the spirit of the river was like talking about the spirit of the asphalt in State Highway 395, the four-lane that slants northeast to Spokane.

To find people in the desert who were eager to talk about the river, I had to ride that monstrous barge with the peas, the lentils, and the angry river men who feared that the Columbia was going to be ruined in favor of fish.

10

Slackwater II

W E SAILED WEST out of the desert, leaving Hanford and the Tri-Cities behind, nudging downstream through low fog that clung like cobwebs to the surface of the river. I emerged from my cabin at dawn to find the wind all but dead, and the air perfumed by shoreline sagebrush soaked with dew. A lone Canada goose, cruising low beside the barge, stamped the glassy river with a fleeting stereoscopic image of its long-necked self. On a small green island in the river, five chubby mule deer grazed on grass that apparently was tasty enough to justify a half-mile swim. Two cargo trains rumbled by in the near distance, also heading west—the Burlington Northern on the Washington State side, the Union Pacific on the Oregon side. It being September, leaves on scattered willow trees along the shore were beginning to yellow. Color fancied up the border between the deep blue river and the dead brown land.

Up in the wheelhouse of the tugboat *Defiance,* Steve McDowell, barge captain and my slackwater impresario, looked poorly. His complexion was pasty, his eyes red and baggy. He wore the same grimy command uniform, blue jeans and a black T-shirt, that he was wearing when I left him in the wheelhouse around midnight. He had been up most of the graveyard shift, standing at the helm of his tugboat until his tow cleared the narrows into which the Snake River funnels before spilling out into the Columbia.

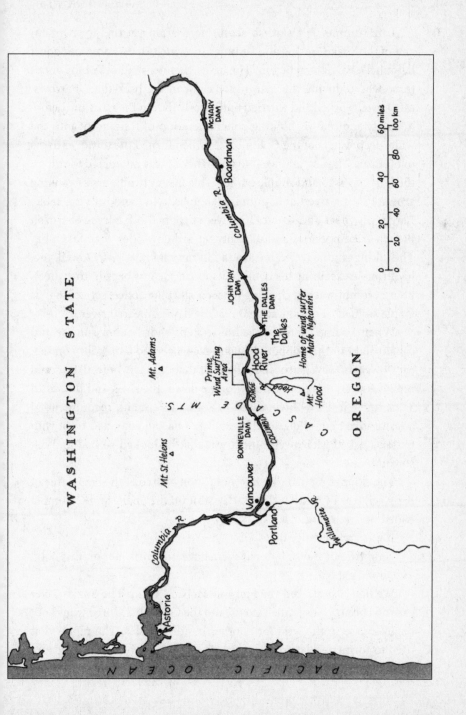

200   Late summer is a skittish season for barging at the downstream end of the Snake. Spring and summer snowmelts have come and gone; fall rains have not yet begun. The barge channel shallows up by about three feet, reducing the margin for error in the rock-lined narrows. McDowell worked and worried until nearly four in the morning before he safely squired his hulking conglomeration of freight out into the wide, deep waters of the Columbia. He then turned the tow over to his pilot, Ernie Theriot, and went to bed. Theriot was instructed to stop in the Port of Pasco and shuffle barges. This meant two hours of yanking around on the riverbank, gunning engines, tying and untying cable. Barges of wheat and wood chips were dropped off; barges of frozen French-fried potatoes and partially tanned cowhides were taken on. The jolting shuffle rolled me around in my cabin bed. McDowell, too, had trouble executing his two-hour snooze. He was back in the wheelhouse promptly at six, chewing tobacco, slurping coffee, scratching his ample stomach, and squinting out at the dawn-smeared river.

When I came up the wheelhouse steps shortly after sunrise and caught sight of the skipper's haggard face, I sensed a bad day coming. McDowell, however, proved far happier than his face. Indeed, he could not have been more delighted with the dawn, the river, and the world as he knew it. He politely asked how I had slept and recommended a restorative high-cholesterol breakfast of bacon, eggs, and toast with butter. I asked McDowell how it was that he looked so bad and felt so good.

The skipper replied that he would soon be free of the barge, free of the river, free of me. His fifteen-day stint on the Snake and Columbia ended this morning.

It was crew-change day.

"For fifteen days, I don't even have to think about this job," McDowell explained.

We had just cleared the locks in McNary Dam. The Snake River canyon country was far behind us, and the Columbia Gorge would not begin to rise in the west for another hundred miles. The rapids that used to torment this stretch of the river had been buried for decades under slackwater. We lumbered through a table-flat, intensely culti-

vated landscape that fed off the puddled-up river. All around us, sprinklers serviced orchards, vineyards, and fields of alfalfa. The flaccid
Columbia was more than two and a half miles wide.

For migrating salmon, this seventy-six-mile-long reservoir that
backs up behind John Day Dam is the deadliest stretch of the commute
to the Pacific. (The last of the big federal dams on the mainstem of the
Columbia, John Day was completed in 1971.) Young salmon often swim
six days to traverse this part of the river, a reach that their pre-dam
ancestors moved through in less than a day. To cut the commuter death
rate, state and federal fish agencies and Indian tribes have proposed
a number of schemes to speed up the river. The least ambitious of
them would lower the level of the reservoir by about nine feet. That
would marginally perk up the flow of the river—without halting barge
traffic—and increase salmon travel time by up to 15 percent. The most
ambitious scheme would lower the river fifty-eight feet, triple the
velocity of the current, and whisk salmon through in about a day and a
half. The latter scheme would require extensive relocation of irrigation
pumps and intake pipes for municipal drinking water supplies. It also
would halt barge traffic on the mid-Columbia. It would put men like
McDowell out of work.

It being a splendid morning on crew-change day, I did not have
the gall to ask the skipper about the possibility that his career might
come to an end so fish could live. McDowell, however, needed no prod-
ding. Sometime in the hours of his night's navigation he had prepared
a valedictory speech, a summing up of the difference between people
who work for a living and people who fret about endangered salmon.
In McDowell's geography of the river, most of the former lived here on
the dry side of the Cascades.

Salmon lovers—a pernicious sub-tribe of the yuppie infidel—lived
over on the wet side. Beyond the mountains, as McDowell explained
it, there was self-delusion, narcissism, and a basic misapprehension of
the human experience.

"These Portland and Seattle people eating berries and twigs and
watching foreign films believe they will live forever. They care more
about the environment than about religion.

202   "People living over here on the East Side, particularly around Hanford, they know damn good and well that they are going to die. They take their religion real serious. They put these fish in perspective.

"We [barge operators] are the ones who keep the export markets alive in the Northwest. Every blow to our industry increases the price of our region's exports. We are pricing ourselves out of the market. For the yuppies, nothing but a good dose of hunger will put their feet back on the ground."

Whatever else might be said about McDowell's little speech, it did have the virtue of good timing. By the end of the day, the barge would enter the Columbia Gorge, cut through the Cascades, and follow the river into a different version of the West.

It is almost impossible to overstate the differences between the two landscapes that are separated by the Cascade curtain yet roped together by the river. I first noticed it when I was nine years old and riding in the backseat of my parents' car.

We were crossing the Cascades, going from Moses Lake to Seattle for the 1962 World's Fair. The passage from brown to green, from sagebrush to trees made me squirm with excitement. No one could possibly have planted all those trees and nobody seemed to be watering them. In Moses Lake, if you did not water something, it died. The West Side, by contrast, was exuberantly alive. Besides trees and wild berries and rain forests choked with ferns, there were cities and freeways and parks full of flowers and spacious split-level houses on hills above lakes alive with sailboats. I remember being resentful when, after a week of the green, glittering city, we had to go back home to emptiness, irrigation ditches, and brown.

The division between the dry and wet sides of the Northwest has grown more pronounced with each passing year. The Columbia River was described in Joel Garreau's *The Nine Nations of North America* as flowing between "essentially different civilizations." The East Side, as Garreau explained it, was on the fringe of the Empty Quarter, which was "the most unpopulated, weakest-voiced, least-developed, who-cares? region of North America. . . ." The West Side, meanwhile, was the heart of Ecotopia, "which is developing the industries of the twenty-

first century: lightweight alloys, computer chips, and ways to use them
that are still in the future. Its natural markets and lessons about living
are in Asia."

The West Side was richer, more attuned to Far East trade, and more
environmentally correct. Technology surpassed timber as the leading
source of jobs in Oregon. Led by Boeing and Microsoft, Washington
State was first in the United States in per capita income derived from
exports. More than 80 percent of the state's trade was with the Pacific
Rim. Washingtonians earned twice as much from exports as Californians. Most of the high-tech growth was on the rainy side of Oregon
and Washington, which accounted for 70 percent of regional population growth and where more than 80 percent of Northwest residents
live. The West Side, as it prospered, spawned New West icons: billionaire Bill Gates, grunge rock, drive-in latte stands, microbreweries, and
the only Major League Baseball team owned by a Japanese company.
Nintendo owned the Mariners and nobody in Seattle thought it was
un-American. Seattle recycled more garbage per capita than almost any
American city. It and Portland ranked near the top in national surveys
of books read per capita. Both cities were also leaders in per capita
numbers of kayakers, hikers, windsurfers, sailors, bird-watchers, skiers,
and mountain bikers. Thus occupied, the residents of these cities had
significantly lower fertility rates than people on the East Side. British
travel writer and transplanted Seattleite Jonathan Raban wrote that
Seattle held a "curious niche" in urban history as a city "to which people
had fled in order to be closer to nature."

I collected personal ads in Seattle and the Tri-Cities newspapers for
the better part of a year. They suggested that the river, as it runs west
through the Cascades, leaves one planet for another.

In the Tri-Cities:

—Widowed WF, 42. Lonely and shy, enjoys movies, walking in the
park, bingo, barbecues. Seeking WM, 40 to 50, for companionship.

—DWM, 50s, 5′10″, 190 lbs. Developing a ranch. Seeks sincere, pretty,
s/dwf for lasting relationship.

In Seattle:

—The finer things in life. Very pretty, thin, happy, financially successful, athletic, 32, SWF, educated health professional seeks intelligent, happy, active, NS, ND or light, no TV, age 32–45, financially successful professional. With a busy schedule I meet few men that I am interested in. I love bicycling, gardening, interior decorating, investing, reading recent Ayn Rand & Michael Talbot, thinking and intelligent conversation. A beautiful city home and country retreat provide a tranquil background for a peaceful, introspective, spiritual life. I am financially successful & strongly emphasize that I seek the same. Photo. Letter only.

—Happy Birthday to Me. A true Cancer, I love water, home life & emotionality. Kayaker, herbalist, cook, hiker, yogi, world-traveler, jazz drummer, sweat lodger, wolf-lover. 6′, height-weight proportional. Back from a "roots" trip to Ukraine, I'm ready. I've been waiting for you, so let's fall in love. But 1st, tell me about yourself. Maybe a photo.

On the East Side, in small towns like Moses Lake or Grand Coulee or Colville, you cannot sit in a coffee shop for more than half an hour without hearing someone in a John Deere cap complain about West Siders with too much money and too little sense telling working people how to live. In Seattle or Portland, you can sit in an espresso bar for weeks on end without hearing a single reference to the East Side, excepting the odd complaint about poison leaking out of Hanford.

East Side communities made a habit in the 1990s of passing anti-gay-rights ordinances that West Side judges and politicians made a habit of declaring unconstitutional. The out-of-doors, on the East Side, is not a holiday destination, but a workplace. And jingoism is nothing to apologize for. On an evening's walk down Main Street in the East Side logging and cattle town of Colville, Washington, I saw a sign in a clothing store that said: "We only sell clothes made for hard-working Americans, by hard-working Americans." Nearby was a taxidermy shop where the display window was crowded with stuffed bears, mountain goats, bobcats, and a buffalo.

Gun shows attract huge, enthusiastic crowds in small towns across the East Side. I attended a show in the Grant County Fair Grounds in Moses Lake where the most crowded booth offered Israeli-made black-matte-finished, field-stock Galil .308-caliber assault rifles for $1,750. Large crowds also pored over the publications booth at the gun show, which offered how-to pamphlets including "Construct the Ultimate Hobby Weapon: Homemade Grenade Launchers" and "Heavy Fire-power: Turning Junk into Arsenal Weaponry." The most prominently displayed poster at the show was of Adolf Hitler. Under his scowling face was a slogan: "When I come back, no more Mr. Nice Guy."

In Portland's fashionable Nob Hill neighborhood a few weeks later, I stumbled upon the West Side antipode to the gun show. A young mother and her two well-dressed children were on their knees on the sidewalk, petting a Dalmatian who was out for an evening's walk on the rhinestone-studded leash of its owner. Before the mother stood and loaded her children into her minivan, she told the dog's owner: "Thank you for letting us enjoy your dog."

The end of the river shift for McDowell and his three-man crew turned out to be Boardman, Oregon, a desert town that smelled strongly, from out on the river, of French fries and cow manure. Barge pilots and deck-hands get on and off the river when their shifts start and end, no matter where the barge may be on the 350-mile run between Lewiston and Portland.

McDowell's wife had driven to Boardman for the shift change, as had the wives of other men on the outgoing and incoming crews. A group of about fifteen waited on the dock. Behind them, a thick column of steam rose in the windless morning from a potato processing plant. After we tied up, incoming and outgoing bargers, along with their wives, girlfriends, and small children, drank coffee, ate doughnuts, and gossiped for about an hour. The shift-change picnic was one of the

206 few social gatherings that barging offers the men and their families, whose homes range from the Oregon coast to northern Idaho. Before leaving for his home in the Columbia Gorge, McDowell graciously took a minute to introduce me to the incoming skipper, Pat Harding.

"He is even more of a redneck than I am," McDowell said, waving goodbye.

By river barging standards, Harding was a clean-liver. He conspicuously lacked the wheelhouse paunch that connotes command on the river. Nor was he divorced, like so many men who work on barges. Nor did he smoke cigarettes or chew tobacco. He was born in Walla Walla, Washington, where he lived fifteen days a month with his wife and young sons. While he was home he slept fitfully, missing the rhythms of the river, finding that his internal clock could not abandon a barge's schedule of six hours on, six hours off. Forty-two years old, short and muscular, with thinning hair and a well-tended mustache, he had twenty years on the river and fourteen years in the wheelhouse as a skipper. As we steamed toward Portland, Harding seemed less redneck than worrier. Problems on the river that annoyed McDowell seemed to make Harding physically ill.

Before chugging back out into the river, we had to pick up more freight. At Boardman, there were barges of fresh Walla Walla sweet onions, cubed alfalfa and frozen peas from around my hometown, and empty garbage containers. Tidewater Barge Lines, the principal barging company on the Columbia-Snake System and my host on the river, has an intermountain garbage arrangement. Tidewater hauls compacted garbage upriver from the far side of the Cascades—from the fast-growing city of Vancouver, Washington, and surrounding Clark County—and dumps it in sparsely populated Morrow County, Oregon, in a landfill about ten miles from Boardman.

This west-to-east migration of garbage—by barge, rail, and truck—had become a growth industry in Oregon and Washington, as the swelling population of Ecotopia (despite strict recycling laws) produced more and more waste and the Empty Quarter remained relatively empty. In nearby Arlington, another small desert town on the

Oregon side of the river, trucks hauled trash to the largest landfill in the Pacific Northwest. Eastern Oregon coveted urban garbage for the same reasons that the Tri-Cities coveted nuclear waste: lots of empty land and the locals had convinced themselves it was both safe and good for the economy. Judge Louis Carlson, chairman of the Morrow County board of commissioners, told me that Tidewater paid his county about two hundred thousand dollars to accept the garbage. For a county of just eight thousand people, Carlson said, two hundred thousand "adds up."

After barges with onions and garbage containers were lashed to the tow and we nudged back out into the river, I climbed down out of the wheelhouse and went for a walk on our two-hundred-yard-long vessel. As the late morning turned warm, the cargo was beginning to ripen. Side by side, just in front of the tugboat *Defiance* (which pushed six barges, tied two-abreast), were warring odors, one seductive, the other sickening.

To the left, the invigorating tang of freshly picked sweet onions. The pride of Walla Walla, the onions are the Northwest's highly competitive answer to gourmet sweet onions grown in Vidalia, Georgia. To the right, the dried-blood, flu-vomit stench of a barge carrying leaky containers of partially tanned cowhide. The hides, bound for a baseball-glove factory in South Korea, wept a salty solution that slickened and corroded the barge's steel deck. As the sun grew hotter on the becalmed river, the smell of the hides overwhelmed the onions. The hides became the fragrance that perfumed my passage through the Columbia Gorge.

Fleeing the smell, I climbed back up to the wheelhouse. It was just before noon. On Tidewater barges, six-hour shifts always change on a fixed schedule. The captain takes the best hours, from six in the morning until noon, from six in the evening to midnight. Harding had been at the helm for only an hour or so, but he was about to give control of the barge over to his pilot. Before doing so, he gave me a simple, quick, and painless (for him) prescription for saving salmon and stopping all this nonsense about removing dams or drawing down the river.

208   "The first thing you do," Harding said, "is you shoot all the seals."

For bargers, nothing symbolized the decline and fall of common sense on the river as neatly as seals. The population of seals and sea lions in the Pacific Northwest has risen sharply since the federal government decided that it had to act to save marine mammals from extinction. For decades, Northwest fishermen had been shooting seals, sea lions, and otters to keep them out of their nets and stop them from creaming off the salmon catch. The Marine Mammal Protection Act made harming these creatures a federal crime. It worked far better than intended.

When the law was adopted in 1972 the population of harbor seals in Washington began growing by 6 to 10 percent a year. By 1999, it had increased to more than thirty thousand. Federal fishery officials said that by 2011 the numbers in Washington and Oregon were at the carrying capacity of both states. California sea lions, much larger mammals that can weigh up to nine hundred pounds and eat forty-five pounds of fish a day, also thrived under the law. These bewhiskered, double-chinned mammals began taking extended vacations in the Pacific Northwest, feasting on threatened salmon in the Columbia River and other waterways.

A few of the sea lions had the bad luck to become celebrities. A group of them, collectively known as "Herschel," began taking their holidays at the Ballard Locks in Seattle, where they decimated a wild run of Lake Washington steelhead. Fish and game authorities bombarded the sea lions with rubber-tipped arrows, rubber bullets, bad odors, firecrackers, and amplified calls from killer whales. Still they stayed on, eating salmon and getting fat. In desperation, fish agencies captured the sea lions and trucked them to California. They swam back and continued to eat more steelhead in front of television cameras.

Harding told me that each spring on the lower Columbia he saw more and more sea lions (as many as four thousand have been counted in the river), even as the numbers of returning adult salmon continued to decline and schemes to remove dams or draw down the Columbia (and ruin his life) gathered steam.

"Just what the hell is going on?" Harding asked, echoing the outrage of barge owners, utilities executives, and irrigators who see salmon-scarfing sea lions as an easily understood and cost-free distraction from the dams and reservoirs that kill 80 percent of the salmon in the Columbia Basin.

Conservationists have been forced by the sea lion imbroglio to concede that mistakes have been made in ecosystem management. At the urging of Washington State lawmakers, Congress acted in 1994 to amend the Marine Mammal Act so that intransigent sea lions, after 180 days of scientific review, could be subject to "lethal removal." But even the congresswoman who wrote the sea-lion-killing amendment made a point of telling the House of Representatives that dams and forestry practices—not marine mammals—were the primary culprits for the decline of salmon. Representative Jolene Unsoeld, whose western Washington district borders the river, said, "we cannot and should not claim that seals and sea lions are what's causing the decline of our salmon runs in the Northwest."*

Having pronounced a death sentence on marine mammals, Harding handed over control of the barge to his pilot and went to lunch. For the next six hours, I stayed on in the wheelhouse with the pilot, Michael Warren, thirty-seven years old, fifteen years on the river, five years in the wheelhouse. We steered clear of any discussion of seals, salmon, or drawdowns. We watched the river as the Columbia Gorge began to rise on both sides.

The irrigated plains gave way to hills of gray rabbit grass streaked with black seams of basalt. The gorge slowly gathered altitude as we moved west through the only sea-level passage in the mountains between California and Canada. A thousand feet above the river, scarred gorge walls showed off the high-water mark of the Ice Age floods that reamed out the gorge. On this stretch of the Columbia, at a

*Unsoeld was soundly defeated in the 1994 election that swept a Republican majority into Congress.

210 distance of more than a hundred miles from the crest of the Cascades, it used to be routine in good weather to see the towering snow-capped volcanic peaks of the Cascades. The most prominent, Mount Hood (elevation 11,235 feet), used to float in the southwest horizon like a child's dream of an ice-cream cone. Lewis and Clark saw Mount Hood from a distance of 150 miles. The peak, in the last decade of the twentieth century, is more often than not shrouded in a bluish haze of smog that rolls east through the gorge from Portland and the heavily populated Willamette Valley. There was not a cloud in the sky, but we could not see Mount Hood.

I asked Warren, who grew up in Heppner, Oregon, a town in the eastern outback of the Columbia Basin, what brought him to the river.

"A paycheck," he said, "and I wanted to get out of the desert."

With the salary he earned on the river, the pilot could afford to live in Seaside, a fashionable resort town on the Oregon coast. Barging on the Columbia, Warren said, allowed him to return regularly to the sagebrush country he grew up in and still loves. More important, he said, it paid him enough money to live someplace less dull.

Speaking of dull, Warren said, piloting a 614-foot-long, 14,000-ton tow in slackwater is among the dullest jobs imaginable—except when something is about to go wrong.

"We have hours upon hours of boredom, and seconds of sheer panic in which you can cause millions of dollars of damage, and maybe even kill some people. If you hit something with 14,000 tons, it gives. You have to treat everything—docks, bridges, other tows—as if it was made from eggshells."

Two days after Warren told me about treating bridges like eggshells, a much smaller river barge in Alabama struck a railroad bridge. An Amtrak train jumped the rails on the damaged trestle and tumbled into Bayou Creek, killing more than forty people.

The unboring part of Warren's life, he said, occurred when he was off the river, chasing women. The twice-divorced, now-single pilot treated me to an extended episode of "As the Barge Turns," the true-life (but possibly wildly exaggerated) sexual antics of river men who have fifteen days a month off the barge to fool around. Throughout the long afternoon, as we followed the sun west into the mouth of the gorge, squinted into a white ribbon of glare, and endured the odd whiff of rank cowhide from the barge below, I learned everything there was to know about a rich, married, well-dressed, and large-breasted woman named Rhonda. He met her on the boardwalk at Seaside. She took him on the road in her red BMW. She seduced him in the garden of the Columbia Gorge Hotel. She paid his way to Vegas. She was a terrific human being, if a bit unstable.

"For health reasons, I had to stop seeing Rhonda," Warren said. "Her husband gave me a call."

After nearly four hours of the Rhonda story, it was shift-change time. I followed Warren to the galley for pork chops with gravy and fresh corn on the cob that one of the incoming deckhands had brought from his farm. Then it was back up to the wheelhouse, to spend the evening with the skipper.

Harding was listening, as he always does on evening shift in the wheelhouse, to conservative talk-radio. Callers complained about tax-and-spend, anti-family feminism, and environmental overkill. The callers inspired Harding to tell me how the Columbia River was being ruined by liberals.

As an example, the skipper pointed to house lights that were beginning to twinkle on each side of the darkening gorge.

"The new lights in the gorge you cannot believe. There are more every week, as these yuppies build their perfect homes with perfect views of the river. With all these new lights, sometimes you cannot tell where the navigation aids are. You can't find the channel. It is more stress for me. I don't need more stress."

The lights reminded Harding that sailboats in the lower river around Portland were multiplying out of control and "they don't seem to think anymore that they have to get out of the barge channel when we come through." Then, he grumbled, there were fishermen who will not get out of the way, even when he honks his foghorn for minutes at a time. The list of stress-producing problems on the river expanded to

212 fill the long evening: "ignorant oil pollution laws," periodic drawdowns of parts of the Snake River that "are supposed to save salmon but make it more dangerous for us to operate," and Indians who fish at night without running lights.

As we sailed into the night, the highways and railroad tracks that line both sides of the gorge bristled with light. A tangle of headlight white and taillight red reflected off the river. The growl of big trucks and the clickety-clack of trains carried well on the water, coming in through the open windows of the wheelhouse to mix with talk-radio rants and Harding's litany of river complaints. As we inched into the locks in John Day Dam, a huge bird, probably a great blue heron, bolted from its perch on the side of the dam and nearly crashed into the windows of the wheelhouse.

"That is stress I do not need," Harding said.

Beyond John Day Dam, we sailed beneath the two most aberrant structures on the entire length of the Columbia. Both were built by a man named Sam Hill, a North Carolinian who married one of the seven daughters of James J. Hill, the railroad tycoon who built the Burlington Northern tracks on the Washington side of the river. High above those tracks on a treeless promontory, Sam Hill built a mansion for his wife, Mary, the tycoon's daughter. She, however, categorically refused to come near Maryhill Castle. So Hill turned it into a museum, and in 1926 he lured a not-very-important European aristocrat, Queen Marie of Romania, out to Columbia Gorge to dedicate the castle. The queen left behind a few pictures of herself and some gilt furniture, which remain on display. Greatly impressed with things European, Sam Hill went on to build a concrete and cut-stone full-size replica of the ancient Druid temple of Stonehenge. It looms above the gorge as a memorial to veterans of World War I who were born in Klickitat County, Washington.

Down on the water we approached what used to be the diciest reach of the Columbia, the part that Captain William Clark described in 1805 as an "agitated gut swelling, boiling & whorling in every direction." Before slackwater, the river was cinched into a narrow, eight-mile-long basalt canyon known as the Dalles.* It squeezed the Columbia from a width of more than half a mile to just 715 feet. The stone girdle provoked violent protest from the river, spitting white water, howling incessantly. At its upriver entrance, the Dalles canyon began with a twenty-two-foot drop called Celilo Falls.

Celilo was the most productive Indian fishing ground in the Northwest. All the adult salmon heading back to spawn on the upper Columbia, the Snake, and their tributaries had to jump the falls, where Indians took them with spear, gaff, net, and J-shaped baskets. The mid-1950s flooding of Celilo behind the Dalles Dam, like the flooding of Kettle Falls behind Grand Coulee, is remembered by local tribes as an act of cultural genocide. Native American poet Elizabeth Woody described what happened after the dam went in.

> There is Celilo,
> dispossessed, the village of neglect . . .
> Drowning is a sensation
> Fishermen and their wives know of.
> Men who fish son after father.
> There are drownings in the Dalles,
> hanging in jails and off-reservation-suicide towns.

The Indians who continue to fish in this stretch of the river use gill nets, stringing them out in the lakes above and below the dams. Nets are constant irritants to barge pilots. Harding dreaded hitting them and provoking tribal complaints to Tidewater Barge Lines that could get him in trouble.

"You see that!" Harding yelped.

We were about twenty miles upstream of the Dalles Dam. It was around eleven and I was going down the stairs of the wheelhouse,

---

*"Dalles" comes from the French word for "flagstones." The name was bestowed by voyageurs who, on their way through the gorge, thought the even slabs of basalt that encased the river resembled flagstones in the courtyards of Montreal.

214 heading for bed, when the skipper saw something alarming. He screamed for me to come back up. Out on the black river, captured in Harding's wheelhouse spotlight, a small motorboat skittered across the Columbia in front of the barge. It had no lights.

"That's some Indian tending his nets in violation of the law. He is supposed to have running lights. Now what am I supposed to do about that? If I hit him, it is my fault. You know what that is? That is more stress for me."

I stayed on in the wheelhouse for almost an hour, grunting sympathetically as Harding told me about how Indians made him anxious.

Finally, I escaped to my cabin. The night was restful. The tow, other than passing through the locks at the Dalles Dam, did not stop. There was none of the torturous bumping—the all-night barge shuffle—that had ruined my previous attempts at sleep on the river.

Beyond the Dalles, the barge chugged past Hood River, Oregon, where, had it been daylight, thousands of windsurfers would have been gamboling on the river—stressing Harding out.

"You certainly don't intend to stress out the barge pilots, but you get very focused on yourself. You are turning the board at high speed in big waves, going back and forth across the river, and all of a sudden you look up and there is this thing in the river the size of a football field. Everybody who has ever windsurfed on that river has had close calls. Eventually somebody is going to die out there."

So predicted Mark Nykanen, a Hood River windsurfer and just the sort of tall, dark, handsome, smart, articulate, affluent, environmentally aware, left-leaning, all-organic New West recreator who made barge skippers shake their heads in disgust.

A couple of weeks before my barge trip I had found Nykanen on a mountaintop not far from Hood River, where he lived in a soaring log house made exclusively of windfall pine. Wearing a T-shirt and running shorts, he invited me to ask him questions as he worked out in his second-floor bedroom, which afforded a sweeping view of nearby Mount Hood and Mount Adams. Lifting dumbbells and stretching a latex exercise band, he was strengthening the rotator cuff in his left shoulder, which he had torn while windsurfing. (He also had broken, while windsurfing, three bones in his foot and two toes.)

"Windsurfing, as it is done here on the river, is a very high performance sport," he said.

Injuries did not keep Nykanen from boarding two or three times a week. He subscribed to a telephone service that reported wind speeds and directions at assorted windsurfing sites along the Columbia Gorge. Nykanen did not put on his black-and-blue neoprene wetsuit and head out to the river unless the wind was blowing at least thirty miles an hour, a velocity that creates large swells on the river. The swells are the display platform upon which expert windsurfers jump and execute high-speed turns called jibes.

"I was a gifted athlete growing up." Nykanen told me, curling a dumbbell with his left arm, as strands of sweat ran down his long, lean face. "When I started windsurfing here in 1987, I devoted myself maniacally to the sport. I went out on the river every day for seven months."

For a while, Nykanen sought out sixty-mile-an-hour winds that whip the surface of the river into an ethereal but treacherous spume that windsurfers call "liquid smoke."

"That was sheer survival. I did it to prove I could do it. It was a kind of macho thing. It is something that I do not seek out any more."

When not on the river, Nykanen recreated in the Columbia Gorge by mountain biking, hiking, all-terrain skiing, acting in local plays, and dabbling in the Hood River real-estate market, the value of which had soared, primarily because of windsurfing maniacs such as himself. Nykanen bought his first house in Hood River for $55,000 in 1985, the early days of the explosion in property values in the Columbia Gorge. When he sold that house four years later, he nearly tripled his investment and bought his ten-acre mountaintop spread. Nykanen explained that his house was on land zoned for forest use and that no other homes could be built on his mountaintop. "The gates are now closed," he said.

Nykanen came to the gorge from Chicago, where he had won four Emmys in seven years as an investigative reporter for NBC News. He saved enough money from network television to subsidize his wind-

216 surfing obsession and to try to launch a new career as a novelist. After six years in the gorge, in addition to high-performance recreating, he had written three unpublished novels (one autobiographical, one historical, and one thriller).

"I haven't watched TV since I left NBC. I quit because I fell in love with windsurfing, and national television news had become a complete joke. Local TV news is a kind of dementia. Also, I did not want to work for a bomb manufacturer [General Electric, an owner of NBC]," Nykanen told me, as he continued to exercise his left shoulder.

A vegetarian, Nykanen drank only organically grown coffee and poured rice milk in his morning bran. He subscribed to *Mother Jones*, *Yoga Journal*, and the University of California *Wellness Letter*. His main source of news was a Pacifica radio station out of Portland. He lived with his girlfriend, Cindy Taylor, also a vegetarian, who worked in the Dalles as a therapist for emotionally disturbed children. Nykanen worried frequently about the quality of the water in the river on which he sails.

"Undoubtedly, the river has been compromised. I have no faith that the government has protected the river from Hanford. Then you have the pesticides and herbicides from the orchards. You hear people grumbling, but they should be screaming."

Nykanen would be happy to pay significantly more for electricity if that would help save endangered Columbia River salmon.

"We are already paying an environment tax that is self-imposed when we pay 20 percent extra for organic foods. So, sure, I would be willing to pay more for utilities to preserve the river and its fish," said Nykanen, who heated his house with a large high-efficiency wood stove.

Before driving up to Nykanen's house, I asked around in Hood River, trying to find out what locals think of well-heeled windsurfers. In a decade, they transformed a depressed logging community of 4,800 people into an international resort where half the housing was owned by people who lived out of state. Store clerks and waiters resented being unable to afford to buy or pay rent in town, where a small apartment went for two thousand dollars a month during the windsurf season. A non-windsurfing auto mechanic who was born in Hood River told me that he kept a windsurf board on top of his car year-round because it allowed him to drink and drive without fear of harassment from local cops who did not want to annoy big-spending, out-of-town "board-heads." Sheriff's Deputy Greg Sandercock, who fished injured and hypothermic windsurfers out of the river, acknowledged that one need not look far to find spiteful locals in Hood River.

"Some of these windsurfers you can compare to spoiled rich kids. They certainly are not criminals, but they are used to doing anything they want. You hear them in the stores or the streets saying that this town would dry up and blow away if they weren't here."

Up on his mountaintop, I asked Nykanen about local anger. What about the indignation of irrigators, barge operators, and utility executives who claimed that imports like him were going to shut down the Columbia so they could jibe around in wetsuits and speculate in real estate?

"When I first moved here, I remember people driving past me and flipping me off. Obviously, I looked different; I wasn't local. But that has begun to fade away. There's been a decrease in antagonism. People sold out for good money and left, or they stayed and prospered from the windsurfing business.

"As for the claim that urban yuppies are taking control of the river, that is complete bullshit. I don't doubt that the perception is there, but it is the perception that industry wants the public to accept. Extractive industry in the Northwest engages very effectively in spin control.

"What people around here don't realize is that this region was dying from a kind of economic leukemia long before the windsurfers showed up. There has been a degeneration of vital fluids, caused by the timber industry, pulp mills, Hanford, and hydroelectric dams. I consider windsurfing to be low impact. We kill no salmon. We dump no heavy metals. We spill no oil."

Speaking of barge pilots in particular, Nykanen apologized for the torment that he and tens of thousands of other windsurfers put them through.

"I totally empathize with them. We don't mean to be such a pain in the ass around the barges. But we are busy sailing, and we just don't see them."*

I woke up on a river cloaked in green. The barren East Side, with its rock-pierced sand, endless sagebrush, and thousand shades of brown, was gone. During the night we had sailed out of the rain-shadow desert and into the wettest slice of the American West. Douglas fir and western hemlock ruled the high shoulders of the gorge, and down by the Columbia there was an uproar of Pacific willow, red alder, black cottonwood, creek dogwood, and stinging nettle. Although the sun shone in a cloudless sky, the air was cool and humid. It softened the morning and deepened the encircling green.

This would be my last day on the barge. We were nearing the locks in Bonneville Dam, the final dam on the Columbia. Portland was a little more than forty-five miles away. There, the tow would be pulled apart, its cargo loaded on ships for the Far East. The empty garbage containers would be refilled with compacted trash and sent back to the Empty Quarter. The tugboat *Defiance*, too, was scheduled for a quick turnaround. It had burial detail. It would push a deactivated nuclear reactor from a U.S. Navy submarine upriver for deposit at Hanford.

Just upriver from Bonneville, the tow hugged the Washington side of the river, following the shipping channel. A few hundred feet off the starboard side, a half-dozen small fishing boats (crowded with families of non-Indians wielding fishing rods and large mugs of coffee) were anchored near the mouth of a small mountain river that spilled into the Columbia. Decked out in rain gear despite the sunshine, they seemed in a foul temper. They did not return my wave. Perhaps it was because the three-foot wake from the tow nearly capsized their boats, forcing

---

*Sometime after I talked to Nykanen, he ran out of money. He went to work in Los Angeles for tabloid television. He helped direct coverage of the O. J. Simpson trial. Nykanen planned to work in tabloid TV just long enough to subsidize another round of fiction and windsurfing in the gorge.

them to drop their fishing rods and coffee mugs and hang on for dear life.

I joined the deckhands in the galley for what proved to be a bracingly impolitic breakfast. Both Jim Richardson, forty-two years old and seven years on the river, and Jeff Blank, thirty-four years old and fourteen years on the river, were in expansive moods. Part of the reason was concrete. Until just a few months ago, at this point on the trip to Portland, the deckhands would have been out on the barges, untying cables and breaking the tow down into smaller pieces that would fit through the narrow locks of the fifty-six-year-old dam. Only two barges and a tug could fit through at one go. For nearly two decades, Bonneville had been the biggest bottleneck on the Columbia-Snake System, forcing deckhands to work outside for hours, unmaking and remaking the tow in a stretch of river often made miserable by rain and wind and cold. New bigger locks at the dam, built at a cost of $340 million, allowed our tow to pass whole through the dam. Deckhands could sit in the galley and eat. Also perking up the deckhands was the good fortune of having snuck around Hood River in the dead of night, thereby eluding the windsurfing hordes.

Since the mid-1980s, deckhands have had to stand out on the bow for daylight passage through the gorge, keeping an eye out for downed windsurfers. A fully loaded barge cannot stop in less than a quarter mile of river, so deckhands can only scream into their walkie-talkies if a windsurfer spills in front of the tow. Mostly, deckhands stand out there in the wind and curse the carelessness of people playing chicken with fourteen thousand tons of freight.

I told the deckhands about the windsurfer who was sorry for being such a pain in the ass. I explained that windsurfers get so self-absorbed they cannot see the barges. The deckhands rolled their eyes; it was not news to them that windsurfers were self-absorbed hazards to navigation.

"I fish those board-heads out of the river all the time. One had his mast snap in the wind. He had hypothermia by the time we got to him and was out of his mind. He was taking off his gloves and throwing

220 them into the river. He couldn't sit on top of his board," said Richardson, who, when he was not on the river, raised sweet corn in Wamic, Oregon, an East Side town south of the Columbia. "We saved his life and he didn't even say thank you."*

Disgust with windsurfers seemed to remind Richardson of how annoyed he was by endangered salmon and the damage they are doing to his career. He made me some pancakes and launched into the single most politically incorrect argument that I heard about endangered fish on the Columbia.

"The biggest mistake they [the federal government] made was putting fish ladders in at Bonneville Dam. If they hadn't done that, all this business about salmon would be over."

With no fish ladders at Bonneville, the entire Columbia River watershed above the dam would have been permanently sealed to migrating adult salmon. All the salmon and steelhead runs above the dam would have been wiped out. All plans for salmon restoration would be moot. Federal judges, Indian chiefs, fish biologists would all stop poking their noses into barge business.

The deckhand's argument was explosive stuff. Given the environmental orthodoxy of the Pacific Northwest, it was hate speech, akin to decrying the end of slavery or denying the Holocaust. No politician, no utility executive, no producer of aluminum, no owner of a barge line that uses public waterways would dare repeat what the deckhand said, at least in public. Certainly, it would be convenient for river users and large industrial electricity consumers such as aluminum companies if salmon disappeared, but saying so—especially on the West Side of the mountains, in Ecotopia—would be a public-relations disaster.

It was not always apostasy to speak openly of destroying all the salmon. Grand Coulee Dam, as we have seen, blocked the upper Columbia River Basin. Hells Canyon Dam, which was completed in

---

*The sheriff's department in Hood River County said that the cold of the Columbia is far more dangerous to windsurfers than the barges. The river's temperature hovers around the mid-50s in the spring and early summer. "They don't realize how cold that is," said one deputy. "They fall in and they cannot get up."

1967, blocked the upper Snake River Basin. It is hardly surprising, then, that had the Army Corps of Engineers had its way back in the early days of the New Deal, Bonneville Dam would have done the same for virtually the entire river, accomplishing precisely what the deckhand suggested.

The chief of the Corps, responding in the early 1930s to fishermen's protests about the proposed dam, reportedly said, "We do not intend to play nursemaid to the fish!"

The Corps has denied that any such thing was said. An official Corps history of Bonneville fuzzes over the question of whether or not the agency wanted to save salmon. However, Milo Bell, a hydraulic engineer who worked for the Corps at Bonneville in the 1930s and who invented its fish ladders, told me that the Corps' original design for the dam would not have allowed salmon upstream. Bell, a professor emeritus at the University of Washington, said that without public pressure the Corps would not have spent the money necessary to make fish passage work and salmon runs would have been destroyed. Corps engineers, Bell recalled, made "a lot of snide comments about salmon."

Before we cleared the locks at Bonneville, I left the deckhands in the galley and climbed up to the wheelhouse, where I overheard the lockkeeper warn Captain Harding on the radio that there were "big doings" downriver. Jodie Foster and Mel Gibson were just downstream, making a movie.

"Watch out," the lockkeeper said, "you don't want to run over a movie star."

Below Bonneville, for the first time since I boarded the barge back in Idaho, the Columbia was not contained between plugs of concrete. Dam makers had found nothing of compelling interest on the river from here to the sea. The steep drop of the Columbia was exhausted. The river went tidal, became flabby, and took on the lazy personality of the Mississippi. Just beyond Bonneville, however, there was one bit of moderately swift water left. We skated over Garrison Rapids (which has no white water and which I would not have recognized as a rapids without Harding telling me it was a rapids) at about ten miles an hour, which is two miles an hour faster than normal for a fully loaded tow,

222 and considerably faster than Harding prefers to travel when hoping that he does not run over a movie star.

"We're scooting," Harding complained, pulling the handle on the tow's warning horn. A stiff breeze was at our backs. The Oregon side of the river was lined with the yellow tents of fishermen. Scores of them were out in small boats, casting for Columbia River sturgeon, bottom fish that can grow up to six feet long and weigh eight hundred pounds. If the fishermen are stupid enough to get in front of him, Harding said, he cannot stop.

A possible celebrity sighting occurred shortly before 9 A.M. We had come abreast of Beacon Rock, a gargantuan black boulder on the north bank of the river that is second in size only to Gibraltar. (The 848-foot-high rock is the central neck of a former volcano.) At the base of Beacon Rock, we saw a freshly painted Old West paddle-wheel riverboat lying at anchor. Then, scampering upstream from Portland, a motorboat approached on the port side of the tow. Sitting in the stern of the boat, out in the bright morning sun, her blond hair blowing in the breeze, her eyes intent on a fluttering script held tightly in both hands, we could conceivably have seen Academy Award winner Jodie Foster on the way to filming one of her most forgettable performances in the movie *Maverick*. Harding, whose binoculars were better than mine, was sure it was she.

Just downriver we came alongside Multnomah Falls, a 620-foot-high rope of white water that wows drivers on Interstate 84 as it sprays out of the Oregon side of the gorge toward the river. Clear across the river on the Washington side, three tiny black-tailed deer drank from the edge of the Columbia. They kept raising their noses between sips, sniffing in the direction of the passing tow, perhaps wondering why the usual smell of diesel exhaust was spiced with onions and cowhide.

We saw our first windsurfer of the day at Rooster Rock State Park, a not very good and not very popular place to sail. He gave the barge an extremely wide berth. Harding said there was a nude beach at Rooster Rock, but binoculars revealed nothing. A luxury cruise ship, the *Sea Lion*, slipped past us, heading upriver. It was packed with mostly white-haired people. On the open back deck, several of them rode stationary bicycles with their noses buried in paperbacks. As Mount Hood lorded over us from the Oregon side, the gorge began to peter out, mountains giving way to high rolling hills.

Handing me his binoculars, Harding pointed to a distant ridge on the Washington side. I saw a three-story mansion with a lawn sweeping down toward the river. There were barns, a gazebo, and twelve llamas grazing on the lawn. It was the home of the man who owned the barge I was riding on and whose Tidewater Barge Lines hauled four out of every five tons of freight on the Columbia-Snake River System. Ray Hickey was a hero to the men on the barges. He started out on the river in 1951 as a ten-dollar-a-day deckhand. By the mid-1990s, he was the sole owner of a company—with holdings in shipping, solid waste removal, docks, and environmental cleanup services—with total assets worth well over $140 million.

"That's where Mr. Hickey lives," Harding said respectfully. "As you can see, he is a wealthy man, but he earned every penny of it. He likes llamas."

Mr. Hickey.

A short, heavyset, intense man with thick glasses and stubby fingers, he granted me an audience at his company's headquarters in Vancouver, Washington, a city across the river from Portland. His public-relations adviser sat in on our forty-minute conversation. Hickey told me four times that he was an environmentalist.

He was an environmentalist who did not buy the generally accepted consensus among fish biologists, environmental groups, fish and wild-life agencies, and federal courts that hydroelectric dams and slackwater reservoirs are primarily responsible for killing salmon in the Columbia and Snake. He was an environmentalist who dominated a shipping industry that is dependent on a river that, as historian Donald Worster puts it, was killed by dams and reborn as money.

"I don't believe they have established what it is that makes the fish disappear," he said. "I think you have to figure out what the problem is before you make a solution. You know the seals at the mouth of the Columbia are eating the fish."

Hickey, who was sixty-five years old when we talked, acknowledged that in his lifetime there has been a wholesale change in the economy and culture of the Pacific Northwest, with the emergence of companies like Microsoft and Nike, which he said "don't need the river and want to protect the appearance of the place.

"The political atmosphere now is that you have to give the impression that you are protecting the environment. It gets you votes here if you are the big savior."

But Hickey said he had to disagree with these cosmetic notions about what is worthwhile on the river and in the West. He said that farmers "are the backbone of the country. They are the ones who have the integrity to go out and make something work."

I asked Hickey, whose company's profits were built on grain transport, how he would describe the river. I mentioned that a prominent lobbyist for the hydropower industry called the Columbia a "damn fine machine."

Hickey closed his eyes for a moment, smiled broadly, and said he found the description "perfect."

"It is a machine," he said with satisfaction, nodding his head vigorously.

Then Hickey caught the eye of his public-relations adviser, who was sending nervous nonverbal signals to the effect that the word "machine" might be a bit too mechanical.

"Maybe 'machine' is the wrong word," Hickey added quickly, "It is more a system. . . ."

After several false starts on organic, non-reductionist descriptions of the river, the barge magnate gave up on describing the river and began speaking of his affection for the Columbia, his lifelong stewardship of it, and how he always has believed that an American businessman should never "forget where you came from." He again said that he regards himself as an environmentalist.

I asked Hickey about the generous federal subsidy that pads his bottom line. Barging companies pay only about a quarter of the operating costs for locks on the Columbia and Snake. They paid none of the construction costs. At the mention of the word "subsidy," Hickey—the self-made millionaire—looked away from me in annoyance.

"The statement that we are subsidized . . . ," he said, shaking his head. "This sort of thing is said by people who do a lot of talking without knowing what they are talking about."

Hickey then conceded that barge companies do receive a substantial subsidy.

"Barge lines don't pay their share," he admitted. "Who does?"

Hickey sold Tidewater Barge Lines a few years after we spoke. He became a philanthropist, giving away more than $20 million to hospitals, land trusts, and the creation of public trails where people can go to walk along the lower Columbia. He died in 2002.

As the *Defiance* slipped into the suburbs of Portland/Vancouver, the only metropolis the Columbia passes through on its run from the Canadian Rockies to the sea, the river was surrounded by handsome new houses. The gentle slope of land up away from the river became a manicured setting for five-bedroom, high-ceilinged, three-car-garaged suburban manses. A few of the finest had private, rock-walled bays that gave suburban sailors access to the river. Through picture windows that faced the river, I saw men and women in their dens, towels around their shoulders, faces flushed from exertion, working out on Nordic Tracks and Stairmasters, watching our barge plod by.

Beyond the suburbs, we entered the port of Portland, a busy freight yard where the Willamette flows into the Columbia, where goods from the interior are hustled off barges and loaded into ocean-going cargo ships. In heavy port traffic, a tug called the *Betty Lou* appeared and began picking our tow to pieces. The *Betty Lou* made off with our peas and onions, then with the cowhides, then with grain barges, and finally the empty garbage containers.

226   Just before I, too, was off-loaded, Mike Warren, the pilot who had regaled me with tales of Rhonda, offered an epitaph for men who work on barges.

"There is a reason why they keep us bargers locked up on the boats for fifteen days at a time," Warren said. "It's so society only has to deal with half of us at any one time."

Portland/Vancouver is where the levers are shifted on the river that Ray Hickey would not for public-relations reasons say is a machine. The levers, quite literally, are shifted in a basement in Vancouver. There, in the Dittmer Control Center, a cavernous computer-filled room that looks like Mission Control in Houston and that was built to withstand nuclear attack, power dispatchers from the Bonneville Power Administration send out signals every six seconds that raise and lower gates on dams, grooming slackwater to system needs.

The power dispatchers in the bombproof Vancouver basement, however, merely execute orders. Those orders are written by a contentious gaggle of river managers—electricity marketers, fish biologists, federal judges, members of Congress, Native American leaders, utility lobbyists, barge companies, irrigators, aluminum companies, and federal bureaucrats. The managers fight with each other endlessly, angling to shape the Columbia according to wildly contradictory notions of what a river should be. They play a kind of multi-dimensional chess game with rules that bend to economic muscle and biological research, environmental law and political fashion.

The fact that fourteen thousand tons of freight had just managed to float downriver to Portland meant that champions of slackwater, for all their hand-wringing about dam removal and salmon and environmentalists, were still winning the game.

In Portland, where many of the players have their offices, I decided to poke around, trying to figure who was winning, who was losing, and why.

11

The River Game

You must never be greedy with [salmon], and you must see to it that no one else is greedy.
—Indian Legends of the Pacific Northwest

THE SIGN ON her office door read, "State Your Business. Avoid Eye Contact. Leave Quietly. And No One Will Get Hurt."

It was supposed to be funny, but her adversaries described the sign as sound advice. The woman who worked behind the door, they said, was a single-minded zealot. Given half a chance, she would hype every memo, monopolize every teleconference, and dominate every meeting. She was a bully, they said, who was ruining the river.

Managing the Columbia was once a gentlemanly pursuit. Men from the Corps of Engineers, the Bureau of Reclamation, and the Bonneville Power Administration could meet in an atmosphere of trust and mutual admiration to make no-nonsense decisions about how best to operate the world's largest hydroelectric system. These men from the federal agencies that built and maintained the big dams were free to extract maximum electricity from the river while preventing floods, keeping barges afloat, diverting water to irrigators, and guaranteeing a slackwater cushion for boaters, windsurfers, and water-skiers.

But that was before Michele DeHart elbowed into the river game.

"She has got a personality that a lot of people have problems with," said Russell George, chief of reservoir control for the Corps of Engineers in Portland. "There is no way to meet her demands unless we completely tear down the system. It seems ridiculous what you have to do. There is no light at the end of the tunnel."

Worse than her personality, according to her adversaries, were her appetites.

"There is no satisfying people like her. She wants more, more, more. Constantly more," said Dan Yibar, a Bureau of Reclamation civil engineer in charge of reservoir oversight in the Columbia Basin.

The power establishment tried to stuff a sock in her mouth. The principal utility lobby in the Pacific Northwest proposed, in an amendment to the Columbia River's fish and wildlife program, that DeHart "will not make decisions or recommendations . . . and will not engage in advocacy and/or lobbying." The amendment failed.

"I don't want this to get too personal," said Al Wright, author of the sock-in-her-mouth amendment and one of the best-known utility lobbyists in the Northwest. "But she has such an extremely strong personality that she grates on people.

"She is one of these fish terrorists who have been in the business a long time. She and her crowd are blinded by their hatred for the power system. They are so obsessed after all these years that they believe anything that destroys megawatts has to help salmon. It is almost a religious sect. They are operating in the Dark Ages. They will kill anyone who disagrees."

The fish terrorist's son, Matt, painted a salmon on a small smooth stone when he was in second grade and gave it to his mother. Indians in the Northwest believe that whoever rubs such a stone acquires the character of a salmon—persistence and determination. DeHart kept the "energy stone" on her office desk in Portland and rubbed it when she was on the phone arguing with the gentlemen from the power side.

"There is something that I do that bothers these men who say I don't play well with others. It is direct confrontation. I say exactly what I think. Many of the men I deal with in the power system are like boys who want to go fishing and don't want girls tagging along. The fact that I am a woman adds to their aggravation.

"Think of what I am doing with the river in terms of the Palestinians. They [the federal agencies that run the Columbia and the utilities that sell its power] are like the Israelis. They have taken over all of the river, and we want some of it back. They give a little bit, and think that is enough. But we want more. It's true what they say, we always want more."

DeHart, a fish biologist in her early sixties, has been playing and winning the river game for more than three decades. Born in Marseilles, France, she came to the United States at the age of three with her mother and sister. After moving around the West from Colorado to California to eastern Washington, she settled in at the University of Washington in Seattle to study biology. A course on the physiology of cold-blooded animals caught her eye. Intrigued by the physiology of salmon, she became obsessed with what happens inside these creatures as they negotiate dams in the Columbia.

"It was not anything peculiar about salmon. It could have been raccoons. It's extinction that bothers me. You have a responsibility to all the people and all the creatures that live on the planet. Your behavior cannot be such that it lacks respect for what is around you. That is what is wrong with the Columbia River. I think it's right to use natural resources, but wrong to destroy them. You are responsible for what comes after you."

I asked DeHart if she, as other players in the river game claim, wanted vengeance on those who dammed the Columbia.

"I don't have personal feelings of animosity and I am not demanding retribution. I am asking them to do something they have a hard time even imagining. I am asking them to undo some of this mammoth river system that they have built and operated and profited from.

"I am simply saying that they cannot have it all anymore. They cannot have maximum economic development and expect salmon to survive. What galls me is that this is fixable. The hydrosystem can make money and fish can get up and down the river.

"It's all about money. No one will actually say that they want salmon to go down the drain because saving them costs too much. That is a horrible moral crime to admit to."

DeHart demanded modifications in the river that would make it a mechanized version of the historic Columbia, the river that rushed

230   to the sea in the spring and summer. She wanted dams to store more water throughout the winter, rather than feed it to turbines to make electricity. From April through August, she wanted more of the river spilled for the salmon migration.

"If we do not have flows, everything else we do to try to rescue salmon in the river is like moving deck chairs on the *Titanic*."

DeHart has long been the director of a Portland-based agency called the Fish Passage Center. Her job and her agency were created as part of a landmark law passed by Congress in 1980. The Northwest Power Act assumed that dams were the principal cause of the decline of salmon in the Columbia and Snake. The law demanded that the hydro-system be changed so that salmon are treated "on a par" with power and navigation and irrigation.

Managers of the river, under the law, were supposed to pay more attention to fish-saving goals than power-production consequences. The expertise of fish agencies and local Indian tribes was supposed to shape the operation of the river. Northwest consumers of electricity, who for half a century had enjoyed America's cheapest power, were expected to foot the bill for salmon recovery through slightly higher electricity rates.

The Northwest Power Act, in theory, spelled out a revolution in western water management. It put longtime inmates of the engineered river—Indian tribes and fish agencies—in a position of power. To administer the revolution, the Power Act created a novel bureaucratic creature. Not quite a federal agency, not a state agency, the Northwest Power Planning Council was made up of two gubernatorial appointees from each of the four states in the Northwest. The Council had powers (rather vaguely defined powers, as it turned out) to change the behavior of the federal agencies that built and managed the hydrosystem. For the first time since the dams were built, the Bonneville Power Administration, the Army Corps of Engineers, and the Bureau of Reclamation were supposed to answer to someone other than themselves.

Passage of the Power Act and creation of the Power Council prompted a celebration among champions of salmon. There was effusive talk about how the Northwest was an environmental showcase for the entire United States. It was said to be an enlightened region where concern about endangered species could be married to economic needs. "The whole climate has changed drastically," enthused the head of the Columbia River Inter-Tribal Fish Commission, one of a score of long-frustrated fish groups. Thanks to the Power Act, said one public-interest fish lawyer in Portland, "Utilities could no longer ride rough-shod over the public interest."

The fish agencies and Indian tribes needed a single articulate voice, a coordinator to monitor salmon survival and speak up at meetings with the men who ran the river. To fill this need, the Council created the Fish Passage Center and chose DeHart to run it.

She took the job with the assumption that the rules of the river game had changed. Congress, after all, had ordered "that no longer [should] fish and wildlife be given a secondary status." When DeHart made demands in the name of the fish agencies and tribes, she expected the power side to do everything it could to cooperate.

Nearly every river user I met insisted that he was on the brink of losing his job and future to "salmon extremists." Barge pilots, irrigators, and business owners all painted a remarkably similar picture of who was to blame for sabotaging their livelihoods and spoiling the pioneer spirit of the American West. It was a uniformly unflattering portrait, and it looked a lot like DeHart.

She was the river user's stereotype of a salmon wacko: A bureaucrat with an energy rock. A West Side paper-pusher who preferred salmon to human beings. An environmental extremist who built her career on the backs of Americans who worked for a living. To push the stereotype to its mean-spirited, misogynistic edge (which was where river users often pushed it), DeHart was a female who took a perverse delight in making men squirm. To repeat a Rush Limbaugh-ism that I often heard on my downriver passage, she was one of those femi-Nazis.

In Portland, where she meets on a weekly basis with the players who run the river, DeHart's adversaries were more careful in their language. Instead of crude sexist attacks, they questioned her grasp of reality.

232   Al Wright, the mouthpiece for the utilities, told me that DeHart's worldview would be acceptable if everyone in the Pacific Northwest was "warm and well-fed and affluent. And you got a BMW and you got a four-thousand-square-foot house and you and your wife's combined salary is a couple of hundred thousand dollars a year."

But the real world, Wright said, was not so cushy.

"I have never once heard of a utility that had an outage and had its customers call and say, 'Well I don't want you to hurt the environment, but sometime in the next two months could you get my lights back on?' I never once heard of a telephone call like that."

Wright's real-world argument, however, did not mention that he and most of the people making it were earning a handsome living from the subsidized river. DeHart's most passionate critics tended to be either federal bureaucrats or well-paid utility executives or wealthy businessmen with shipping or irrigation interests.

Despite passage of the Northwest Power Act, salmon continued to decline. The most severe drop-off was among Idaho salmon, the fish forced to run the gauntlet of eight federal dams on the Columbia and Snake. Many fish biologists saw a momentum toward extinction that they feared was irreversible. Across the Pacific Northwest, wild salmon were only about 20 percent as abundant as they were historically.

Downstream from Portland, in a century-old fishing village called Skamokawa, Washington, I spent two sad days with a family that had been forced to give up fishing in the Columbia. Kent and Irene Martin's annual gross income from river fishing had fallen in five years from sixty thousand dollars to one thousand dollars. The strictest fishing restrictions in the history of the river, along with "virtually no fish to catch," convinced the Martins in 1994 to abandon a way of life that had served their family for four generations.

"The thing that has been most difficult to accept is that it's our own fault. We in the Pacific Northwest have crapped in our own nest," said Kent Martin, a bulky bald man with muttonchop whiskers. He found it difficult to keep his voice down and his anger under control.

"It is extermination for us. We have lost the guts of our fishing season. We have not been allowed to catch summer chinook since 1964, but their population continues to go down. You tell me where the fish are dying. Of course, most of it is the dams. But the utilities and the aluminum companies and the federal power agencies continue to tell anybody who will listen that it is everybody's fault but their own.

"I call them poachers in pinstripes. They ought to be in jail. They don't have the will, the intention, or the desire to save the fish. If they were serious, they would not be stooging around about our harvest."

The Pacific Fisheries Management Council, a federal agency that regulates fishing, agreed with Martin. Jim Coon, a staff officer for the Council, told me that if "you took away all the ocean fisheries and took away all the river fisheries, you would see an immediate [upward] blip in the number of adult salmon reaching the dams. But it would be very small and it would not reduce the downward trend. What is happening is not harvest. What is happening is with the river."

About seven hundred miles upstream from the Martins, on the upper Grand Ronde River in northeast Oregon, wild salmon had all but disappeared by the mid-1990s.

When Michael Farrow, a forty-six-year-old Cayuse and Walla Walla Indian, was a boy, fifteen thousand of those spring chinook salmon returned to that tributary of the Snake. Farrow told me that the absence of the fish made him ashamed of himself and his country.

"When I found out that no one had seen a salmon, I stopped and looked for a long time at the river. I never had such a lonely feeling. I had wanted to train my boys to hook salmon there. My boys are the first generation in ten thousand years that have never fished there. Those fish in the upper Grand Ronde are all but gone, and it is nothing but a sin. Those stocks are so ancient. They were created by someone higher than us. It really ticks me off."

The confederated tribes of the Umatilla Indian Reservation, for which Farrow worked as director of natural resources, decided unilaterally in 1974—twenty years before there were no spring chinook in the upper Grand Ronde—to suspend all tribal fishing in the river, as well as

234   other streams and rivers in the area. The tribes made the decision after widespread in-stream habitat destruction by wheat farmers, ranchers, and timber operators had combined with Snake River dams to reduce adult returns to a level that alarmed the Native American fishermen.

"The tribes took that action on their own. If you had seen similar good-faith actions by the hydrosystem, as well as by the farmers and the timber companies, we wouldn't be in the fix we are in," Farrow said.

There was a dreary familiarity in these fish stories. They were part of a poisonous pattern I experienced on the river. Whether it was making electricity, irrigating the desert, or making plutonium, the pattern held: The federal government moved in on the river with urgent goals, lofty motives, and expensive machinery. It succeeded quickly, beyond anyone's expectations. It put people to work and won public approval. The Biggest Thing on Earth. The Planned Promised Land. It's Atomic Bombs!

Then, out along the Columbia, the federal machinery quietly came under the control of narrow interests. Irrigation farmers wrote special rules that allowed them to waste water and pad their subsidies. The keepers of the plutonium factory poisoned their neighbors. Dam builders bullied, cheated, and dispossessed river Indians. And salmon died in dams.

With salmon, though, there was far more transparency. Their decline was an event that everyone witnessed, like a public hanging. Everyone who wanted to know, knew. In a region that consumed twice as much electricity per capita as the rest of the nation, at rates half the national average, everyone with a light switch was a collaborator.

The downwinders were covertly poisoned by a national security apparatus. It was a crime for which there was little or no local responsibility. With salmon, everyone was to blame.

We did it—to save on our monthly electricity bill.

Alarms first went off in the 1930s. Commercial fishermen, Native Americans, and fish biologists warned that the first dams were seriously degrading the world's largest inland run of salmon. They predicted that more dams would ruin a major regional industry.*

The Colville Indians were the first to see what dams actually do to fish. They noticed a drastic drop in adult salmon jumping Kettle Falls as soon as the first mainstem dam was finished on the Columbia in 1933. Rock Island Dam near Wenatchee, a small dam built by a local utility, had fish ladders. But they did not work well.

"Our total catch at the falls . . . after this dam was completed, was only four hundred salmon [compared to fifteen hundred the previous year]," Pete Lemry, spokesman for the Colville Indians, told a congressional subcommittee in 1933. "And the most salmon we saw this year was two hundred and fifty in one day; we used to see that many in half an hour before the dam was built. The white people ask me what is the matter with the salmon? I say I do not know unless the Rock Island Dam has stopped them."

By the mid-thirties, warnings from fish biologists and fishing associations in the lower Columbia pressured the United States Senate to pass a resolution that ordered the federal commissioner of fisheries to assess the effect of Bonneville Dam and recommend steps "to attain full conservation of such fish."

By the forties, with Grand Coulee and Bonneville complete and the salmon catch in the Columbia down to half its thirty-year average, Northwest fish scientists, commercial fishermen, and Indian tribes demanded a moratorium on all new dams. A study by the U.S. Fish and Wildlife Service had found that at least 15 percent of juvenile migrants in the Columbia were killed at Bonneville Dam. Although the secretary of Interior forbade publication of this information, it leaked out. Fishermen could add. Each new dam meant fewer juvenile fish going to sea

---

*When the dams began going in the thirties, fishing was not an insignificant matter. The Army Corps of Engineers, in a massive document laying out a scheme for dams on the Columbia, noted in 1932 that salmon fishing was the fourth largest industry in the Northwest, after farming, ranching, and timber. It employed about thirteen thousand fishermen and earned about ten million dollars a year. It is worth noting that in the Corps' magnum opus on dams, a document running to 1,280 pages, just two and a half pages dealt with fish.

236 and fewer catchable adults coming home. The fishermen wanted the Corps and the Bureau to slow down, think things through, and figure out how to design safer dams.

The fish lobby was allowed one high-noon confrontation with the builders of dams. It came in Walla Walla, Washington, in June 1947. Fish agencies and Indian tribes were, at the time of the meeting, desperate to head off the building of McNary Dam. Representatives of the power side showed up in force in Walla Walla, along with advisers to the region's governors. But before they came, they demonstrated who was calling the shots on the river. Two months before the meeting, construction started at McNary.

The chief of fisheries for the Oregon Fish Commission foretold the future in Walla Walla. "The plans of the dam builders, if completed, will completely ruin for all time some of the richest fishery resources of this nation," Paul Needham said. What particularly alarmed Needham and other biologists were plans to dam the lower Snake. "The finishing touch will be the four-dam plan now being recommended by the Army Engineer Corps for construction on the Snake River to provide slack-water navigation to Lewiston, Idaho. All western biologists with whom I have talked agree that this plan, if followed, will spell the doom of the salmon and steelhead migrations up the Snake. . . ."

The power side, in response, argued that fish passage worked fine. The federal agencies that were building dams, as well as barging companies, the Northwest Development Association, and all the leading Northwest utilities, ignored early research showing that migrating juvenile salmon were dying in turbines. Nearly every member of Congress from the Northwest sent a letter to the meeting, urging that the dams be built as fast as possible—to meet growing power demands and open up slackwater navigation. Choosing to believe what was economically expedient over what was biologically ruinous, the lawmakers invoked a soothing nostrum: "We can have fish and power too."

The Bureau of Reclamation, however, did not see a need to mince words. It had the courage, or perhaps the arrogance, to admit that fish and power do not mix.

"The Department [of the Interior] feels that the Columbia River

fisheries should not be allowed indefinitely to block the full development of the other resources of the river," said a Bureau press release
in advance of the Walla Walla meeting. "The overall benefits to the
Pacific Northwest from a thoroughgoing development of the Snake and
Columbia are such that *the present salmon run must, if necessary, be
sacrificed* [italics are mine]."

After the Walla Walla meeting, the proposed moratorium on new
dams was bumped upstairs to the Federal Interagency River Basins
Committee, which unanimously rejected it on the grounds that "facts
and evidence presently available do not substantiate the fear" that dams
will "result in major loss or extinction of fish life" in the Columbia and
Snake.

There is always reasonable doubt about who or what is to blame for
disappearing salmon.

"The science, unfortunately, has never been black or white. And
the gray has always been marketable, it has always been worth a lot of
money," said Bert Bowler, a fisheries biologist who works for the state
of Idaho. "The utilities spend a lot of time and money to exploit the
gray and push uncertainty. Politicians like the gray because it means
they don't have to make decisions that will raise voters' electricity bills."

DeHart put it more bluntly: "With salmon, you have a dead body
and nobody's fingerprints are on it."

Here is a memorandum written at Basic American Foods, a large
processor of potatoes in the Columbia Basin and a huge consumer
of electricity. The memo was sent to the management of the Grant
County Public Utility District, a utility that owns two dams on the mid-
Columbia and sells electricity at rates that have been advertised as the
cheapest in America. The salmon advice was listed in the memo under
"some ideas on attack strategies"*:

---

*The Grant County Public Utility District, as it turns out, did not need the advice. For at
least ten years before the memo was written, as it continued to use cheap power rates to lure
heavy industrial users of electricity to the Columbia Basin, the utility resisted installation of

Reinforce the cost avoidance policy for salmon reclamation and environmental expenditure. Require a mandate, test it by lawsuit, require *proof* of technical viability and negotiate a long-term implementation schedule prior to implementation [italics are mine].

Salmon themselves encourage corporate obfuscation and interest-group finger pointing. The life cycle of the fish makes controlled scientific experiments—and irrefutable proof of what is responsible for wiping them out—all but impossible. A salmon run, like a chain breaking at its weakest link, can collapse anywhere. From gravel to gravel, from hatching in a mountain stream to dying four or five years later in the same stream after spawning, an Idaho salmon must negotiate up to 1,800 miles of slackwater and figure out how to get around sixteen dams. The fish also has to survive up to four years and more than 4,000 miles of travel in the ocean. Salmon are perhaps the most complex creature ever addressed by the Endangered Species Act.

"People have not awakened to the difficulties of saving these fish," said Bill Bakke, head of a Portland-based environmental group that helped force the federal government to put Idaho salmon on the endangered species list. "We don't have a rational scientific program for salmon. All we have is a lot of enviros and business interests fighting each other."

Dams are clearly not the only problem. Salmon runs on Northwest rivers with no dams are often in as poor shape as runs in the Columbia and Snake. Sorting out the decline of salmon inevitably leads to a recitation of the four H's: habitat, hatcheries, hydropower, and harvest. The relative sin committed by each H is inversely proportional to how much money you happen to make off the H in question.

Logging and farming have ravaged the gravel streambeds that are both birthplace for young salmon and grave for spawned-out adults. To reproduce before they die, salmon must find clean, permeable

salmon bypass screens at its dams on the Columbia. After a decade of delay, the utility was finally ordered by a federal judge to build and install the screens.

gravel beds in their home stream. They dig nests (redds), deposit eggs, fertilize them, and then cover the redds with gravel. If sediment from nearby logging or farming covers the gravel, survival of eggs in the redds drops precipitously.

Hatchlings must quickly find pools of clean water where they can hide, safely protected from fast water that might flush them downstream too soon. Spreading out in the stream, tiny salmon become territorial, staking out a patch of quiet water near swifter currents that deliver drifting food. The young fish need shade to survive hot summer temperatures. They also need fallen trees, boulders, and other large debris that divide streams into secluded spaces where fish can rest and grow and not be seen by predators. As they begin to migrate toward the sea (a journey that can begin anywhere from a few days to four years after emerging from gravel nests), juveniles tend to travel in groups close to the edges of a stream or river, weaving through rocks and fallen timber.

Logging and farming can ruin all this, stripping streams of their complexity, turning them into erosion troughs without food, shade, or hiding places. By the 1990s, the Grand Ronde River was an example of all that could go wrong. Windblown dirt from wheat fields buried gravel beds. Diking of the river, removal of streamside trees, and draining of adjacent wetlands had transformed much of the Grand Ronde into a murky irrigation ditch. Below the few spawning grounds that remained in the upper river, streamside cattle grazing, road construction, and loss of shade created thermal kill zones where summer water temperatures often reached a lethal 82 degrees Fahrenheit.

The plight of the Grand Ronde was similar to that of many rivers in the Columbia Basin. But damaged riverbanks can be nursed back to health. Since the 1990s, costly efforts have been made across the Columbia Basin to do exactly that. The Grande Ronde has been singled out for triage. More that $20 million has been spent to stabilize stream banks, keep cattle away from the river, and plant trees to provide cooling shade to juvenile salmon. So far, though, the benefits of habitat restoration for endangered wild salmon have been under-

240 whelming. Wild salmon runs in the Grande Ronde and many other rivers upstream from dams in the Columbia and Snake remain at high risk of extinction.

A popular treatment for proliferating dams and sick habitats is the salmon hatchery. It has been prescribed since Grand Coulee Dam blocked off the upper Columbia and the dosage grew larger with each passing decade. About 150 million hatchery salmon and steelhead a year are pumped per year into the Columbia and Snake Rivers above Bonneville Dam. A half century ago, nine out of ten of migrating juvenile salmon in the Columbia were wild. Now, more than nine of ten are born in hatcheries.

While hatchery fish have helped prevent a total collapse of the sport, commercial, and Indian catch in the river, they tend to create as many problems as they solve. For starters, about 99 percent of hatchery smolts carry an infectious kidney disease that some fish biologists speculate may drastically reduce their chances of coming back from the sea. The kidney ailment has infected wild salmon, with which migrating hatchery fish share streams and rivers. Cramped conditions on barges and trucks that the Corps of Engineers uses to transport salmon around dams are also responsible.

More important, the genes of hatchery fish are suspect. The federal government's rush to make up for salmon losses encouraged fish agencies to ignore or fudge the distinct genetic traits that salmon adapted to survive in specific streams. Hatchery managers interbred salmon without regard for geographic origin. They selected for fish that would grow fat and hearty in the concrete confines of the hatchery. For decades, managers measured their success and won promotion on the basis of how many baby fish they put in the river, while paying little attention to the percentage of adults that returned from the sea.

It turned out that hatchery fish were about ten times less likely than wild salmon to come home. To beat these odds, hatchery managers force-fed more and more concrete-cradled smolts into the river system. Tens of millions of hatchery fish were dumped into streams and rivers at the same time that dwindling numbers of wild juveniles were trying to migrate. Hatchery fish, as young migrants, were usually bigger and stronger than their scrawny wild cousins. At McNary Dam, while I was looking at the machines that remove fish from the river for transport on barges, I saw a half-swallowed wild chinook in the mouth of a much larger hatchery steelhead. A fish biologist at the dam told me it was a common sight.

When wild and hatchery fish do manage to return as adults to the same stream, they often interbreed. This degrades the genetic robustness of wild stocks and dramatically reduces the chance that their not-so-wild offspring will find their way home from the sea.

Once young salmon reach the ocean (where, depending on species, they stay for one to four years), questions about what may or may not be killing them become even more difficult. There is the El Niño effect, a periodic fluctuation in the prevailing winds around the Earth that raises the temperature of the coastal waters into which the Columbia River empties. The unhealthful warm water, along with mackerel and other predators that come north with it, reduces survival for young salmon. The unexpectedly severe decline of Pacific salmon in the 1990s is believed to have been caused, in part, by a lethal blend of El Niño with an unusual reduction in an ocean phenomenon called upwelling, which occurs when strong winds churn up the sea and bring up beneficial nutrients from the ocean floor. Ocean conditions sometimes do change in favor of salmon survival. Around 2004, scientists began to monitor an increase in upwelling in the Pacific and returns of adult salmon suddenly exploded. For some species, the number of salmon in the Columbia and Snake jumped to levels not seen since before the dams were built. Stunned by these numbers, fish scientists conceded there was still much about salmon survival rates that they did not understand.

The final major killer of salmon is harvest, which means fishing. Here there is more certainty in assessing blame. Salmon runs in the Columbia were decimated by a fishing free-for-all in the late nineteenth century. Commercial fishermen used fish wheels, nets, and traps to satisfy a hugely profitable canning industry. In 1883, the peak

242 year of river fishing, the commercial catch of just one salmon species, chinook, totaled forty-three million pounds. That was larger than the pre-settlement Indian catch for all salmon species.

"The helpless salmon's life is gripped between these two forces—the murderous greed of the fishermen and the white man's advancing civilization—and what hope is there for salmon in the end?" asked Dr. Livingston Stone of the U.S. Bureau of Fisheries in an 1892 rebuke to the fishing industry.

As concerns the greed of fishermen, hope has come in the form of fishing limits and shorter fishing seasons. The rules have steadily become more restrictive and more strictly enforced. Outright fishing bans on several endangered runs of salmon have been in place for decades.

But fishing regulation, too, is beset by the complexity of salmon behavior. It is illegal to catch the three Snake River species that have been declared endangered. But the fish do not segregate themselves for protection. They swim upstream in the Columbia along with their more numerous relatives who spawn in the Hanford Reach. Gillnetters (either commercial operators or Indian tribes) who go after the abundant Hanford Reach run are likely to catch fish that are on the brink of extinction.

Confusion about what exactly kills salmon has spawned a new salmon-related industry. Cynical fishermen call it biostitution. River users hire teams of marine biologists, ecologists, and natural-resource economists who spend months or even years gathering and analyzing data about the river. These experts—the biostitutes—produce lengthy, chart-ridden reports that invariably suit the financial interests of the river users who hired them.

The Oregon Forest Industries Council hired two eminent fisheries biologists to produce a 328-page tome that came to the not surprising conclusion that logging practices, while bad for fish "in the past," have improved a lot. The study said that loggers are less guilty than fishermen, dams, or farmers of killing salmon.

The Army Corps of Engineers paid for a study that found that dams do not kill all that many salmon. Pacific Northwest utilities paid for a study that maintained that transporting salmon is better than letting them swim.

The Northwest Power Act was to have blown a whistle on biostitution and stopped the finger pointing. After it was passed in 1980, Indian tribes and regional fish agencies were supposed to call the shots for remaking the river. Neither had been paralyzed by uncertainty. Having watched the steady disappearance of the fish for half a century, Indian tribes and fisheries biologists had always agreed that the principal cause was dams. They also agreed that salmon needed more water in the river. To reduce mortality for juvenile salmon in dams, the agencies and tribes jointly demanded installation of screens and bypass systems. They also wanted to spill more of the river and its fish over dams rather than feeding them through turbines.

When DeHart joined the river game at the Fish Passage Center, she believed that federal law empowered her to act as an agent for the tribes and agencies. She assumed that salmon would receive "equitable treatment."

Her assumption was wrong. For more than a decade, DeHart was an irritating but ineffectual presence at meetings that decided how the river would be operated. Decisions were made behind her back. Spill requests were denied or ignored.

DeHart's direct boss, the Northwest Power Planning Council, shied away from challenging the gentlemen from the power side. It demanded increased spill for salmon, but did not make a fuss when the power side said no. It ordered prompt construction of fish screens, but set no deadlines and tolerated long delays. Most important, the Council, which had been instructed by Congress to "heavily rely" on the opinion of fish agencies and Indian tribes, kept questioning, revising, and rejecting that advice. Again and again, the agencies and tribes asked for more water for fish. Each time the Council found reasons why water was too expensive and delivering it, too complicated.

"It breaks my heart. The Power Council could have worked," DeHart said. "In the end, it turned out to be just eight politicians appointed by

244 four politicians [the governors of Washington, Oregon, Montana, and Idaho]. They respond to special interests and short-term thinking. The tribes and the fish agencies lost out in the bars and restaurants of Portland as the utilities wined and dined."

Staff members working for the Council, who did not care to speak publicly, agreed. Under Council rules, it was easy for utilities to lobby for delay; they only needed to win over three Council members. Three votes could stop the eight-member body from making any decision.

"By God, yes, the utilities have had control of this apparatus," said Ted Hallock, himself a Council member from Oregon who retired in 1995. "We were an implicit captive or actual captive of the goddamn utilities."

A federal appeals court also agreed with DeHart. The U.S. Court of Appeals for the Ninth Circuit in San Francisco ruled in 1994 that the Power Council had, in effect, fallen into bed with utilities, aluminum companies, and other power interests. The court found that the Council had ignored both the letter and spirit of the Northwest Power Act.

The court concluded that Columbia River salmon and the people who depended on them had been betrayed for the sake of the status quo. The river game, the court found, had been rigged.*

By this time, Indian tribes and environmental groups had given up on the Northwest Power Act. Searching for a stronger weapon to protect salmon, they tried the Endangered Species Act, a sweeping law which, at least in theory, ignores all "nonbiological" factors in protecting endangered creatures.

A petition from the tribes and agencies forced the federal government to invoke the act in 1991 to protect Snake River salmon. To enforce this law, yet another federal agency entered the river game. The

---

*The appeals court wrote: "The Council's approach seems largely to have been from the premise that only small steps are possible, in light of entrenched river users' claims of economic hardship. [Claims that the court found to be unsubstantiated.] Rather than asserting its role as a regional leader, the Council has assumed the role of a consensus builder, sometimes sacrificing the [Power] Act's fish and wildlife goals for what is, in essence, the lowest common denominator acceptable to power interests and [aluminum companies]."

National Marine Fisheries Service (later called the National Oceanic and Atmospheric Administration [NOAA] Fisheries Service) had the authority, if it chose to use it, to demand sweeping changes in river operations.

Genuine alarm erupted among river users. The last thing they wanted was for the salmon crisis to go the way of the spotted owl. For that bird, a federal judge, acting under authority of the Endangered Species Act, closed five and a half million acres of federal forests until the federal government could come up with a credible protection plan.* River users said the Northwest could not afford such interference. The salmon issue was "orders of magnitude more complicated than the owl," and should be kept in the hands of responsible local agencies that knew the river and the regional economy.

Seeking to head off draconian enforcement of the Endangered Species Act, river users began talking about regional cooperation to protect salmon. In language that sounded suspiciously like the rhetoric generated earlier when the Northwest Power Act was passed, there was talk of a new era in river management. Farmers, fishermen, utilities, bargers, and industrial users of electricity all stated they were "committed to a solution."

At first, signs of change were promising. The federal government ordered more water spilled through the hydrosystem. The Corps of Engineers rushed to put in more screens on federal dams. Before long, however, the gentlemen from the power side found that the federal fisheries agency, an arm of the Commerce Department, was not a ferocious advocate of costly change. In announcing its first plan for running the river, it did not demand major systemic changes in the operation of dams. Its biological opinion found that endangered Snake River salmon were not in jeopardy from routine workings of the hydrosystem.

---

*The spotted-owl issue is often caricatured as an example of environmental extremism. But the owl was a symptom of irreplaceable habitat destroyed by pollution and development. Before a federal judge halted logging in federal forests in the Northwest, 90 percent of the spotted owl's old-growth habitat had already been destroyed.

The "no-jeopardy" ruling halted regional cooperation before it began. Environmental groups and Indian tribes immediately sued. And a federal judge in Portland intervened.

U.S. District Judge Malcolm Marsh said he was taking this "rare opportunity to tell all of these players" that the federal government was not standing up for salmon. The judge said, in effect, that DeHart was right: The power side was shuffling deck chairs on the *Titanic*.

". . . the situation literally cries out for a major overhaul," Marsh wrote. Federal agencies "have narrowly focused their attention on what the establishment is capable of handling with minimal disruption."

The "establishment" that no one wanted to upset was the Bonneville Power Administration, along with its attending court of utilities and aluminum companies.

Since the river game began in the 1930s, this federal agency has had a genius for getting its way. It was the BPA that hired Woody Guthrie to convince the American people that damming the Columbia was an act of national salvation. The BPA went on to receive credit for what John Gunther, in his 1946 book *Inside U.S.A.*, called "one of the most striking pieces of social legislation in the history of the United States."

The agency pioneered the "postage-stamp rate," which made electricity available across the Northwest at one low rate, whether the user lived beside a dam or on a farm five hundred miles away. The BPA forced down power rates charged by all private utilities in the region. It also made the Northwest a national leader in the percentage of farms with electricity.

Bonneville was so efficient at selling "power at cost" that for forty years, between 1940 and 1980, the inflation-adjusted cost of electricity in the Northwest went down. Amazingly, the price dropped nearly fourfold.* A large slice of the American aluminum industry came to

---

*The inflation-adjusted price fell from 2.74 cents a kilowatt-hour in 1940 to 0.65 cent in 1980.

the Northwest for cheap electricity. Bonneville became what its first director, J. D. Ross, called a "superpower" of electricity.

By the 1970s, Bonneville was so intoxicated with success that its vision began to blur. The head of the agency at the time, Don Hodel, who would later become secretary of energy under Ronald Reagan, gazed into the future and spotted what he thought was a dark cloud. He became convinced that severe electricity shortages were in store for the Northwest. To guarantee a future of unlimited electricity at a bargain price, Hodel demanded the construction of an armada of nuclear and coal-fired power plants.

The nuclear plants, five in all, were peddled to ratepayers in the Northwest as a rebirth of the New Deal. They would carry on the bold pioneer vision of the men who built Grand Coulee Dam. Without nuclear plants, Hodel warned, "homes will be cold and dark or factories will be closed or both. . . ."

In a celebrated speech that came back to haunt him, Hodel exhorted residents of the Northwest not to surrender their prosperity to weak-kneed, no-growth naysayers who preferred conservation to increased generating capacity.

"I call [them] the Prophets of Shortage. They are the anti-producers, the anti-achievers. The doctrine they preach is that of scarcity and self-denial. By halting the needed expansion of our power system, they can bring this region to its knees."

There were a number of eminent energy experts who said the Northwest did not need five nuclear plants. But Hodel, boldly pressing ahead, committed the BPA to six billion dollars in bond obligations to pay for three of the plants. He made the commitment before researchers from his own agency had conducted studies to see if they were really needed.

Just a year after the "Prophets of Shortage" speech, the draft of a BPA-commissioned study concluded that conservation was six times cheaper than new nuclear plants and could be carried out with "no significant changes in life style." Word of the study leaked to many of the small, publicly owned Northwest utilities that Hodel was rounding

248   up to guarantee bonds for his nuclear plants. Hodel kept the utilities on board by denouncing his own agency's study.

With Hodel leading the way, Bonneville and nearly one hundred public utility districts in the Northwest joined together in the Washington Public Power Supply System or WPPSS, which became infamous as WHOOPS. Together they walked off a cliff, taking electricity consumers from across the Pacific Northwest with them.

The result was the greatest municipal bond default of all time, a financial catastrophe that spawned sixty lawsuits, including the nation's largest security fraud case. By the time WHOOPS defaulted in 1983, the estimated price tag on the five nuclear plants (only one of which ever produced electricity) had ballooned to a staggering twenty-four billion dollars. Oregon congressman James Weaver called it "the greatest scandal in the history of the Northwest."

WHOOPS and the BPA became a regional laughing stock, synonyms for fiasco and incompetence. Back in Washington, D.C., Bonneville lost the protected status it had enjoyed since the New Deal. Ronald Reagan's budget director, David Stockman, condemned the agency's "preposterous mythology" that BPA was paying back its eight-billion-dollar dam-building debt to the U.S. Treasury in a timely manner.

"Nothing," Stockman said, "could be further from the truth." BPA had finessed a swindle, the budget director said, postponing all payment of principal on its debt to the last year of a fifty-year loan agreement. Stockman called it "the antithesis of sound business principles and loaded with hidden taxpayer subsidies."

Most damaging was the debt. Payments on one ailing and two stillborn nuclear power plants forced whopping increases in Northwest electricity rates. Rates went up sixfold in just five years (but still were about half the national average). About one-quarter of the average monthly electric bill across the Northwest went to pay for BPA's nuclear mistakes.

Higher rates meant that the BPA, for the first time in its existence, faced stiff competition. Before WHOOPS, the agency could sell electricity for a tenth of the price of private competitors. After WHOOPS most of that price advantage disappeared. Gas-fired turbines owned by private companies could generate a kilowatt-hour of electricity for about three cents—same as Bonneville. Bonneville's customers began defecting in the mid-1990s, turning to private suppliers of electricity.*

After WHOOPS, the river game had a new dynamic. Bonneville became a financial weakling at precisely the time that the Northwest Power Act was demanding that it shoulder the cost of saving salmon. Initially, Bonneville tried to escape its responsibilities, joining in a lawsuit that challenged the authority of the Power Council. However, a federal appeals court ruled that there was no reason why the Council could not give direction to a federal power agency.

With legal challenges blocked, Bonneville resorted to what it had always done when it came to salmon—it dissembled and delayed. It balked at providing salmon with the spill that fish agencies and tribes demanded, giving priority instead to energy sales and reservoir refill. When the BPA did spill water for salmon, it exaggerated the cost, even blaming salmon spills for costs that were caused by drought.

---

*Since WHOOPS. Congress has begun picking at BPA's budget, its padded payroll, and its cozy relationship with traditional clients, especially aluminum companies and irrigators.

Aluminum companies paid substantially less for electricity than other customers. The rationale for the discount was that they helped the hydrosystem by using power at night when demand is low. Also, their power supply could be cut in times of drought. But aluminum companies got special considerations that weren't remotely related to the workings of the hydrosystem. The price they paid Bonneville for electricity went up and down with the world price of aluminum. If things were bad for the industry, as they were after the collapse of the Soviet Union caused a glut of cheap aluminum on the world market, then Northwest plants did not have to pay so much for power.

What all this added up to, according to congressional reports, was a sweetheart deal. The cost of babying aluminum companies with special rates was just under $1 billion between 1986 and 1995. But the industry went bust anyhow. Unable to compete with higher technology and lower labor costs in other countries, nearly all of the aluminum smelters in the Northwest stopped operations by 2001.

Bonneville's discounts for irrigators also raised eyebrows at a time of rising electricity rates for household consumers. If farmers in federal irrigation schemes in the Northwest paid the same rate for power as other BPA customers, the power agency could increase its revenues by about $32 million a year. If farmers on non-federal irrigation schemes paid the going rate, that would raise another $27 million a year. If all irrigators left their water in the river, Bonneville would have between $150 and $300 million more electricity to sell.

At the very least, according to a congressional report called "BPA at a Crossroads," raising power rates for farmers would provide a powerful incentive for irrigators to conserve water. That would keep more water in the river for salmon and for power generation.

250   The old accounting biases of the engineered river remained. Salmon were a burdensome expense, irrigation a sacred duty. When Bonneville did spend money on salmon, it was sloppy. A federal audit found that it paid for hatchery construction, predator control, and poaching enforcement that were never done.

Bad faith on salmon recovery tarnished the BPA's image almost as much as WHOOPS. Public hearings on salmon and the power agency became sixties-style protest rallies. There were chants of "Hey, Hey, BPA, How Many Fish Did You Kill Today?" The Sierra Club called the agency the "Jeffrey Dahmer of the salmon world," a reference to the serial killer who himself was murdered in prison after killing and cannibalizing seventeen people.*

Weakened by WHOOPS and stung by public disapproval on the salmon issue, BPA was forced to acknowledge mistakes.

"Sure we are perceived as arrogant. We are aware we are not trusted by many people. We want to change that," Bonneville spokeswoman Dulcy Mahar said in the mid-1990s. "It is no longer the case that we are a power business and [protecting] fish got tacked onto it. We have got to let our employees know that we see [salmon] goals as so intertwined with generating electricity that you can't achieve one without the other. We are changing our culture."

But the power side did not change all that much. A decade after saying it was seeking public trust and shifting priorities toward salmon, the BPA tried to fire DeHart and dismantle the Fish Passage Center. The power side was sick of DeHart's data, which year after year documented how federal dams kept killing salmon.

*The Bonneville Power Administration was not the only power agency to fall from grace. The Army Corps of Engineers, long worshipped in Northwest newspapers for its dam-building and job-creating prowess, was accused by Senator Mark Hatfield of Oregon of hiding "behind a bureaucratic curtain and pretend[ing] it has no responsibility to change the very operations that are killing these fish." Hatfield said that "this can-do agency is becoming a don't-know agency." When the Corps dedicated its state-of-the-art fish bypass center at McNary Dam, protesters showed up dressed as the Grim Reaper.

Senator Larry Craig, a Republican from Idaho, gave the BPA congressional cover for its effort to throw DeHart out of the river game. In Washington, D.C., Craig inserted unusual language into a 2005 committee report on a bill to fund federal spending on energy and water. BPA "may make no new obligations in support of the Fish Passage Center," it said. It also said the center should be closed and its responsibilities transferred to other agencies.

"Data cloaked in advocacy creates confusion," Craig thundered in a speech on the Senate floor. "False science leads to false choice."

Shortly after the speech, I talked to DeHart in Portland, asking her if she was mad at the senator from Idaho.

"I have never met the man," she said. "No one from his office ever contacted me. I guess I am flabbergasted. We are biologists and computer scientists, and what we do is just math. Math can't hurt you."

But salmon math had clearly riled up Craig, a long-time champion of utility companies in Idaho. In his 2002 election campaign, he received more money from electric utilities than from any other industry. The National Hydropower Association named him legislator of the year.

A few months before Craig's angry speech on the Senate floor, salmon math, as promulgated by DeHart, had been a decisive factor in a federal court decision that infuriated Craig, Northwest utilities, and the BPA. In Portland, Judge James A. Redden ordered that large amounts of water be spilled over federal dams to increase salmon survival. This meant less water to spin hydropower turbines. Less electricity for BPA and utilities to sell. And, perhaps, less campaign money for Craig.

"Idaho's water should not be flushed away on experimental policies based on cloudy, inexact assumption," Craig said in a news release.

The senator justified zeroing out the Fish Passage Center on the grounds that "many questions have arisen regarding the reliability of the technical data." He quoted from a report of an independent scientific advisory board that reviewed work done by the Fish Passage Center. When I contacted an author of that report, he said that Craig had neglected to mention that the board found the work of the center to be "of high technical quality."

252   "Craig was very selective in reflecting just the critical part of a quotation from the report," said Charles C. Coutant, a fishery ecologist who worked on Columbia salmon issues for sixteen years. "It did give a misleading impression. . . ."

In the Senate, Craig also said that "most" of the data collected by the Fish Passage Center duplicated work already done by other institutions and that shutting down the center would save money. This claim was false, according to fish and game agencies in Oregon, Washington, and Idaho; Indians with fishing rights on the Columbia; and the governors of Oregon and Washington. They all said that eliminating the Fish Passage Center was a bad idea that would reduce the quality and quantity of data on Columbia River salmon. The head of the Washington State Department of Fish and Wildlife wrote a letter saying that getting rid of the center would "actually increase salmon recovery costs, as the states and tribes will need additional staff to replace lost functions."

Still, the BPA embraced Craig's thinking. It attempted to dismantle the Fish Passage Center and put DeHart out of work, even though the Senate committee report language that zeroed out the center was not included in federal law. In 2006, BPA hired two private groups to do the work of the center.

DeHart's defenders sued in federal court, and in 2007 the U.S. Court of Appeals for the Ninth Circuit stopped BPA and Craig. It saved the Fish Passage Center and DeHart's job. The court ruled that BPA "acted contrary to law in concluding that the congressional committee report language carried the force of law." It said that BPA failed to "cogently explain" why it had ignored its obligations under the Northwest Power Act to fund the center. The San Francisco–based appeals court ordered BPA to halt its "arbitrary and capricious" behavior and to continue funding the center.

About nine months after the court ruling, Craig himself was thrown out of the river game. He reluctantly quit the Senate in disgrace after his Republican colleagues told him to go and after weeks of crude jokes on late-night television. Craig had been arrested in a Minneapolis airport men's room after an undercover officer monitored conduct by the senator that was "often used by persons communicating a desire to engage in sexual conduct." Craig, a vocal opponent of gay rights in Congress, pleaded guilty to disorderly conduct. He later insisted that he was not gay. He said he had done nothing wrong in the men's room when his foot touched that of an undercover officer in the next stall ("I have a wide stance when going to the bathroom"). He said he should not have pleaded guilty.

DeHart, meanwhile, continued to play the river game. Her agency's data tormented the gentlemen from the power side. Between 1998 and 2010, it showed that spilling water over dams did more to improve salmon survival than any other manipulation of the hydropower system.

"We knew that spill was going to be good for fish," DeHart told me when I last spoke with her in 2011. "We never knew it was going to be this good."

Fish scientists, Indian tribes, and, most importantly, the federal judge in charge of enforcing the Endangered Species Act came to rely on the center's numbers in making decisions about the future of the engineered river. The power side conceded that some spill helped fish, but insisted that it be limited.

DeHart expected the fight over spill to go on indefinitely.

"Water that does not go into turbines does not make electricity," she said. "It's about money."

Uncle Sam took up the challenge in the year of '33
For the farmers and the workers and for all humanity.
Now river you can ramble where the sun sets in the sea,
But while you're rambling river you can do some work for me.

—WOODY GUTHRIE
"Roll, Columbia, Roll"

MICHELE DEHART SHOULD spend more time out on the river. If she did, she might save more salmon. She would not make so many enemies. She would come to accept the inexorable sadness of concrete.

This opinion came from an Indian chief who wears his long black hair braided and tied at the end with green rubberbands. Rex Buck, Jr., led the Wanapums or river people, a tribe of about fifty men, women, and children who live in the rain-shadow desert of eastern Washington, encircled by the machinery of the river. They survived—and, in a curious sense, they prospered—by accepting the unacceptable.

To their immediate south, behind a razor-wire fence, lies the Hanford site. In 1942, the Manhattan Project ordered the Wanapums off this land where they had lived for thousands of years. They were forbidden to fish in the river as it flowed past the nuclear reservation.

To their immediate west, up over the lip of a five-hundred-foot-high basalt bluff, lies the U.S. Army's Yakima Firing Range. The army ordered the Wanapums off their hunting and root-gathering territory so that it could be periodically shelled and so that soldiers could play war games.

To their north, corporate orchards and resort communities with names like Desert Aire creep down the river valley. Each year, bulldozers come closer, pushing aside the sagebrush to make way for neat rows of irrigated apple trees and mobile-home parks with concrete boat ramps. The newcomers sustain themselves and their apples by extracting water from the river. Looters periodically raid Wanapum burial grounds.

And, finally, to their immediate east, spanning the Columbia River, sits Priest Rapids Dam. The dam is so close to the village that its electric whine is a given in the lives of the Indians, like the nagging wind in the river canyon. The dam was built on top of the Wanapum's sacred island, a burial ground and shrine where they had carved stones and painted pictographs of salmon. As compensation for the dam and the flood that came with it, the Wanapums were allowed to occupy forty acres next to the dam. They receive free electricity and free alcohol counseling.

The Wanapums prefer not to be visited by strangers. The entrance to their village is a one-lane concrete passageway on the spine of Priest Rapids Dam. The passageway is marked by a sign that says: WARNING—DANGER AREA—UNAUTHORIZED PERSONS KEEP OUT—NO PUBLIC THOROUGHFARE.

The route across the dam zigzags around fish ladders, bumps over rail tracks, and crosses under high-voltage lines. Upstream from the dam, the wind whips up whitecaps on the blue-green surface of the swollen, impounded river. Just downstream, an almost invisible web of stainless-steel filament—bird wire—dangles above the water that boils up out of the dam. The wire keeps seagulls from feasting on juvenile salmon stunned by passage through turbines. On the far side of the river, a rocky cliff jolts up, its face blemished by sagebrush and scree. The Indian village, wedged between the dam and the foot of the cliff, amounts to ten small houses, one long shed made of corrugated steel, and a scattering of pickup trucks and old cars.

I drove across the dam to meet with Buck. He lived in a small one-story house with a red-shingled roof and a basketball hoop in the driveway. His son answered the door. The boy said his father did

256   not want to talk to me in the house. He pointed to the shed of corru-gated steel, which was across a gravel yard. It had a shaded porch and a wooden bench. The boy told me to wait there.

Buck walked slowly across the yard and sat down beside me. He was a stocky, barrel-chested man. When he sat down, he tucked his braids behind his ears. They tailed across his chest and stomach to just below his navel. He wore new blue jeans, a red-and-blue checked sports shirt, a beaded Indian belt, and a very large Seiko watch. He seemed wary of me and avoided looking me in the eye.

It was his day off. Like nearly everyone in his tribe, he worked at the dam. He had started out as a "utility person" eighteen years earlier, while still attending community college in nearby Yakima. He had worked his way up to electrician foreman, the highest-ranking and best-paid job that any Wanapum holds at the dam. He works four ten-hour days a week, heading up a maintenance shift that takes care of pumps and motors and installs new equipment. In the village, he was the leader of all religious ceremonies and the one designated to talk to strangers.

I asked Buck if, considering his radioactive, shell-shocked, and hydro-electrified neighborhood, it was fair to describe this place as the most peculiar Indian settlement in the American West. He smiled, shook his head as if in disgust, and asked me to consider the alternative to living here.

"If we had lost this, we wouldn't have anything. We would be like everybody else in America. The dam and the firing range and Hanford came here. Sure, we didn't want them. But we could do nothing about it. Sure, we would prefer not to have these terrible things as neighbors. But we had to try to make it work.

"We often hear the rounds of artillery in the evenings. It is kind of like the dam. We got used to the humming from the dam. We got used to the artillery.

"Are you going to cry about things the rest of your life?"

To make it work, Buck had made deals with his pestilential neigh-bors. The Army agreed to silence its artillery, on special occasions, so the Wanapums can hunt and gather roots. Arrangements had also been

made—after years of Wanapum complaints that low-flying Army heli-
copters drown out drums during religious ceremonies—for a one-mile,
no-fly zone around their village. Buck had a special phone number to
call when an Army pilot violated tribal space.

Wanapum chiefs were not always willing to negotiate from a position of weakness. For the better part of a century, leaders of the tribe
taught the river people to expect a violent cataclysm that would wipe
out the white settlers whom they called *Upsuch*, the greedy ones.

Buck's great-great uncle, Smohola, told Wanapums to stay away
from white ranchers and farmers who took land beside the river. He
told them to wear long braids, eat only the old Indian foods, and seek
truths in lonely places. Smohola was the founder of the Dreamer religion, which in the late 1800s attracted a considerable following among
dispossessed Indians in the Pacific Northwest. Be patient, Smohola
taught, a miraculous punishment of the greedy ones would soon
come.

The Wanapums did as Smohola instructed, with debilitating consequences. They chose not to be a party to any agreement with the United
States government. They disavowed a treaty that the Yakimas, a much
larger neighboring tribe, signed with the first governor of Washington
Territory. The Wanapums were left with no reservation and no legal
standing as an Indian nation. When Lewis and Clark encountered the
tribe in 1805 at the confluence of the Snake and Columbia, they were
estimated to number between two thousand and three thousand. By the
early 1950s, there were only eight full-blooded Wanapums left. They
lived near the river in a village of tule mat houses without running
water or electricity. They held no legal title to the land they occupied.
And the Grant County Public Utility District (the utility that serves my
hometown) wanted to build a dam that would flood the Indians out.

The coming dam forced Rex Buck's grandfather, Puck Hyah Toot,
the last priest of the Dreamer religion, to decide in 1953 that it was
time for the Wanapums to stop pretending that the greedy ones would
go away.

Ever since whites began taking the river, Puck Hyah Toot said,
"there was never a place we could really call home. . . . The cattlemen

258 let us live along the river awhile and then told us to move. The government came to build its big medicine plant at [Hanford] and again we had to move. The Army Firing Center closed in from where the sun sets. Then came the dam builders. Now there is no place left. . . ."

Puck Hyah Toot was the first Wanapum leader to sign a piece of paper that formally acknowledged the right of whites to occupy land along the river. In the document, the tribe promised not to challenge the federal license that allowed Grant County Public Utility District to build Priest Rapids Dam. In return, the Wanapums were guaranteed the right to occupy a small parcel of land that could never be taken away from them. The utility also agreed to build three private houses and a ceremonial long house for the tribe, as well as pay them twenty thousand dollars. Grant County PUD saw to it that the Wanapums would have licenses to fish in the Hanford Reach of the Columbia, just downstream from the dam.

The Wanapums made an irrevocable decision to cooperate with their former enemies. They chose to build a future for themselves based on what the Columbia River is, not what the Wanapums wished it would be. Buck told me that whites who played the river game today could learn from what the Wanapums did.

Do not try to resurrect a river that is gone, he said. Make a realistic bargain that preserves what can be saved of the Columbia and its salmon and its spirit. Make an agreement and abide by it honestly.

"Our relationship with the Grant County PUD is unique, one of a kind," Buck told me. "It is built on mutual trust. They have a dam. We have a place where we can teach our children. That is all that grandfather ever asked for.

"We can fish for ceremonial purposes and for our subsistence. We eat fish every day like our grandfather did. We smoke it, freeze it, can it, and dry it. We barbecue the fish. We boil up the heads. Boy, that is good, the heads. We boil the eggs, we like the eggs. I eat salmon every day. I always got to have salmon. I don't know what I would do without it."

Buck pointed up at the barren rocks on the cliff above the village.

"You look around and you don't see anything. Do you? This place is our sacred and holy place that outside eyes cannot see. We look around and we feel our past, we draw from everything that is around here. We understand that we can't live like we did two or three generations ago. We also understand that this land is important. The Wanapums are here. Our prayers are being answered."

The engineered West, Buck acknowledged, was an exceedingly strange land. He and his people had all the salmon they needed because vast ponds of radioactive goo kept fish-killing civilizers away from fishing sites on the Hanford Reach. The Wanapums had jobs and housing and alcohol counseling and free electricity because of a concrete structure that flooded their sacred island. They could hunt and gather roots, if they called ahead and asked the Army to postpone artillery practice.

Sharp disagreements, of course, remained between the Wanapums and white people. Buck resented researchers who came to ask questions about his tribe's religion, particularly about the "vision quests" that young boys make to the hills above the river. He did not want researchers to know what the boys do up there, how long they go without food, or what they imagine among the rocks.

"If we turn this over to the colleges or somebody else, it would not be right. It is really sad when children don't go to their elders, but to the professors for their own culture. This knowledge doesn't belong in Seattle or Boston."

And the tribe was implacably opposed to the wind turbines strung out along the ridges of the river valley.

"It is sad that now they want to trap the wind. It is easy to do, I guess, but they don't know what the effect will be. It is like the nuclear and the dams. The wind has got his own spirit. He knows how things were set up. Now that they want to capture him, I don't know what is going to happen."

In the matter of windmills, I told Buck that the Wanapums, oddly enough, had allies in nearby Richland. The atomic town had organized to stop a plan to generate electricity with windmills constructed on

260   Rattlesnake Mountain, the basalt summit on the nuclear reservation. Richland's campaign, "Save Our Rattlesnake Heritage," had succeeded. Hanford's nuclear waste was not surmounted by wind turbines.

Buck had not heard about this, but he nodded approvingly. He said that Rattlesnake Mountain was a sacred Wanapum religious site and the tribe wanted it back.

When we finished talking, Buck walked back to his house and I headed for my car. I was trying to remember, as I walked, what name the Wanapums have given to this village squeezed between Hanford, the firing range, and the dam.

"Mr. Buck, what do you call this place?" I shouted across the gravel yard.

"Home," Buck said, above the whine of the dam. "I call it home."

1: Slackwater

Page

29 "something . . . thrilling about a river": Wallace Stegner, *Beyond the Hundredth Meridian* (New York: Penguin Books, 1992), p. 47.

31 "eight lumps of concrete": Associated Press, November 19, 1993. In *Tri-City Herald*, Kennewick, Wash., p. A11.

32 With dams, it could be as long as two weeks: These travel-time estimates come from Jim Lazar, "Resource Evaluation for Improved Fish Migration," a paper prepared for the Pacific States Marine Fisheries Commission, January 31, 1991.

33 all the salmon were dead: James Baker, of the Sierra Club's Northwest Salmon Campaign. Quoted by the Associated Press, August 11, 1993.

37 10 percent of the nation's entire public-works budget: Carlos A. Schwantes, *The Pacific Northwest: An Interpretive History* (Lincoln: University of Nebraska Press, 1989), p. 344.

41 That moist air . . . races downhill: This is based on an interview with Ora Gifford, director of the National Weather Service's station on the Hanford site, July 26, 1993.

42 "Board-heads" from around the world: Windsurfing statistics come from David Povey, "Columbia River Gorge Windsurf Economics, 1990 Season," University of Oregon, Community Planning Workshop, 1990.

44 "needless red tape": State senator Nat Washington of Ephrata, Washington, as quoted in the *Columbia Basin Daily Herald,* January 11, 1974, p. 1.

44 Before the treaty, the river spent most of its power in the summer: "Power System Coordination," Columbia River System Operation Review, Portland, Ore., U.S. Bureau of Reclamation, February 1993, p. 7.

45 and so did the newspaper: "Nuclear Power Park," *Columbia Basin Daily Herald*, January 11, 1974, p. 1.

45 burned in effigy: Schwantes, p. 373.

45 "We don't have to tolerate people in the government": Moses Lake farmer David Sparks as quoted in the *Columbia Basin Daily Herald*, January 30, 1974, p. 1.

46 "The rewards of acquiescence are so high": Donald Worster, *Rivers of Empire* (New York: Pantheon, 1985), p. 330.

2: Better Off Underwater

51 Truckers routinely blew out their brakes: Margaret Day Allen, *Lewiston Country. An Armchair History* (Lewiston, Idaho: Nez Perce County Historical Society, 1990), p. 217.

54 less than a quarter of the system's annual operating . . . costs: This comes from an August 31, 1993, speech to the American Fisheries Society annual meeting in Portland, Oregon, by Ken L. Cassavant, a transportation economist from Washington State University who later became a member of the Northwest Power Planning Council, a federal agency that monitors the Columbia River.

61 "not a cozy river": Stewart H. Holbrook, *The Columbia* (New York: Rinehart and Co., 1956), p. 7.

3: Machine River

65 "And it is a damn fine machine": Al Wright, executive director, Pacific Northwest Utilities Conference Committee, interview with author in Portland, Oregon, September 1, 1994.

67 "most uncomfortable, abominable places": Lieutenant Thomas W. Symons, "Report of an Examination of the Upper Columbia River" (Washington, D.C.: U.S. government, 1882).

67 "even more thorny and troublesome than any we have yet seen": *The History of the Lewis & Clark Expedition*, edited by Elliot Coues (New York: Dover Publications), Vol. 2, p. 637.

67 river Indians usually acting as middlemen: From interview with Barb Kubic, a Kennewick, Washington, historian who worked for the Washington State Parks Department at Sacajawea Park, the point of land at the confluence of the Snake and Columbia, May 20, 1994.

67 reduced the Indian population on the coast by half: Eugene S. Hunn, *Nchi'i-Wana "The Big River": Mid-Columbia Indians and Their Land* (Seattle: University of Washington Press, 1990), p. 27.

68 "a history of the ravages of disease": Hunn, p. 32.

68 "and our joy at finding ourselves surrounded by our children": Coues, p. 636.

70 a stupefying 2.3 pounds of fish per day per person: Discussion of various estimates of Indian salmon catch in Charles F. Wilkinson, *Crossing the Next Meridian* (Washington, D.C.: Island Press, 1992), p. 185.

71 The energy released by the largest of the floods: The account of the catastrophic floods is based on John Eliot Allen, *The Magnificent Gateway* (Forest Grove, Ore.: Timber Press, 1984), and John Eliot Allen, Marjorie Burns, and Samuel C. Sargent, *Cataclysms on the Columbia* (Portland, Ore.: Timber Press, 1986).

73 "agitated gut": *The Journals of Lewis and Clark*, edited by Bernard DeVoto (Boston: Houghton Mifflin, 1953), p. 264.

77 three-quarters of the Columbia's annual flow raced to the Pacific in the warmest and driest half of the year: "Power System Coordination," Columbia River System Operation Review (Portland, Ore.: U.S. Bureau of Reclamation, February 1993), p. 7.

77 the river's power potential would have been spent in just three balmy months: "The Columbia River System: The Inside Story," Columbia River System Operation Review (Portland, Ore.: U.S. Bureau of Reclamation, September 1991), p. 4.

4: The Biggest Thing on Earth

85 "we got a dead man over here": Interview with Mary Oaks, retired phone operator, in her home in Coulee Dam, Washington, April 12, 1993.

86 "everyone found with disease": Dr. George Sparling quoted in Wenatchee *Daily World*, September 16, 1936, p. 7. This quote and some of the details in this paragraph are found in Paul C. Pitzer, "Grand Coulee—The Dam," unpublished manuscript, 1992. Portland, Oregon, p. 296.

86 laced their drinks with knockout drops: Hu Blonk, *Behind the Byline Hu: A Feisty Newsman's Memoirs* (Wenatchee, Wash.: Hu Blonk, 1992), p. 76.

86 "I got canned because I was drunk": Ibid., p. 141.

86 "the biggest thing on earth": Richard L. Neuberger, "The Biggest Thing on Earth," *Harper's Magazine,* February 1937, p. 247.

88 "socialistic, impractical dam-foolishness": Murray Morgan, *The Dam* (New York: Viking, 1954), p. 28.

88 "a grandiose project of no more usefulness than the pyramids": Ibid., p. 29.

89 "Superlatives do not count for anything": This quote and many of the statistics and facts in the above paragraph are found in Pitzer, pp. 225–34.

89 "Roll On Columbia, Roll On": Rights to the songs are held by Ludlow Music, New York.

264 *Page*

90 "one of the best investments Uncle Sam has ever made": Frank J. Taylor. "The White Elephant Comes into Its Own," *Saturday Evening Post*, June 5, 1943, p. 27.

90 nearly 750 big ships: Gene Tolletson, *BPA & the Struggle for Power at Cost* (Portland, Ore.: Bonneville Power Administration, 1987), p. 218.

91 "It's going to be a working pyramid": Morgan, p. xviii.

93 "'bowels open and your mouth shut'": L. Vaughn Downs, *The Mightiest of Them All: Memories of Grand Coulee Dam* (Fairfield, Wash.: Ye Galleon Press, 1986), p. 39.

98 "not the preservation but the remaking": Wallace Stegner, *Where the Bluebird Sings to the Lemonade Springs* (New York: Penguin, 1992), pp. 85, 88, and discussion on pp. 80–98.

98 "of unending economic growth": Donald Worster, *Rivers of Empire* (New York: Oxford University Press, 1985), p. 57.

98 "ultimate power over nature": Ibid., p. 52.

101 "did not kill off the salmon resource in the river": Downs, p. 98.

102 "some grand old ruined roofless hall": Quoted in *Cataclysms on the Columbia*, p. 114.

102 "It is the wonder of Oregon": Alexander Ross, *Fur Hunters of the Far West* (Norman: University of Oklahoma Press, 1956), pp. 31–32.

105 "No one, however, had the courage to go out and say very much about the idea": W. Gale Matthews, from a typed manuscript written in 1952, reprinted by *Reclamation Era*, April 1983.

105 "the most unique, the most interesting, and the most remarkable": Rufus Woods, *Wenatchee World*, June 7 and December 16, 1920.

106 "he is mentally unbalanced and headed for the insane asylum": *Wenatchee World*, December 17, 1934.

106 "to get the government to do it" and "at the same time protect the interest of the locality": Quoted in Robert Ficken, *Rufus Woods, the Columbia River, and the Building of Modern Washington* (Pullman: Washington State University Press, 1995).

106 Woods never got over the loss of local control: This observation owes much to the generosity of historian Robert Ficken, who allowed me to read the manuscript of his excellent authorized biography of Rufus Woods.

106 "treated as though it was a scrub": Ficken.

107 "Every drop of water that runs to the sea": Ibid.

Page
114 "Power becomes faceless and impersonal . . . so much so that many are unaware it exists": Donald Worster, *Rivers of Empire* (New York: Pantheon, 1985), p. 52.

115 "a ruthless disregard for Indians as human beings": Verne Ray, speaking in *The Price We Paid,* a 1979 film made by the Colville tribe.

115 "drowned the culture it had nourished": Verne F. Ray, "Ethnic Impact of the Events Incident to Federal Power Development on the Colville and Spokane Indian Reservations," consulting report prepared for the Colville Reservation and Spokane tribe, Port Townsend, Washington, 1977.

115 "as the water lapped at our heels": Donald Collier, Alfred E. Hudson, and Arlo Ford, *Archeology of the Upper Columbia Region* (Seattle: University of Washington Press, 1942), p. 12.

118 "as completely as possible away from home and family life": Institute for Government Research, *The Problem of Indian Administration* (Baltimore: Johns Hopkins Press, 1928), p. 403.

118 "a violation of labor laws in most states": Ibid., pp. 375–76.

123 "This dam comes in here and we are wiped out": Pete Lemry in *Congressional Committee Hearings Index,* Part III, 69th Congress–73rd Congress, December 1925–1934, p. 17113.

123 "careful and prompt attention so as to avoid any unnecessary delay": Harold Ickes signed his approval on December 22, 1933, to a letter containing this language that was sent to Bureau of Reclamation officials responsible for building Grand Coulee Dam. The letter is in the files of Harry Sachse, a Washington, D.C., attorney who represents the Colville Indians.

6: Ditches from Heaven

128 About four thousand landowners in the Columbia Basin Project use about a third as much water: The estimate of the number of farmers in the Columbia Basin Project is from Jim Cole, project director for the Bureau of Reclamation. The average amount of water delivered to urban customers in California is 8.8 million acre-feet, according to the California Department of Water Resources.

128 blessed with at least $2.1 million in federal infrastructure subsidies: Bureau of Reclamation letter to the Subcommittee on Water and Power Resources of the Committee on Interior and Insular Affairs. February 23, 1988, p. 3.

128 More than nine of every ten dollars . . . came from federal taxpayers or electricity consumers: Unpublished National Resources Defense Council paper on Columbia Basin Project, November 11, 1986, p. 2. Also author interview with Jim Cole, Bureau of Reclamation director for the Columbia Basin Project.

129 The more water they sucked out of the river, the more profits they had.: This is supported by "Taking from the Taxpayer: Public Subsidies for Natural

Resource Development," majority staff report, Subcommittee on Oversight and Investigations, House Committee on Natural Resources, August 1994, p. 73.

130 "reap harvest from the desert": Michael W. Strauss, commissioner of the Bureau of Reclamation, as quoted in Murray Morgan, *The Dam* (New York: Viking, 1954), p. 61.

130 "a happier and more secure life on the land": Quoted in Marc Reisner, *Cadillac Desert* (New York: Viking), 1986, p. 154.

136 "prevent monopoly and concentration of ownership": Quoted in Richard W. Wahl, *Markets for Federal Water* (Washington, D.C.: Resources for the Future, 1989), p. 22.

136 the tightest land ownership regulations in the history of federal reclamation: Paul Pitzer, "Visions, Plans, and Realities: A History of the Columbia Basin Project," Ph.D. dissertation, University of Oregon, June 1990, p. 67.

139 The highest percentage subsidy: This section relies on a remarkably thorough analysis by Wahl in *Markets for Federal Water,* pp. 28–46.

140 "so long as someone else is paying the bill": Pitzer, "Visions, Plans, and Realities," p. 323.

142 from 18 to 12 percent: Mark Svendsen and Douglas Vermillion, "Irrigation Management Transfer in the Columbia River Basin Project, USA," paper for the International Food Policy Research Institute, October 20, 1993, p. 32.

143 the amount of water the Project diverted from the Columbia River increased substantially: Rick Gove and William Bean, "Water Conservation of Instream Recapture on the Bureau of Reclamation's Columbia Basin Project," paper submitted to the Subcommittee on Oversight and Investigations of the House Committee on Natural Resources, July 19, 1994, p. 8.

143 "quite rational for [farmers] to increase their water orders": Svendsen and Vermillion, p. 65.

144 Gross returns to Project irrigators rose steadily for thirty years. Farm profits also seemed to rise: Ibid., p. 66.

144 reduce by one-third the price per acre they paid for water from the Columbia: Ibid.

7: A Noble Way to Use a River

145 98 percent of its costs were paid by taxpayers who lived somewhere else: Walter R. Butcher, "Distribution of Impacts from the Second Half of the Columbia Basin Project," paper presented by the Washington State University agriculture economist to the Washington State legislature, September 24, 1984, p. 7.

148 "It's hard for me to understand how the work that went into this Project": Representative Curt Smith quoted in *Columbia Basin Daily Herald*, Moses Lake, Washington, March 8, 1984, p. 1.

150 Project's annual cost to Washington State exceeded its direct benefits by sixty-three million dollars: Eric Ernest Elder, "Economic Impacts of Irrigation on Development in Washington," doctoral dissertation, 1985, as quoted in Paul Pitzer, "Visions, Plans, and Realities: A History of the Columbia Basin Project," Ph.D. dissertation, University of Oregon, June 1990, p. 318.

151 "Program benefits are shared in a very unequal fashion": Craig Lynn Infanger, "Income Distributional Consequences of Public Provided Irrigation: The Columbia Basin Project," unpublished doctoral dissertation, Washington State University, 1974, p. 133.

152 "water from the Columbia Basin Project was delivered to an estimated forty-two thousand to fifty-three thousand acres of ineligible lands": U.S. Department of the Interior, Office of Inspector General, "Audit Report: Irrigation of Ineligible Lands, Bureau of Reclamation," Report No. 94-I-930, July 1994, p. 8.

152 "the extremely low price" farmers pay for electricity encourages them to waste water: House Committee on Natural Resources, "BPA at a Crossroads," majority staff report, BPA Task Force, May 1994, pp. 20–21.

152 "Every drop of water added to the canals provides more profit": "Taking from the Taxpayer: Public Subsidies for Natural Resource Development," majority staff report, Subcommittee on Oversight and Investigations, House Committee on Natural Resources, August 1994, p. 73.

153 The multinational potato processors also failed . . . to shoulder the social costs: William Bean and David Runston, *Value Added and Subtracted: The Processed Potato Industry in the Mid-Columbia Basin* (Portland, Ore.: Columbia Basin Institute, 1993).

153 Bean's study said: Ibid., p. 94.

153 thumbing their noses: Rick Gove and William Bean, "Water Conservation of Instream Recapture on the Bureau of Reclamation's Columbia Basin Project," paper submitted to Subcommtee on Oversight and Investigations of the House Committee on Natural Resources, July 19, 1994, p. 9.

155 The schemes were found to represent an inefficient use: Bureau of Reclamation letter to the Subcommittee on Water and Power Resources of the Committee on Interior and Insular Affairs, February 23, 1988, p. 2.

155 inefficient use of land, water, capital, labor, and materials: Richard W. Wahl, *Markets for Federal Water* (Washington, D.C.: Resources for the Future, 1989), p. 45.

8: Wild and Scenic Atomic River

159 "an area with almost no people": Franklin T. Matthias quoted in S. L. Sanger, *Hanford and the Bomb* (Seattle: Living History Press, 1989), p. 7.

162 "fingers were burning with blue flames": This description and other descriptions of the effects of the Hiroshima and Nagasaki bombs come from Richard Rhodes, *The Making of the Atomic Bomb* (New York: Simon & Schuster, 1986), pp. 714–47.

165 Hanford documents show that biologists secretly discussed the "advisability of closing" a downstream stretch of the river to public fishing and hunting: This paragraph relies on Michele Stenehjem Gerber, *On the Home Front: The Cold War Legacy of the Hanford Nuclear Site* (Lincoln: University of Nebraska Press, 1992), pp. 113–30.

166 "the green stuff is just raining down from heaven": Bill Richards, "Nuclear Site Learns to Stop Worrying and Love the Boom," *Wall Street Journal,* August 28, 1992, p. 1.

169 Three-quarters of eastern Washington residents did not believe the government had been honest about Hanford's dangers: Survey results reported in Pat Moser, "Many Feeling Deceived about Hanford, Survey Results Show," *Tri-City Herald,* July 21, 1994, p. A12.

169 Asked if the government should pay compensation to downwinders affected by radiation from the plutonium factory, nearly 60 percent of respondents said no: "It's Your Call," *Tri-City Herald,* May 21, 1994, p. A3.

174 enough dirt to cover a football field to a depth of seven hundred feet: Doug Garr, "Too Hot to Handle," *Popular Science,* August 1992, p. 54.

174 "it's as though you had a party every night for forty-five years": Thomas Grumbly quoted in *Newsweek,* December 27, 1993, p. 18.

175 Swanson's TV dinners: Matthew L. Wald, "The Only Sure Thing Is Peril." *New York Times,* June 21, 1993, p. A1.

175 The original builders at Hanford had guessed it would take up to 180 years: Karen Dorn Steele, "Hanford: America's Nuclear Graveyard," *Bulletin of the Atomic Scientists,* October 1989, p. 19.

176 Rules prohibited the publication of statistics about how much ice cream was consumed on the site: "1942–1945: Wartime Construction Boom," *Tri-City Herald,* May 23, 1993, p. G3.

176 "If I could have caught that joker three days after I got here, I would have killed him": Ibid.

177 "There was nothing to do after work except fight": Leona Marshall Libby, *The Uranium People* (Washington, D.C.: Crane Russak, 1979), p. 167.

179 brawl-ending canisters of tear gas: Rhodes, p. 499.

179 The head of Hanford's dose reconstruction project has said that some eastern

Washington downwinders were exposed to twice as much radiation as civilians who lived downwind of atomic testing in Nevada: Keith Schnieder, "New View of Peril from A-Plant Emissions," *New York Times*, April 22, 1994, p. A21.

179 "a very serious health problem": Gerber, p. 208.

179 Alice Stewart . . . has found a correlation between cancer deaths and worker exposure to low levels of radiation at Hanford: Matthew L. Wald, "Pioneer in Radiation Sees Risk Even in Small Doses," *New York Times*, December 8, 1992, p. A1. Also Len Ackland, "Radiation Risks Revisited," *Technology Review*, February–March 1993, p. 56.

9: Born with No Hips

188 "I was born a year after my stillborn brother": Tom Bailie, "Growing Up as a Nuclear Guinea Pig," *New York Times*, July 22, 1990, p. E19.

191 "discharge standards . . . are at a rate so low that no damage to plants, animals or humans has resulted": Michele Stenehjam Gerber, *On the Home Front: The Cold War Legacy of the Hanford Nuclear Site* (Lincoln: University of Nebraska Press, 1992), p. 66.

192 Vegetation samples taken not far from Mesa . . . showed radiation counts as high as one thousand times the then-tolerable limit: Ibid., pp. 90–91.

192 "Nothing is to be gained by informing the public": Ibid., p. 100.

195 "I didn't expect this level of anger. We perhaps didn't handle this very well": Karen Dorn Steele, "Downwinders Lash Out," *Spokesman-Review*, May 12, 1994, p. A1.

10: Slackwater II

202 "essentially different civilizations": Joel Garreau, *The Nine Nations of North America* (Boston: Houghton Mifflin, 1981), p. 4.

202 "the most unpopulated . . . who-cares? region": Ibid., p. 302.

203 Technology surpassed timber as the leading source of jobs in Oregon: Timothy Egan, "Oregon, Foiling Forecasters, Thrives as it Protects Owls," *New York Times*, October 11, 1994, p. A1.

203 Washington State was first in the United States in per capita income derived from exports: Mike Fitzgerald, Washington State Department of Trade and Economic Development, quoted in "Local Firms Capitalize on Asian Trade," *Spokesman-Review*, November 14, 1993, p. A1.

203 books read per capita: Elaine S. Friedman, *The Facts of Life in Portland* (Portland: Portland Possibilities Inc., 1993), p. 104.

203   the residents of these cities had significantly lower fertility rates than people on the East Side: Chart in *Time,* January 30, 1995, p. 69.

203   "people had fled in order to be closer to nature": Jonathan Raban, "The Next Last Frontier," *Harper's,* August 1993, p. 33. Although Raban makes this point only about his hometown of Seattle, it is equally true of Portland.

213   "Drowning is a sensation": Elizabeth Woody, *Hand into Stone* (New York: Contact II Publications, 1993).

221   "We do not intend to play nursemaid to the fish!": This quote is found in Anthony Netboy, *The Columbia River Salmon and Steelhead Trout: Their Fight for Survival* (Seattle: University of Washington Press, 1980), p. 75.

221   "a lot of snide comments about salmon": Author interview with Milo Bell, October 27, 1994.

223   killed by dams and reborn as money: Donald Worster, *Rivers of Empire* (New York: Oxford University Press, 1985), p. 276.

11: The River Game

227   "You must never be greedy with [salmon], and you must see to it that no one else is greedy": Ella E. Clark, *Indian Legends of the Pacific Northwest* (Berkeley: University of California Press, 1953), p. 95.

231   "The whole climate has changed drastically" and "Utilities could no longer ride roughshod over the public interest": Both of these quotes are found in Ed Marston, ed., *High Country News, Western Water Made Simple* (Washington, D.C.: Island Press, 1987), p. 105.

232   a momentum toward extinction "that is most likely irreversible": Ibid.

232   only about 20 percent as abundant as they were historically: Wilderness Society, "Pacific Salmon and Federal Lands: A Regional Analysis" (Washington, D.C.: October 1993).

235   "The white people ask me what is the matter with the salmon?": Pete Lemry, letter submitted to the Senate Subcommittee of the Committee on Indian Affairs and to the Commissioner of Indian Affairs, following a hearing on the proposed Grand Coulee Dam in Nespelem, Washington, October 25, 1933.

235   "to attain full conservation of such fish": Quoted by Judge Thomas Tang, U.S. Court of Appeals for the Ninth Circuit, in opinion in *Northwest Resource Information Center v. Northwest Power Planning Council,* September 9, 1994, p. 10875.

236   "the doom of the salmon and steelhead migrations up the Snake. . . .": Paul Needham's article from the June 1947 *Oregon Business Review* is quoted in Anthony Netboy, *The Columbia River Salmon and Steelhead Trout: Their Fight for Survival* (Seattle: University of Washington Press, 1980), p. 83.

236 "We can have fish and power too": Netboy, p. 81. This section on the Walla Walla meeting is described thoroughly in Netboy.

237 *"the present salmon run must, if necessary, be sacrificed* [italics are mine]": Department of the Interior Information Service press release, Boise, Idaho, June 13, 1947.

237 "facts and evidence presently available do not substantiate the fear" that dams will "result in major loss or extinction of fish life" in the Columbia and Snake: Netboy, p. 82.

238 "Reinforce the cost avoidance policy for salmon reclamation": Memorandum from Basic American Foods to Grant County Public Utility District commissioners, October 5, 1994, p. 4.

240 99 percent of hatchery smolts carry an infectious kidney disease: This figure came from an interview at Lower Monumental Dam on the Snake River with Jim Congleton, a fish biologist with the Idaho Cooperative Fish and Wildlife Research Unit, May 1993.

240 managers measured their success and won promotion on the basis of how many baby fish they put in the river: This is according to an interview with Peter Bergman, a former salmon program director for the Washington State Department of Fisheries. Bergman was a member of the Salmon Recovery Team appointed by the National Marine Fisheries Service to come up with a rescue plan for endangered salmon in the Snake River.

242 "the murderous greed of the fishermen and the white man's advancing civilization": Quoted in Charles F. Wilkerson, *Crossing the Next Meridian* (Washington, D.C.: Island Press, 1992), p. 191.

242 logging practices, while bad for fish "in the past," have improved a lot: V. W. Kaczynski and J. F. Palmisano, *Oregon's Wild Salmon and Steelhead Trout* (Portland: Oregon Forest Industries Council, April 1993).

242 The Army Corps of Engineers paid for a study which found that dams do not kill all that many salmon: The results of the study are briefly summarized in John Stang, "Dams Aren't Only Danger to Salmon, Study Says," *Tri-City Herald*, April 30, 1993, p. A5.

243 transporting salmon is better than letting them swim: D. W. Chapman, "Is 1995 the Last Chance for Snake River Spring / Summer Chinook?" (Boise, Idaho: Don Chapman Consultants Inc., October 31, 1994), p. 8.

245 they were "committed to a solution": John D. Carr, executive director of an association of aluminum companies, quoted in Tom Kenworthy, "Sacrificing for Salmon," *Washington Post*, January 14, 1992, p. A1.

248 "the greatest scandal in the history of the Northwest": Representative James Weaver, quoted in Chip Brown, "Nuclear Frontiersmen Blazed Errant Trail in Northwest," *Washington Post*, December 3, 1984, p. A1.

Page

249 It balked at providing salmon with the spill that fish agencies and tribes demanded, giving priority instead to energy sales and reservoir refill: Michael C. Blum and Andy Simrin, "The Unraveling of the Parity Promise: Hydropower, Salmon, and Endangered Species in the Columbia Basin," *Environmental Law*, Northwestern School of Law, Lewis and Clark College, Portland, Vol. 21, 1991, p. 689.

249 even blaming salmon spills for costs that were caused by drought: "BPA at a Crossroads," majority staff report, House Committee on Natural Resources, BPA Task Force, May 1994, p. 37.

250 The old accounting biases of the engineered river remained: Congress found that the BPA counted salmon spills as a $300 million budget drain in 1993. It refused, however, to treat irrigation withdrawals as an annual expense. "BPA at a Crossroads," p. 37.

250 "Jeffrey Dahmer of the salmon world": Bill Arthur of the Sierra Club speaking at a Portland meeting of Columbia River power players. Quoted by the Associated Press in the *Tri-City Herald*, June 20, 1994, p. A5.

Epilogue

258 "Now there is no place left. . . .": Click Relander, *Drummers and Dreamers* (Seattle: Northwest Interpretive Association, 1986), p. 281.

Acknowledgments

I am grateful to the Alicia Patterson Foundation, which helped make this book possible by subsidizing my travels along the river. I also owe thanks to the *Washington Post* for granting me a longer leave of absence than I had solemnly promised I would need. My editor at Norton, Carol Houck Smith, worked very hard to clear cobwebs from my head and give this book shape. Mary Battiata, who among her many talents is an extraordinary reader, helped me put the book together.

A number of people at the Northwest Power Planning Council, especially John Harrison, gave generously of their time and expertise. At the Fish Passage Center in Portland, Michelle DeHart and Larry Basham spent many hours teaching me about salmon in a machine river. I also want to thank Tidewater Barge Lines for giving me a long ride on the river, as well as the pilots and deckhands who fed me and endured my questions, and who will endure what I have written about them. Jerry Erickson and his family in Richland, Washington, were invaluable in explaining what there is to love about a plutonium factory. Tom Bailie, on the downwind side of Hanford, showed me what there is to hate. Farmer Ted Osborne and his wife Barbara welcomed me into their kitchen, where they introduced me to the peculiar world of western irrigation. Norm Whittlesey of Washington State University explained how federal subsidies make that world possible. On the

274 Colville Indian Reservation, Vern Seward, Martin Louie Sr., and tribe historian Adeline Fredin helped me understand my neighbors.

Finally, I thank my family: my parents and my sisters, Debbie and Mary. They supported this project, never once showing impatience with my endless jabber about the river. My mother listened when she was ill and my father opened up his life for me to write about. More than ever, I am proud to be their son.

Index

Page numbers in *italics* refer to maps.

Adolph, Joe, 119

Agency for Toxic Substances and Disease Registry, 165

aggregate, 103–4

agribusiness, 72–73, 136*n*, 161

aluminum companies, 22, 26, 90, 220, 244, 246–47, 249*n*

American Agriculture Economics Association, 149

American Rivers, 49

American Society of Civil Engineers, 88

americium, 183

Andrus, Cecil, 31

apples, 127, 254, 255

Army Corps of Engineers, U.S.:
    autonomy of, 46
    cost estimates by, 32
    dams built by, 20, 21, 33, 77, 160*n*, 221, 235*n*, 236, 242, 245
    drawdown testing by, 32, 33
    Hanford barracks constructed by, 176
    Marmes site flooded by, 56
    river management by, 73, 74, 76, 106, 227, 230, 236, 250*n*
    salmon transported by, 79–81, 243

atomic bomb, 162–63

Atomic Cup, 75*n*

Atomic Energy Commission, 46, 179, 191

Atomic Harvest, 190

Bailie, Linda, 188

Bailie, Matt, 190

Bailie, Tom, *158*, 168, 187–88, 195, 196–97

Bakke, Bill, 238

bald eagles, 30, 157

Banks, Frank A., 102–3

Banks Lake, 103, 132

barge operators, barges, 29–43, 50–51, 54–57, 198–226
    author's journeys on, 23–24, 29–43, 50–51, 54–57, 109, 131, 197, 198–226
    cargo of, 31, 34, 54–57, 200, 206–7, 218
    collisions of, 41, 210
    cost effectiveness of, 31, 55
    deckhands of, 23, 29–31, 33–34, 35, 38–39, 40, 219
    drawdown opposed by, 32–33, 43, 52–53, 55, 80, 208, 209, 212, 226
    environmentalists vs., 30, 201–2, 220, 223–25, 226
    federal subsidies for, 225
    firms for, 22, 38, 40, 41–42, 50–51, 59, 63, 206, 213, 223–25
    garbage transported by, 206–7, 218
    locks navigated by, 30, 50–51
    Native Americans vs., 30, 60–61, 213–14
    oil spills and, 42, 43, 63, 212, 217
    pilots of, 23, 29–31, 39–43, 50–51, 54–57, 59–61, 200–202, 205
    romantic problems of, 30, 35, 40, 43, 210–11
    salmon preservation and, 23, 30, 31–33, 43, 58, 201, 207–8, 212, 220, 223–24, 226, 231

barge operators, barges (*continued*)
  slackwater for, 23, 35, 52, 53, 54, 73, 223, 226, 236
  tow of, 29, 34–35, 41–42, 54, 59, 61, 200, 214, 218–19
  tugboats for, 29, 35, 38, 39–40, 54, 57, 198, 218, 225
  winds and, 34, 40–42, 43, 58
  windsurfing and, 30, 42–43
basalt, 70–71, 101, 103, 209, 254
Basic American Foods, 237
bass, 37, 53
Beacon Rock, 222
Bean, Bill, 152–53
Bell, Milo, 104*n*, 221
Ben Franklin Dam, 160*n*
Betty Lou, 225
Beyond the Hundredth Meridian (Stegner), 29
Big Jack (bartender), 85
biostitutes, 242
birth defects, 164, 187–88, 191, 196
Blair, Matt, 74
Blank, Jeff, 219
Blue Bridge, 76
blue herons, 157, 212
Boardman, Ore., 205
Boeing, 90, 203
Bonneville Dam, *10,* 25, 79, 104, 235, 240
  locks of, 218, 219
  Native Americans displaced by, 123–24
  size of, 99
  in World War II, 90
Bonneville Power Administration (BPA), 125
  hydroelectric control by, 73, 75–76, 90, 94–95, 152
  river management by, 106, 226, 227, 229–50
  salmon preservation and, 249–50
  WHOOPS default and, 248–50
Bowler, Bert, 237
"BPA at the Crossroads," 249*n*
Brauer, Don, 173–83
Bretz, J. Harlen, 71*n*
B Street, 83–86, 92, 94, 97, 100, 101, 121
Buck, Rex, Jr., 254–60
Burbank, Wash., 73
Bureau of Land Management, U.S., 98
Bureau of Reclamation, U.S., 88
  annual report of (1937), 115

  autonomy of, 46
  budget of, 145
  canals maintained by, 38, 137, 139
  criticism of, 97–98, 99, 145
  engineers of, 98–107
  environmental impact statement by (1975), 116
  environmentalists vs., 99, 145
  hierarchy of, 98, 100
  irrigation supervised by, 110–12, 128, 141–43, 150–52
  public-relations efforts of, 87–90, 111–12, 129–31
  river management by, 98, 100, 106–7, 110, 123, 189, 227, 236
  slogan used by, 26
Burlington Northern Railroad, 198, 212
Bush, George W., 15, 16
Buske, Norm, 160–62

Caldwell, Glyn, 195, 196
cancer, 163*n*, 164, 179–80, 187, 193, 195
Cargill, 72–73
Carlson, Louis, 207
Cascade Mountains, 24, 36, 66, 67, 71, 210
cattle, 239
Cavanagh, Ralph, 150
Cayuses, 68, 233
Celilo Falls, 61, 213
cesium, 176, 181
Chelyabinsk-65 site, 169
Chernobyl nuclear plant, 171–72
Chevron Pipeline Company, 72
Chief Joseph Dam, *11,* 76, 124*n*, 125
Chung, Connie, 190
Clapp, Billy, 105, 134–35
Clark, William, 23, 65–70, 72–73, 82, 159, 210, 212, 257
Clinton, Bill, 48, 54, 159
cofferdams, 91
Cole, Jim, 128
Collier's, 88
Columbia Basin, 23, 24, 38, 44, 70, 112, 127–28, 141
Columbia Basin Development League, 107
Columbia Basin Institute, 153
Columbia Basin Irrigation Project, *11,* 14, 127–56
  construction of, 136, 142, 146–47

costs of, 136–37, 146–48, 154

criticism of, 145–50

drainage of, 127–28

dust in, 130

farmer-controlled districts of, 140, 154–55

farm failures in, 130–31, 138–39, 147, 188–89

farming in, 129–32, 134–40, 147, 150–53, 154–55, 188–89, 224

federal management of, 20, 22–23, 45, 128, 145, 147, 150–54, 234

federal study for, 135

land use in, 45, 97–98, 137

map of, 126

produce of, 127, 132, 134, 145, 148, 153, 154, 155–56

public-relations effort for, 129–31

repayment obligations for, 137, 138, 141–43

size of, 112, 145–50, 152

soil fertility of, 127, 135

as symbol of engineered West, 127

water conservation problems of, 23, 98, 112, 136n, 152, 153–54, 156, 234, 249n

water rights for, 133, 141–42, 154

Columbia Gorge, 42, 72, 200, 202, 209–14, 215, 223

Columbia Ice & Cold Storage, 20

Columbia Plateau, 70–71

Columbia Rediviva, 65

Columbia River:

    agro-industrial sprawl on, 72–73

    artificial branch of, 126, 127

    Big Bend of, 70

    coldness of, 38, 63, 77, 220n

    controlled flow of, 73–76, 80, 94–95, 113, 226, 228, 229–30, 245, 249–50

    coulees of, 71, 101–2

    current of, 31, 32, 63, 73

    drainage of, 25

    drawdown of, 32–33, 43, 58, 80, 166, 201, 208, 209, 212, 226

    drop of, 25, 70, 221

    economic potential of, 20, 21–22, 26, 85, 90–94, 96–97

    erosion barrier (riprap) for, 124

    federal control of, 251–53

    freezing of, 30

    landscape around, 66–67, 87, 88, 101–2

    Lewis and Clark's exploration of, 23, 64, 65–70, 72–73, 82, 159, 210, 212, 257

    as "machine," 13, 17, 20, 25, 29, 49, 65, 75, 76, 77, 80, 81–82, 109, 157, 224, 226

    management of, 22–25, 30, 32–33, 46–48, 77–79, 97, 100, 106–7, 111, 122–23, 189, 216–17, 226, 227–46, 249–52

    Mississippi River compared with, 25, 31, 58, 61, 70, 221

    as "most endangered river," 48–49

    as natural resource, 103, 229

    origins of, 70–72

    as pool, 23, 73–76

    power of, 25, 70–72, 97

    radioactivity in, 164–65, 175, 182

    rapids of, 31, 70, 72, 73, 200, 221

    redevelopment of, 22–23, 24, 30–31, 227–46

    return of salmon to, 125

    seasonal flow of, 44–45, 77, 80

    Short Narrows of, 72

    size of, 25

    Snake's confluence with, 23, 28, 35, 61, 63, 65, 66–67, 68, 71, 72–73, 198–201, 257

    strangeness of, 61–62, 66, 70

    surges in, 76

    temperature of, 164, 241

    water quality of, 48–49, 63, 128, 139, 216

    West symbolized by, 22–23, 27, 113, 127, 259

    wind on, 34, 40–43, 58, 62, 72

Columbia River Inter-Tribal Fish Commission, 231

Colville, Wash., 204

Colville Indian Reservation, 84, 108–25

Colville tribe, 84, 101, 104, 108–25, 235

"constant full pool," 73–74

Coon, Jim, 58, 233

Coutant, Charles C., 252

Crab Creek, 134

Craig, Larry, 251–53

crappies, 37

"criticality," 163n

Curly (crooner), 85

Dalles, 10, 213–14

Dalles Dam, 10, 213–14

Dam, The, 91
dams:
    construction of, 20, 21, 32, 33, 54, 77–78,
        160*n*, 220–21, 235–36, 235*n*, 242, 245
    fish bypass systems of, 51–52, 104, 124*n*,
        140, 220, 235, 237*n*–40*n*, 243, 245,
        255
    flooding by, 55–57, 62, 73, 108–25, 213
    hydroelectric power generated by, 14–15,
        32, 44, 73, 76, 78, 90, 94–95, 152
    irrigation provided by, 36, 88, 101,
        111–12, 114, 132, 135
    locks of, 30, 44, 45, 50–51, 54, 218
    nature conquered by, 25, 44
    as obstacles for salmon, 16, 32, 43,
        44–45, 48–49, 51, 77–81, 101, 104*n*,
        107, 112–13, 120, 122, 124, 197,
        208, 209, 220, 223, 229, 232–43,
        250*n*, 255
    proposed demolition of, 32–33
    slackwater from, 23, 35–36, 52–53, 54,
        73, 212, 223, 226, 236
    spilling of, 81, 94–96, 230, 245, 249
    turbines of, 32, 78, 94
    see also individual dams
DeFazio, Peter, 153–54
Defense Nuclear Facilities Safety Board, 166
Defiance, 39, 40, 54, 57, 198, 207, 218, 225
DeHart, Matt, 228
DeHart, Michele, 227–32, 237, 243–44, 246,
    250–53, 254
Deliverance, 168–69
Depression, Great, 19–20, 26, 27, 86, 87, 93,
    113, 134
DeVoto, Bernard, 22
dioxin, 48
Dittmer Control Center, 226
Downs, L. Vaughn, 99–104, 121
Downs, Margaret Savage, 99, 100
downwinders, 21, 164, 167, 168, 177–78, 179,
    188–97, 234
drainage wind, 41
Dreamer religion, 257
drought, 19, 20, 36, 112
"dual-purpose" nuclear plants, 171
Dunn, Deanna, 129
Dunn, Donald D., 129–30
Dunn, Sally Ann, 129
Dunn, Vernetta Jean, 129–30

DuPont, 176–77
dust storms, 134, 177

earthquakes, 71
East Columbia Basin Irrigation District,
    140, 155
East Low Canal, 132
Eisenhower, Dwight D., 47
EL-18 lateral canal, 132
electricity, *see* hydroelectric power
electricity, wind-generated, 41
El Niño effect, 241
Emmanuel Lutheran Church, 21
Empty Quarter, 202, 206, 218
Endangered Species Act, 32, 151, 238, 244,
    245, 253
Energy Department, U.S., 46, 160, 166, 174,
    186, 190, 194
environmentalists:
    barge operators vs., 30, 201–2, 220,
        223–25, 226
    Bureau of Reclamation vs., 99, 145
    dam removal supported by, 32–33
    drawdown supported by, 33, 226
    endangered species supported by, 24–25,
        33, 48–49, 81–82, 150, 151, 154,
        154*n*, 232–33, 238–39, 242, 244–45,
        250–53
    Hanford Atomic Works criticized by,
        167–69
    irrigation criticized by, 98, 133, 145, 146,
        153–54
    public relations of, 48
    river management and, 16, 22, 47, 227–
        32, 238–39, 243, 244, 246, 250–53,
        254
Erickson, Bernie, 49
Erickson, Dick, 155–56
Erickson, Jerry, *158,* 169–86, 196
Erickson, Peggy, 171
Erickson, Tim, 170, 183–85, 197
Evans, Dan, 148
"Expedited Response Action," 162
Exxon Valdez oil spill, 42

Farmer's Home Administration, 189
"Farm-in-a-Day," 129–31
farming, farms:
    failures of, 130–31, 138–39, 147, 188–89

family, 98, 135–36, 140
  income from, 137, 143–44
  irrigation, 129–31, 134–40, 147, 150,
    151–53, 154–55, 188–89, 224
  irrigation districts controlled by, 140, 155
  land for, 72, 98, 136
  rainfall and, 37
  salmon preservation vs., 234, 238–39
  self-reliance of, 21–23, 27, 45, 49, 53–54,
    55, 181
  tax burden of, 135
Farrow, Michael, 233–34
Fat Man bomb, 162–63
Faulkner, Dave, 40
Federal Bureau of Investigation (FBI), 163
Federal Interagency River Basin Committee,
    237
Federal Power Act, 122–23
fertilizers, 38, 146
fish:
  hatcheries for, 37–38, 81, 125, 240–41,
    250
  predator, 32, 78, 241
  "trash," 43n
  see also salmon
Fish and Wildlife Department, Washington
    State, 252
Fish and Wildlife Service, U.S., 98, 159, 235
Fish Passage Center, 230, 243, 250–52
fish-pounding stones, 56
Flatland tribe, 118
Foley, Thomas, 46, 142
Forbes, Larry, 176
Foster, Jodie, 221, 222
Four Winds Guest House, 111
Franklin D. Roosevelt Lake, 108
Frazier, Lynn Joseph, 123

Gable Mountain, 183
Garreau, Joel, 202–3
Garrison Rapids, 221
Gates, Bill, 203
General Electric, 216
George, Russell, 227
Gibson, Mel, 221
gill nets, 58, 60, 242
glaciers, 102, 105
Glen Canyon Dam, 91
global warming, 14

Government Accountability Office, U.S., 165
Grand Coulee, 101–2
Grand Coulee, Wash., 83–86, 95, 97, 100,
    110, 121
Grand Coulee Dam, *11,* 83, 86, 107, 235
  author's job at, 24, 95–97, 110
  concrete used in, 87, 88, 91, 92, 101, 105,
    111
  construction of, 13, 20, 25, 37, 82, 83–86,
    115, 120–22, 247
  criticism of, 88, 90
  design of, 98–107
  federal control of, 37, 38, 87, 95, 105–7,
    113, 123
  fish ladders lacked by, 104, 124n, 140,
    220
  flooding by, 108–25
  granite base of, 91, 101, 103
  as gravity dam, 91–92
  height of, 71
  hydroelectric potential of, 44, 87–88, 90,
    101, 106, 112, 113, 116, 120, 122,
    138, 139
  idea for, 105–7, 134
  irrigation provided by, 88, 112, 114, 132,
    135
  jobs provided by, 83, 91–94, 96–97, 167
  laser light show at, 111–12
  local control of, 105–7, 123
  local understanding of, 110, 113–14
  location of, 88, 101, 104–5
  Native Americans displaced by, 101, 104,
    108–25
  press coverage of, 88, 90, 105–6
  public-relations efforts for, 87–90
  public-works budget for, 37
  replica of, 88
  Roosevelt's visits to, 87–89
  safety problems of, 91–92, 96
  salmon preservation and, 104n, 107, 120,
    122, 124
  size of, 25, 71, 87–89, 91, 99, 107
  spillway of, 94–96, 111
  as symbol of engineered West, 113
  as symbol of Manifest Destiny, 86–87, 89
  "total use" ethic for, 103
  turbines of, 94
  worker housing for, 83–86
  in World War II, 90, 112n, 135

Grand Ronde River, 233, 239–40
Grant County, 135
Grant County Fair Grounds, 205
Grant County Public Utility District, 76, 237,
    257, 258
Gray, Robert, 65–66
Great Recession, 166
Green Run experiment, 191–92
Grover, Leslie R., 159n
Grumbly, Thomas, 174
Grunlose, Mattie, 108
Gunther, John, 246
Gustafson, Carl, 55, 56
Guthrie, Woody, 19, 89–90, 246, 254

Hallock, Ted, 244
Hanford Atomic Works, 11, 157–86
    atomic weapons research at, 46–47, 75n,
        90, 112n, 159, 162–64
    B Reactor at, 180
    cleanup of, 165–66, 172, 174–75, 180–85
    construction of, 20, 159–60, 176–77
    criticism of, 167–69
    downwind population and, 21, 164, 167,
        168, 169, 177–78, 179, 188–97, 234
    economic impact of, 167–69
    electrical demand of, 90, 106, 112
    engineers for, 160, 169–86
    environmental problems of, 21, 24,
        160–62, 164–70, 172, 204, 216, 234
    federal management of, 44–46, 167–69,
        234
    groundwater under, 112, 160n, 175–76,
        185
    Hanford Reach site of, 157–62, 166–67,
        258, 259
    K East Reactor at, 181–82
    landfills at, 174–75
    leakage from, 21, 160–62, 174–76,
        178–79, 180, 181–82
    "mulberry syndrome" of, 161–62, 177
    Native Americans displaced by, 254, 256,
        258
    N Reactor at, 160, 164, 169, 171–72, 178,
        181, 182–83, 184, 196
    N Springs at, 160–61, 162
    as part of engineered West, 166, 167
    plutonium finishing plant (PFP) of,
        183–84
    plutonium uranium extraction (PUREX)
        plant at, 178, 181–82, 183–84
    press coverage of, 166, 182, 184, 188, 190
    public-relations effort for, 112n, 157, 171
    radiation from, 21, 112, 164, 165, 167–
        81, 185–97, 234
    radioactive waste from, 21, 23, 160–62,
        164–66, 174, 185–86
    REDOX plant at, 192
    salmon preservation and, 165, 168
    security for, 172–73, 177, 183–84
    soil contamination at, 174–75
    stabilization run for, 167
    Tank 101–SY at, 185–86
    "200 Area" of, 178, 183
    waste tanks for, 177–78, 185–86
    wildlife at, 157, 160
    workers at, 167–69, 176–77, 179–82,
        185, 186
Hanford Downwinders Coalition, 190
Hanford Engineering Works, 160
Hanford Health Information Network, 193, 194
Hanford High School, 177
Hanford House Red Lion Inn, 167, 168
Hanford Patrol, 177
Hanford Reach, gillnetters in, 242
Hanford Reach National Monument, 159
Hanford Story, The, 157
Hanson, Frank "Tub," 148–49
Harden, Albert, 83, 85, 93
Harden, Alfred, 19, 93
Harden, Arno, 13, 19–20, 21, 24, 26, 27, 30,
        62–63, 82, 83, 85, 91–97, 100, 110,
        117, 122, 129, 140
Harden, Betty Thoe, 94, 129
Harden, James Arno, 44
Harden, Joe, 19–20
Harden, Mary, 129–30
Harding, Pat, 206, 211–14, 221–23
Hastings, Doc, 17
Hatfield, Mark, 250n
Hells Canyon Dam, 220–21
Heraclitus, 13, 17
herbicides, 125, 216
Herschel (sea lion group), 208
Hickey, Ray, 223–25, 226
Hill, James J., 212
Hill, Mary, 212
Hill, Sam, 212

Hiroshima bombing, 71, 162–63, 189, 191
Hitler, Adolf, 86, 90, 159, 205
Hodel, Don, 247–48
Hodgkin's disease, 195
Hood River, Ore., 42, 214, 217, 219
Hoover, Herbert, 107
Hoover Dam, 91–92, 99
House Committee on Natural Resources, 152
Howard, Barbara, 194–95
Hudson's Bay Company, 108
Hunn, Eugene S., 68
hydroelectric power:
    control of, 73, 76, 90, 94–95, 152, 234
    electric rates for, 106, 112, 116, 120, 122,
        230, 246, 248, 249*n*, 253, 255
    generation of, 14, 32, 44, 73, 76, 77, 80,
        81, 90, 94–95, 152
    potential for, 20, 22, 23, 25, 44, 77,
        87–88, 90, 101, 106, 112, 113, 116,
        120, 122, 138, 139
    power grid for, 76
    subsidies for, 49, 106, 113, 116, 128–29,
        143–44, 146, 147–48, 150, 152, 153,
        249*n*
hydrogen, 185
hydromechanics, 81
hydroplane racing, 65, 73–76
hypothyroidism, 193*n*

ice age, 71–72, 101–2, 209
Ice Harbor Dam, *11*, 61, 76
Ickes, Harold, 122–23
Idaho National Engineering Laboratory, 51
Idaho Territory, 52
individualism, 27, 47, 53, 54, 133, 181, 182
Infanger, Craig Lynn, 151
Inside USA (Gunther), 246
in-situ vitrification, 165, 174
Interior Department, U.S., 112*n*, 151, 236–37
International Food Policy Research Institute,
    143–44
iodine-131, 179, 188, 191, 193, 194, 195
Iron Triangle, 46–47
irrigation, 127–56
    canals for, 20, 24, 36–38, 53, 129–31,
        132, 137, 139, 189
    dams built for, 36, 88, 101, 112, 114, 132,
        135
    ditches for, 35, 36, 131, 137, 188

electrical subsidies for, 49, 116, 128–29,
    143–44, 146, 147–48, 150, 152, 153,
    249*n*
environmental impact of, 98, 133, 145,
    146, 154
farming with, 129–32, 134–40, 147,
    150–53, 155, 188–89, 224
lobbying for, 133, 145–50, 156
Native American rights and, 115–16,
    133, 136*n*, 140–41, 150
salmon and, 80, 133, 140, 146, 147, 150,
    151–52, 154, 196–97, 231
soil salinity and, 98
sprinkler systems for, 127, 133, 143
"theology" of, 132–33
water subsidies for, 23–27, 36, 116, 127,
    128–29, 133, 136, 141–44, 151–56,
    181, 234, 249*n*
water wasted by, 23, 98, 136*n*, 152, 153,
    155, 156, 234, 249*n*
wells for, 45
see also Columbia Basin Irrigation
    Project

Jackson, Henry M., 37, 45, 46, 141–42, 145,
    148
Jackson, Johnny, 61
Japan, 58, 162–63, 189
Japan Airlines, 131–32
Jefferson, Thomas, 65, 135
jibes, 215, 217
John Day Dam, 201, 212
John Day tribe, 67
Johnson, Lyndon B., 56

Kennedy, John F., 171
Kennewick, Wash., *11*, 72, 163, 166
Kerr, Andy, 47–48, 81–82
Kettle Falls, 115, 116, 119, 213
Klamath River, 16
Klickitat tribe, 61
Korth, Jeff, 114

Laborer's Union, 96
Lake Roosevelt, 94
landslides, 70, 72
Lemry, Pete, 123, 235
Lewis, Meriwether, 23, 65–70, 72–73, 82, 159,
    210, 257

Lewiston, Idaho, *11*, 26, 32, 44, 51–54, 236
Lewiston Hill Grade, 51
Libby, Leona Marshall, 163*n*, 177
Liddy, G. Gordon, 56–57
Limbaugh, Rush, 56, 154, 231
"liquid smoke," 215
Little Boy bomb, 162
logging industry, 45, 48, 238, 246*n*
"Lonesome Larry," 31–32
Longmeyer, James, 170
Los Angeles, Calif., population density of, 48
Louie, Baptist, 120
Louie, Martin, Sr., 108–10
Louisiana Purchase, 65
Lower Granite Dam, 50, 52
Lower Monumental Dam, 55
Lyon's Ferry bridge, 55

Mackenzie River, 25
Magnuson, Warren G., 37, 45, 46, 141–42,
     145, 148
Mahar, Dulcy, 250
Main Canal, 132
Majeski, Greg, 33–35, 40
malaria, 67
"managed oasis life," 46–47
Manhattan Project, 159, 162, 176, 180, 254
Manifest Destiny, 86–87, 89
Marie, Queen of Romania, 212
Marine Mammal Protection Act, 208, 209
Marmes site, 55–57
Marsh, Malcolm, 246
Martin, Irene, 232, 233
Martin, Kent, 232–33
Maryhill Castle, 212
Matthews, W. Gale, 105
Matthias, Franklin T., 159
Maverick, 221, 222
McClosky, Harold, 149–50
McDonald's, 127, 153
McDowell, Steve, 39–43, 50–51, 54–57,
     59–61, 198–202, 205–6
McGinn, Francis, 86
McMurray, F. Ron, 52–53
McNary Dam, *11*, 73–76, 77, 78, 80, 200, 236,
     241, 250*n*
McNary Pool, 73–76, 80
measles, 68
Mesa, Wash., 190, 191–92

Microsoft, 156, 203, 224
Mightiest of Them All, The (Downs), 101
Miss Budweiser, 74, 75, 76
missionaries, 68
Mississippi River, 25, 31, 58, 61, 70, 221
Mormon Church, 189
Morrow County, Ore., 206
Moses, Chief, 36–37
Moses Lake, 36–38
Moses Lake, Wash., *11*
     author's upbringing in, 21, 27, 38, 62–63,
          95–97, 109–10, 129, 202
     irrigation for, 20–21, 24, 36–38, 49, 53,
          129–31, 189
Moses Lake airfield, 132
Mount Hood, 214, 223
"mulberry syndrome," 161–62, 177
Multnomah Falls, 222

Nagasaki bombing, 112*n*, 163, 189, 191
National Forest Service, U.S., 98
National Hydropower Association, 251
National Marine Fisheries Service, U.S., 245
National Park Service, U.S., 98
Native Americans:
     alcoholism of, 60, 108, 110, 113, 115,
          122, 141, 255, 259
     anthropological evidence on, 55–56, 108,
          110, 115
     barge operators vs., 30, 60–61, 213–14
     blood quantum for, 116
     burial grounds of, 115, 255, 259
     congressional hearing on (1933), 123
     as dam laborers, 95, 117, 120–21, 256
     displacement of, 22, 67–69, 101, 104,
          108–25, 234, 254–60
     education of, 118–19
     electricity rates for, 116, 120, 122, 255
     epidemics among, 67–68, 113, 118
     federal rulings in favor of, 45, 60
     genocide against, 109
     income distribution for, 116
     irrigation denied to, 115–16, 133, 136*n*,
          140–41, 150
     radioactivity exposure of, 165
     religious traditions of, 102, 108, 116,
          157, 183, 257, 259–60
     reservations for, 68, *84*, 108–25, 256,
          257

river management and, 17, 230, 233–36, 242–46, 252, 253
   salmon as important to, 16, 26, 45, 56, 60, 67, 69–70, 104, 108–9, 111, 112–13, 114–15, 117, 119–20, 122, 124, 140–41, 197, 201, 213–14, 227, 234–36, 240, 258, 259
   skiffs of, 60
   suicide rate of, 108–9, 113, 115
   trading by, 67, 68, 73
   treaties of, 45, 256–59
   water rights of, 116*n*
   whites vs., 36–37, 45, 60, 67–68, 108–12, 113–14, 115–16, 121–22, 140–41, 170, 254–60
   see also individual tribes
Needham, Paul, 236
New Deal, 37, 83, 87, 135, 136, 145, 153, 167, 221, 247
Newlands, Francis G., 136
New York Times, 188, 190
Niagara Falls, 96
Nielson, Allen, 114
Nine Nations of North America, The (Garreau), 202–3
Nixon, Richard M., 184
Northwest Development Association, 236
Northwest Passage, 66
Northwest Power Act, 230–31, 232, 243, 244, 245, 249, 252
Northwest Power Planning Council, 230–31, 243–44, 249
nuclear energy, 44–45, 57, 164, 171, 192, 218, 247–49
Nykanen, Mark, *199,* 214–18

Oak Ridge, Tenn., 159*n*, 161–62, 163
Oaks, Mary, 85
Obama, Barack, 16
oil spills, 42, 43, 63, 212, 217
Operating Engineers Union, 122
Oregon Forest Industries Council, 242
Oregon Natural Resources Defense Council, 82
Osborne, Barbara, 131, 136–37, 154
Osborne, Donald, 132
Osborne, Ted, 126, 131–44, 146, 148, 151, 154–55
Outlaw, 29, 35, 38
Ozbun, Jim, 149

Pacific Fisheries Management Council, 58, 233
Pacific Northwest:
   British vs. U.S. control of, 66
   East Side vs. West Side of, 24, 36, 41, 47–48, 52–53, 180, 201–5, 217–18
   economic transformation of, 22, 24, 26, 48, 203, 223, 232
   extractive industry in, 217
   old-growth forests of, 21, 202, 246*n*
   urban areas of, 47–48, 155–56, 201, 203–5, 218, 225, 226
   see also Washington
Pacific Northwest Grain and Feed Association, 33
Pacific Northwest Utilities Conference Committee, 82
paper mills, 48, 52
Parker, Herbert M., 192
Pasco, Wash., *11,* 72, 163, 166
Patt, Ralph, 175–76
Pengelly, Mary, 193–94, 195
pesticides, 196, 216
pheasants, 37, 48
Philco, 171
phosphorus, radioactive, 165
Pitman, Dexter, 43*n*
Pitzer, Paul, 90*n,* 140
plutonium, 20, 23, 26, 44, 47, 106, 112, 157–74, 178–84, 191, 196
Popular Mechanics, 100
Portland, Ore., 201, 203–5, 218, 225, 226
"postage stamp rate," 246
potatoes, 127, 153, 200, 237
Potholes Reservoir, 38, 126, 128
Potlatch paper mill, 52
power lines, 73, 131
Priest Rapids Dam, *11,* 76, 255, 256, 258
"Prophets of Shortage" speech, 247
Public Works Administration (PWA), 123
Puck Hyah Toot, 257–58
Puget Sound Naval Shipyard, 57

quartzite, 115

Raban, Jonathan, 203
radionuclides, 175, 179, 189
rads, 179*n,* 195
railroads, 31, 55, 198, 212

rainfall, 112
Rattlesnake Mountain, 157, 260
Ray, Verne, 114–15
Raynaud's disease, 194
Reagan, Ronald, 184, 247, 248
Reclamation Act, 136, 138
Redden, James A., 16–17, 81, 251
Redfish Lake, 31–32
reservoirs, 44, 78, 103, 114, 166
Reynolds, Hiram, 122
Reynolds, Johnny, 122
Rice, Esther, 100
Richardson, Jim, 219–20
Richland, Wash., *11*, 72, 163, 164, 166–67,
        173, 184, 186, 196, 259
riprap (erosion barrier), 124
Rivers of Empire (Worster), 46, 98, 114
Rock Island Dam, 235
Roessler, Genevieve, 190–91, 195
"Roll, Columbia, Roll," 254
"Roll On Columbia, Roll On," 89–90
Roosevelt, Franklin D., 25, 45, 87–88, 93, 99,
        106, 117, 120–21, 135, 148
Rooster Rock State Park, 222
Ross, Alexander, 102
Ross, J. D., 247
Royal City, Wash., 151
ruthenium, 192

Sacajawea State Park, *64*
St. Lawrence River, 25
Salish language, 116–17
salmon:
        barges and, 23, 30, 31–33, 43, 58, 201,
                208–9, 212, 220, 224, 226, 231
        bypass systems for, 51–52, 104, 124*n*, 140,
                220, 235, 237*n*–40*n*, 243, 245, 255
        chinook, 69, 80, 114–15, 120, 125, 154,
                154*n*, 157, 182, 233, 241, 242
        coho, 69
        dams as obstacles for, 16, 32, 43, 44–45,
                48–49, 51, 77–81, 101, 104*n*, 107,
                112, 120, 122, 124, 197, 208, 209,
                220, 223, 229, 232–33, 250, 255
        decline of, 241
        distillation of, 79–81, 242
        as endangered species, 24, 33, 49, 81–82,
                150, 151, 154, 154*n*, 232–33, 238–
                39, 242, 244–45, 250–53
farming vs., 49, 234, 238–39
fish agencies for, 230–33, 242–46, 250–
        51
fishing for, 58, 60–61, 69–70, 98, 116–17,
        119–20, 141, 213–14, 233, 235, 240,
        241–42, 258, 259
"four H's" of, 238–43
genetic strains of, 240
hatchery, 81, 125, 240–41, 250
imprinting process of, 81
irrigation and, 80, 133, 140, 141, 146,
        147, 150, 151–52, 154, 196–97, 231
juveniles of, 31, 76–81, 104*n*, 182, 235–
        36, 239–41, 243, 255
legal rulings on, 244, 245–46, 249, 252
migration of, 31, 32–33, 76–79, 81, 196–
        97, 201, 230, 232, 235–36, 238–40,
        241
myths about, 43*n*
Native American need for, 16, 26, 45,
        56, 60–61, 67, 69–70, 104, 108–9,
        111, 112, 114–15, 116, 119–20, 122,
        124, 140–41, 197, 201, 213–14, 227,
        234–36, 240, 242, 258, 259
nests (redds) of, 239
passive integrated transponder (PIT)
        tags for, 79
physiology of, 77–78, 229
as political issue, 243–44, 249–53
preservation of, 21–22, 31–32, 45, 49,
        165, 168, 216, 217, 220, 227–32, 253
return to Columbia River of, 125
river management and, 22–24, 30,
        77–79, 227–32
sockeye, 31–32, 43, 43*n*
spawning by, 31–32, 43, 159, 213, 232,
        238–39, 241
spearing of, 98, 116–17, 120
water temperature and, 32, 77, 78, 80,
        239
wild, 80, 81, 232, 239–40, 241
Salmon Days festival, 104
salmon math, 251
Sandercock, Greg, 217
"sanitary lagoons," 73
Saturday Evening Post, 90
Savage John Lucian, 100
scarlet fever, 68
Schleuter, Jonathan, 33

Schneider, Mark, 74–76
Sea Lion, 222–23
sea lions, 208
seals, 208, 209, 224
Seattle, Wash., 201, 203–5
Seattle Times, 182
Senate Agriculture Committee, 149
Sever, Lowell, 195–96
Seward, Vern, *84,* 116–22, 124–25
Shannon, Whitey, 85
Shasta Dam, 99
Sheffler's Elevator, 59
shipyards, 90
Sierra Club, 33, 81, 250
Silver Dollar Saloon, 85, 121
Silverthorn, Archie, 118–19
Simons, T. W., 102
Simpson, O. J., 202*n*
single-pass reactors, 165
sinkholes, 95
Sjogren disease, 193
Skamokawa, Wash., 232
Slocum, Harvey, 86
smallpox, 67
Smith, Curt, 148
Smohola, 257
Snake Basin, 221
Snake River:
    archaeological sites under, 55–56
    canyon of, 35
    Columbia's confluence with, 23, *28,* 35,
        61, 63, 65, 66–67, 68, 71, 72–73,
        198–201, 257
    current of, 31, 32
    drawdown of, 32–33, 51, 52–53, 208, 212
    freezing of, 30
    shipping channels in, 31, 40
Sommers, Helen, 148
"Song of the Great Coulee Dam, The," 89
sonic booms, 132
Sons of Norway, 21, 131
Sparling, George, 85
Spokesman-Review, 80
spotted owl, 21, 245
steelhead, 69, 208, 220, 236, 241
Stegner, Wallace, 29, 97–98
Stewart, Alice, 179
stillbirths, 164
Stockman, David, 248

Stone, Livingston, 242
Strauss, Michael W., 130
strontium, 161, 176, 181
sugar beets, 37, 48, 189
Sutherland, Kay, 193–95
Swanee Rooms, 86, 92

"Taking from the Taxpayer," 152
"Talkin' Blues, The," 19
Taylor, Cindy, 216
Taylor, Dick, 111
Teals, Brenda, 113, 127
Tex (foreman), 96–97
Theriot, Ernest, 57–60, 200
Three Gorges dam, 87*n*
Three Mile Island nuclear plant, 192
thyroid disease, 164, 179, 187, 193, 194, 195,
    196
Tidewater Barge Lines, 38, 39, 40, 41–42,
    50–51, 59, 63, 206, 213, 223–25
Toaster, 76
Tri-Cities, 72, 163, 164, 166–67, 168, 171,
    180, 189, 197, 203, 207
    "environmental mission" of, 166
Tri-City Herald, 169
Tri-City Industrial Council, 166, 168
tritium, 175, 181
trout, 37, 43*n,* 124
trucks, 31, 51
Truman, Harry S., 90, 162
tuberculosis, 118

Umatilla tribe, 67, 233
Union Pacific Railroad, 198
Unsoeld, Jolene, 209
upwelling, 241
uranium, 163, 163*n,* 174–75, 178, 180, 181
Utah & Idaho (U&I) Sugar Company, 37, 189
utilities, private:
    lobby for, 228–29, 244
    monopolies by, 86, 87, 88
    river management and, 22, 32, 216–17,
        228–29, 231, 232, 237, 242–43, 244,
        246, 250–53
    WHOOPS default and, 248–50

Vantage, Wash., 62
veterans, 129, 140
Veterans of Foreign Wars, 129

286

Vietnam War, 44
vision quests, 259
Volpentest, Sam, 166

Walla Walla, Wash., 193, 207, 236, 237
Walla Walla tribe, 67, 68, 233
Wall Street Journal, 166
Wanapum Dam, 20, 54, 62
Wanapum tribe, 67, 183, 254–60
Warren, Earl, 90
Warren, Michael, 209–11, 226
Washington:
    Fish and Game Department of, 37
    Health Department of, 85–86, 161
    legislature of, 44, 146–48
    Palouse region of, 71
    political representation of, 37, 46, 49
    scabland of, 72
Washington, University of, 48, 115, 171, 229
Washington Post, 20
Washington Public Power Supply System
    (WPPSS), 248–50
Washington State University, 55, 139, 146,
    149, 151, 169
Washington Territory, 257
water:
    conservation of, 23, 98, 136n, 152, 153,
        156, 234, 249n
    drinking, 201
    ground-, 112, 141, 148, 153, 160, 167,
        175–76, 185
    rights to, 116n, 132–33, 141–42, 154
    scarcity of, 19, 20, 36, 112
    subsidies for, 23–27, 36, 116, 127, 128–
        29, 133, 136, 141–44, 151–56, 181,
        234, 249n
    temperature of, 32, 77, 78, 80, 239
Water Follies Columbia Cup Unlimited
    Hydroplane Race, *64,* 65, 73–76
"water spreading," 151–52
Wayampam tribe, 67

Weaver, James, 248
welders, 20, 93–94, 96, 122
Wenatchee, Wash., 19–20, 26, 105–7
Wenatchee World, 86, 105–6
West:
    Columbia River as symbol of, 22–23, 27,
        113, 127, 259
    engineered, 113, 117, 127, 166, 167, 259
    individualism in, 27, 47, 53, 133, 181
    land use in, 97–98
    natural resources of, 87, 103, 229
    New, 47–48, 214
    population density of, 47–48
    wilderness in, 156
    see also Pacific Northwest
Westinghouse, 173–74, 184
wheat, 31, 34, 45, 55, 57, 127, 137, 191, 200
Wheeler, Burton K., 123
"White Elephant Comes into Its Own," 90
Whitman, Marcus, 68
Whittlesey, Norm, 146–50
whooping cough, 68
WHOOPS, *see* Washington Public Power
    Supply System
wildlife, 30, 124–25, 137, 157, 159, 160,
    208–9, 212, 222, 223
Willamette River, 225
windmills, 14, 259–60
windsurfing, 30, 42–43, *199,* 214–18, 222
wind turbines, 41
Woods, Rufus, 105–7
Woody, Elizabeth, 213
World War II, 26, 86, 90, 112n, 122, 135, 159,
    162–63
Worster, Donald, 46, 98, 99, 114, 223
Wright, Al, 65, 82, 228, 232

Yakima Firing Range, 254, 256
Yakima River, 170
Yakima tribe, 67
Yibar, Dan, 228

ABOUT THE AUTHOR

BLAINE HARDEN, a reporter for PBS's *Frontline* and a contributor to the *Economist*, was bureau chief for the *Washington Post* in eastern Europe, sub–Saharan Africa, and northeast Asia. He is the author of *Africa: Dispatches from a Fragile Continent* and *Escape from Camp 14: One Man's Remarkable Odyssey from North Korea to Freedom in the West*. Harden lives in Seattle.